WITTGENSTEIN — THE EARLY PHILOSOPHY

An Exposition of the *Tractatus*

WITTGENSTEIN-

THE EARLY PHILOSOPHY

An Exposition of the "Tractatus"

by

HENRY LE ROY FINCH

HUMANITIES PRESS

New York   1971

Library of Congress No. 73-135985

SBN 391-00123-X

Printed in the United States of America

It is strange how you can look at
something and never see it.

WITTGENSTEIN

Dedicated to

M. R. F.

and to

E. G. and G. G.

who taught us to keep looking until we see

Preface

Despite the fact that it is nearly half a century since Wittgenstein's *Tractatus* was first published it remains largely an enigmatic book, ironically honored as much for what we do not understand about it as for what we do. A great deal of work has been done in the attempt to explicate it, but this has not succeeded in clearing up fundamental difficulties. As a consequence some students have been led to deny that there is any coherent system of thought in the *Tractatus*, while others have tried to impose various forced interpretations.

The understanding of Wittgenstein's later philosophy has in turn also been impaired by this failure to understand the *Tractatus*. There is an integral development of Wittgenstein's ideas which cannot be recognized until we have a clear comprehension of his starting point. To remain content with a *Tractatus* which is seen as a compendium of "hints and guesses" is to condemn the foremost philosopher of our age to remain half-understood.

A careful study, however, following the text sufficiently closely, reveals that the *Tractatus* is throughout, indeed, a coherent and systematic whole and that its obscurities arise, for the most part, from failing to pay the necessary attention to Wittgenstein's own language. The book, it will be found, presents a single integrated vision of the world, even though this becomes apparent only when a detailed examination has been completed.

Alexander Maslow was correct in his judgment when he wrote in one of the first full-length studies of the *Tractatus:*

> I feel that, if one could only, to use a metaphor, strike the right key from the beginning and give the proper meanings to Wittgenstein's essential terms, such as atomic fact, object and form, one could go on without much trouble into the rest of this syncopated philosophical composition.[1]

---

[1] *A Study in Wittgenstein's "Tractatus"* — written in 1933, published in 1961, (Berkeley and Los Angeles, Calif.), p. xiii.

The "key" which is needed, but which has been missing, lies in Wittgenstein's central distinction between *objects* and *things*, the distinction by which he attempted to bring together in the *Tractatus* the conflicting points of view of his teachers Frege and Russell. This distinction between *objects* (which is a logically-oriented term) and *things* (which is an empirically-oriented one) has been overlooked mostly because it is so pervasive. (In the chapter entitled *Objects and Things* in the present book twelve fundamental differences indicated by Wittgenstein between *objects* and *things* are discussed.)

The vision which finally emerges in the *Tractatus* is that the *things* of the world are, from the unavoidable and necessary point of view of logic, formal *objects* and that the world has whatever structures it has only in terms of such objects. This vision is arrived at largely through an "immanent" conception of *logical form* in language, as mirroring the possibilities of existence and non-existence of such structures, functioning as the formal equivalents of the material properties of the world.

The mark of "objectivity," as the *Tractatus* sees the world, is *structure*, and the basic principle of language and thought is *structural picturing*. The book is concerned mainly with what this supposes about the nature of the world and the way in which such structural picturing is present in ordinary language. Close to the center is the ancient problem of the relation between possibility and existence, or, as it also appears here, between meaning and truth.

Because of its extreme condensation the *Tractatus* requires a close attention to every word. Important distinctions, for example, are drawn between *objects*, *objects of pictures*, and *objects of thought*, between *propositions*, *completely analyzed propositions* and *elementary propositions*, between *configuration*, *situations (Sachlagen)* and *states of affairs (Sachverhalte)*. The meanings of these and other terms have to be carefully distinguished if all the pieces of Wittgenstein's analysis are to fit into place.

The general principle which has to be accepted (and which is borne out in practice), is that in the *Tractatus* every different word may be counted upon to have a different meaning. As in a mathematical treatise, there are no synonyms. The consequences are that we cannot be too scrupulous in following the text and that when errors creep in, it will almost always be because we have overlooked some small, but crucial detail.

I have throughout followed the Pears and McGuinness translation

(London and N.Y., 1961, with corrections of 1963). In accordance
with the *one-word-one-meaning* principle, however, there are three
translations in particular accepted by Pears and McGuinness which can
be misleading:

(1) the translation of both *Wirklichkeit* and *Realität* by the English
    word *reality;*
(2) the translation of both *Bestehen* and *Existenz* by the English word
    existence; and
(3) the translation of both *Verneinung* and *Negation* by the English
    word *negation.*

In these cases Wittgenstein had in mind specific distinctions which
are valuable clues to his thought. I have, nevertheless, chosen, with
some hesitation, to accept the Pears and McGuinness readings for con-
venience of reference and because it is possible to call attention to the
distinctions in other ways when this is needed.

The same cannot be done, however, in another case—the failure of
the Pears and McGuinness translation to preserve the three words *Gegenständen, Dingen* and *Sachen* as having different meanings (at 2.01,
2.15, 2.1514, 4.1272B). Here are three different meanings which must
be kept, and the earlier Odgen English translation was more accurate
in using the three words *objects, things* and *entities.*

The epigraphs which I have put at the beginnings of the chapters
are an important part of the book. They sum up in the languages of
different traditions and disciplines some of Wittgenstein's most fundamental ideas, showing their universality and timelessness. I wish
to thank particularly my colleagues Horace Gregory and Joseph Camp-
bell for the quotations respectively from John Wilmot, Earl of Rochester, (preceding the chapter on *Negation*), and from the *Dryg-Drya
Viveka,* (preceding the chapter on the *Self*), and also my former student Miss Nancy Grove for the stage direction from the medieval
morality play (quoted at the beginning of the chapter on *The Ethical
and the Religious*).

For permission to quote at length from the *Tractatus* thanks are
due to its publishers Routledge and Kegan Paul and The Humanities
Press, and for permission to quote from Wittgenstein's other books, and
especially from *Notebooks 1914-1916,* to Basil Blackwell, Oxford.

I also wish to acknowledge my debt to the *"Tractatus" Index—
Terms in Their Propositional Context in Wittgenstein's "Tractatus"*

by George Kimball Plochman and Jack B. Lawson, (Southern Illinois University Press, 1962), and to Max Black's *A Companion to Wittgenstein's "Tractatus,"* (Cornell University Press, 1964). Both of these are invaluable tools for studying the *Tractatus.*

Finally I wish to express my appreciation to my dear friends Gotthard Günther and Harold Isaacson for many hours of stimulating conversation and to my wife and family for their patience and helpfulness during the years this book was being written.

HENRY LE ROY FINCH
Sarah Lawrence College
June, 1970

Acknowledgments

Acknowledgment is made to the following publishers for their kind permission to quote from books published by them: Harry N. Abrams, Inc. for the quotation from Paul Klee in Will Grohmann—*Paul Klee;* Cambridge University Press for the quotations from G. S. Kirk and J. E. Raven—*The Presocratic Philosophers;* Dover Publications, Inc. for the quotations from Heinrich Hertz—*Principles of Mechanics,* edited by Robert S. Cohen; George Allen & Unwin Ltd. for the quotations from K. N. Jayatilleke—*Early Buddhist Theory of Knowledge,* Herbert Giles—*Chuang-tzu Taoist Philosopher* and Bertrand Russell—*Logic and Knowledge;* Grove Press for the quotation from Samuel Beckett— *Malone Dies;* the Belknap Press of Harvard University Press for the quotations from Charles Peirce—*Collected Papers,* edited by Charles Hartshorne and Paul Weiss; Horizon Press for the quotations from Paul Engelmann—*Letters from Ludwig Wittgenstein with a Memoir* and from Eric Gutkind—*The Body of God,* edited by Lucie B. Gutkind and Henry Le Roy Finch; Levin & Munksgaard for the quotation from Jorgen Jorgensen—*Treatise on Formal Logic;* the Museum of Modern Art for the quotation from Giorgio de Chirico in James Thrall Soby— *Giorgio de Chirico;* the Philosophical Library for the quotations from Edward Conze—*Buddhist Texts Through the Ages* and from Gottlob Frege—*The Foundations of Arithmetic,* translated by J. L. Austin; Princeton University Press for the quotations from Soren Kierkegaard— *Philosophical Fragments,* originally translated by David Swenson, revised translation by Howard V. Hong and from Hermann Weyl—*Philosophy of Mathematics and Natural Science;* Routledge and Kegan Paul for the quotations from Simone Weil—*The Notebooks of,* translated by Arthur Wills in two volumes; Sanskrit Press, Calcutta for the quotations from Gaurinath Sastri—*The Philosophy of Word and Meaning;* St. John's University Press for the quotation from *The Platform Scripture,* translated by Wing-tsit Chan; Stuart and Watkins Ltd. for the quotation from L. C. Beckett—*Movement and Emptiness;* the University of Chicago Press for the quotations from Leibniz—*Philosophical Papers,* edited by Leroy E. Loemker; the University of Wisconsin Press for the quotation from Richard H. Robinson—*Early Madhyamika in India and China;* Yale University Press for the quotation from John Wilmot, Earl of Rochester—*The Complete Poems of,* edited by David M. Vieth. I wish also to acknowledge with especial thanks the kindness of Basil Blackwell, Publisher, for their permission to quote from Wittgenstein —*Notebooks 1914-1916* and *Philosophical Investigations.*

Contents

WITTGENSTEIN — THE EARLY PHILOSOPHY

PHILOSOPHY

An Exposition of the *Tractatus*

THE ANIMALS

They do not live in the world,
Are not in time and space.
From birth to death hurled
No word do they have, not one
To plant a foot upon,
Were never in any place.

For with names the world was called
Out of the empty air,
With names was built and walled,
Line and circle and square,
Dust and emerald;
Snatched from deceiving death
By the articulate breath.

But these have never trod
Twice the familiar tracks,
Never never turned back
Into the memoried day.
All is new and near
In the unchanging Here
Of the fifth great day of God,
That shall remain the same,
Never shall pass away.

On the sixth day we came.

EDWIN MUIR
(by permission of Oxford University Press
and Faber Ltd.)

Introduction

The very ideas of Truth, of Fact, of Rationality, the very essence of cognition and logic, will have to be scrutinized in order to gain the thread that can lead us out of the world-labyrinth into a kingdom and an order which ought to be our human world.

DIMITRIJE MITRINOVIC

διὸ δεῖ ἕπεσθαι τῶι κοινῶι· ξυνὸς γὰρ ὁ κοινός.
τοῦ λόγου δ' ἐόντος ξυνοῦ ζώουσιν οἱ
πολλοὶ ὡς ἰδίαν ἔχοντες φρόνησιν.

(Therefore it is necessary to follow the common; but although the Logos is common, the many live as though they had a private understanding.)

HERACLEITUS (frag. 2)

That which is not expressed through speech, but that by which speech is expressed, that, verily, know thou is Brahman, not what people here adore.

Kena Upanishad I-5

CHAPTER 1

Introduction

There are four basic terms in the *Tractatus* which have to be distinguished clearly at the outset, though a full understanding of the way they work together can only be found at the end of our study. They are:

> *things (Dingen)*
> *objects (Gegenständen)*
> *situations (Sachlagen)*
> *states of affairs (Sachverhalte)*

Unless these terms are clearly distinguished the book as a whole becomes incomprehensible. We begin, therefore, with a preliminary indication of what they mean:

> *Things* are empirical complexes, whatever can be both named and described. They are what we *experience, see* and *can describe.* (5.634) Unlike objects, which have forms, they have a "form of independence," for the possibilities of their occurrences in situations are limited only by the possibilities of states of affairs. (2.0122) *Things*, when named, function as objects, but, when described, turn out to be facts, or conjunctions of further existing combinations of objects.

> *Objects* are logical simples, or what can only be named. They are what we *know, mean* and *think.* (2.0123, 3.2, 3.203) They are essentially simple (not factually simple), which means that they have only one form and one content each. They are the ontological coordinates for the descriptions of different kinds of properties. In having only one form an object is unlike any thing we are acquainted with, but in any completely analyzed proposition we name things in just that way.

> *Situations* are empirical occurrences of things. They are the

1

ways in which things occur with properties or with each other.
It is *situations* which are represented by the words and sentences of everyday language. But situations have to be possible, and it is this which links them with objects. (2.014) We
distinguish between a possible situation and an impossible one.
(*The book is leaning against the wall* is a possible situation;
the ball is leaning against the wall is an impossible one.) The
possibility of situations is determined by states of affairs.

States of affairs are the fixed possible structures of a world.
They define possibility. A single state of affairs is always one
of all possible combinations of its objects, since if any objects are given, all objects are always given (5.524A), and with
all objects always go all their possible combinations. (2.0124)

These four terms indicate the two aspects of the world in the
Tractatus. On the one side is the "empirical" aspect *(things-in-situations)*, and on the other the "formal" aspect *(objects-in-states-of-
affairs)*. It is by means of the latter that it is possible to experience,
think about, and talk about the former.

The pivotal conception of the *Tractatus* is that we represent *things-
in-situations* by means of *objects-in-states-of-affairs*, and the nature of
the world is such that we *can* represent it this way, and *can only* represent it this way.

Two points have to be emphasized immediately in order to forestall
possible misunderstandings: (1) this is not a question of what we can
do in a perfect language, but of the way in which ordinary language
is able to function at all, and (2) we do not *impose* this method of
representation on the world, but rather the world itself has just the
character that it *can* only be represented this way. This is part of what
Wittgenstein means by saying that a proposition is *essentially* connected
with a situation by being its logical picture, (4.03) (i.e. by representing it as a state of affairs).

What brings *things-in-situations* and *objects-in-states-of-affairs* together is the threefold circumstance that (1) things themselves have to
be able to combine in structures; (2.011) (2) in *pictures* when we
depict *possible relations of things*, we are picturing facts (or existing
structures of objects) because the elements of a picture "correspond

Note: In the references to the *Tractatus* letters refer to paragraphs under a
given entry, and not to sentences. Thus 2.0121C is the third paragraph in the entry
numbered 2.0121.

to" objects (2.1, 2.13) and (3) in *propositions* the elements of a propositional sign can be expressed in such a way that they also "correspond
to" objects (in this case the "objects of a thought"). (3.201)

Wittgenstein's clear understanding is that both representable sense
experience (*pictures*) and thoughts (*logical pictures*) represent *things-
in-situations* in a structural way, and this same way of representing
them can be expressed in propositions by the use of names. Hence he
says that a proposition "presents" (*vorstellen*) a structure or state of
affairs in order to "represent" (*darstellen*) a possible situation. (4.0311,
4.031) The situation can be represented in this way just because the
parts of a situation are treated as "objects of a thought" when in a
completely analyzed proposition they are treated in such a way as to
be named. (3.2)

Pictures and propositions both function according to the same principle of representing "possible occurrences of things" as "possible structures of objects." The difference is that a picture "presents" a situation
in logical space to do this, (2.11) while a proposition "presents" a state
of affairs to do it. (4.0311) But both rest upon the same "logic of picturing." (4.015) As Wittgenstein says, a proposition can represent a possible situation only by being a description of a state of affairs (4.023)
or because the situation is "put together" as it were, experimentally in
a proposition in logical space. (4.031, 4.023E)

Things-in-situations are, in effect, external relatednesses between
things or between things and properties, and Wittgenstein's pivotal
thought is that *all representation depends upon being able to depict
these external relatednesses of things as internal structural relatednesses
of objects*. And this is only possible because this is at bottom what
they are.

Behind the possibility of every representation there are objects.
Pictures and *thoughts*, Wittgenstein says, "contain" the possibility of
the situations they represent. (2.023, 3.02) (Their elements, he says,
are the "representatives" of objects. (2.131)) And, somewhat similarly,
propositions "contain" the possibility of expressing sense, which is the
same as representing situations. (2.13, 4.031) (Propositions are only possible, he says, because of "the principle of the representation of objects by signs" and because a thought can be expressed with names, and
"a name represents an object in a proposition." (4.0312, 3.22))

While propositions can only represent situations by presenting them
as states of affairs (i.e. by using signs which stand for objects), Witt-

genstein emphasizes (and calls it "my fundamental idea" (4.0312B))
that *there are no signs which stand for the logic of what is represented.*
This is a far-reaching idea and means, among other things, (as will be
seen in detail later), that, when we have completely analyzed propositions, things, properties and relations are all represented as objects, and
the differences between what is represented being a thing, or being a
property or being a relation is conveyed entirely by syntax. The "distinguishable parts" of a situation are represented by "distinguishable
parts" of a proposition. (4.04) What cannot be so represented is the
"logical articulation" of the parts, which *includes* whether what is represented is a thing, or a property or a relation. What is referred to as
the particularities of things, properties and relations are all represented
in a proposition by names as "objects of a thought." (3.2) The difference between a thing and a property or a thing and a relation is just
what, after analysis, shows itself entirely in the syntax.

Besides the requirement that we can only represent the world in
terms of fixed structures, there is a second general requirement for both
pictures and propositions, as well as for the world, and this is that the
world must be able to be represented in such a way that the representation can be correct or incorrect, true or false. In order to meet this requirement we have to represent the world as what Wittgenstein calls
reality (Wirklichkeit) or with the additional dual possibilities of existence and non-existence for every state of affairs. The term *reality* means
this polarity as available for every possible structure. Every situation must be seen in this way too, because every situation takes place
against the backdrop of its possible non-existence. It has, in other
words, when factually seen both a "positive" and a "negative" version
(analogously to the way in which a spatial shape, for example, while
remaining one and the same shape, can be described either "positively"
in terms of the space which it occupies or "negatively" in terms of the
space which surrounds and bounds it).

Pictures and propositions must not only represent situations structurally, but also "logically," or in terms of the "form of reality," or
the possibilities of existence and non-existence of these structures. We
have to consider not merely all possible combinations of objects, but
the further possibilities of these in each case in the form of one-existing-
and-all-others-of-the-same-form-not-existing. In an ordinary picture the
possible structures represented (*pictorial form*) can be distinguished
from the possibilities of existence and non-existence of these structures

(*logical form*). But in a logical picture or thought these two are fused, so that the "form of the object" which is "known" (2.0123) has to accomplish what the pictorial form does in the picture.

ii

How does language succeed in representing *things* as *objects* and so *things-in-situations* as *objects-in-states-of-affairs?* The answer to this question lies in the special role of *names* in the *Tractatus*.

It will be seen that, in a general way, *words-in-ordinary-propositions* run parallel with *things-in-situations*, while *names-in-completely-an-alyzed-propositions* (which "hang together" in the same way as names-in-elementary-propositions[1]) run parallel with *objects-in-states-of-affairs*. But this does not tell us anything until we know what *names* are and how they work.

Names (along with *words, signs, symbols, propositional elements* and *expressions*) are able both to *designate (bezeichnen)* and to *mean (bedeuten)*. In the *Tractatus* we can designate just about anything— *objects,* (3.322) *things,* (4.243) *complexes,* (3.24) *numbers,* (4.126) *concepts,* (5.476) *formal concepts,* (4.127) and *generalizations* (4.0411) But it should be noted that *names* are only said to *designate* things and objects, (4.243, 4.126) and they are only said to *mean* objects. (3.203)

What is peculiar about names then is this: that they are signs which designate only things and objects; but they do not mean things, they only mean objects. It is, first of all, the distinction between *designation* and *meaning* which enables us to distinguish between things and objects and between ordinary words as names and real names. What is this distinction?

The clue to the difference between *designating* and *meaning* is that, while there are different "ways of designating" (or "modes of signifying"), there are *no different ways of meaning.* Meaning, in other words, is *what* is designated when this is taken independently of anything added by a *way* of designating, or by the use or employment of a sign. Meaning might be called *proto-designation,* or sheer reference as such, just what is left to be referred to when everything conveyed by syntax has been removed.

---

[1] Completely analyzed propositions, which still have syntactically different parts, must not be confused with elementary propositions, which have only combinatorially different parts, a point to be discussed further. See especially Chpt. 2, sec. iv; Chpt. 4, sect. ii; Chpt. 7, sect. i; Chpt. 11, sect. ii.

Ordinary words and names have something in common because Wittgenstein calls them both "simple signs," (4.026, 3.2, 3.201) but they differ in two important respects: (1) ordinary words designate in different ways, while names all designate in the same way; and this is what is meant by saying that names (as well as being "simple signs") are also "simple symbols"; (3.24D, 4.24) and (2) ordinary words can be further defined, while names cannot be further defined; and this is what is meant by saying that names (as well as being "simple signs" and "simple symbols") are also "proto-signs" (*Urzeichen*). (3.26)

(The difference between *simple signs* and *proto-signs* is that the meanings of *simple signs* can be explained by "translating" them as the dictionary does, (4.025) while the meanings of *proto-signs* can only be explained by "elucidations," which are propositions already containing the proto-signs. (3.263))

Names, it may be said, unlike ordinary words, have both syntactic and semantic simplicity, since they have no conventional syntax (but only a combinatorial one) and since they only mean objects. Syntactically they are *simple symbols;* semantically they are *proto-signs*. The question which arises, however, is what is the justification for calling the "simple signs employed in propositions" names and then indicating (in parentheses) that ordinary words are also simple signs? (4.026, 3.2, 3.201)

The justification is the same as for saying that a state of affairs is a combination of *objects* and then indicating (also in parentheses) that it is a combination of *things* (*Dingen*) and of *entities* (*Sachen*). (2.01) It is that ordinary words are subject to the same logic names are, in the same way that things are subject to the same ontology objects are. What makes it possible to talk about things at all is just what makes it possible to use ordinary words to talk about them—namely, the structure of language, which is just as much the structure of ordinary language as it is the structure of completely analyzed language. Ordinary words are already functioning as simple signs in referring to things, as the things referred to are already functioning as objects when they are so referred to.

The parallel between what Wittgenstein tells us about language and what he has earlier told us about the world is virtually complete and may be outlined in this way:

(1) Ordinary words occur in ordinary propositions in the same way that things occur in situations.

(2) A word does not have a completely independent meaning apart from the meaning it has in propositions any more than a thing has a nature completely independent of the situations it can occur in. (2.0122)

(3) Words must be able to be names in a completely analyzed proposition in the same way in which things must be able to be parts of states of affairs. (3.2, 2.032)

(4) These names, meaning objects, are in a "hanging together" (*ein Zusammenhang*) in a proposition in the same way that objects "hang together" (*zusammenhang*) in the structure of a state of affairs. (4.22, 2.032)

What Wittgenstein is telling us is that if words can occur together at all, and if things can occur together at all, then both must be able to occur together structurally, which means ultimately in terms of the immediate kind of connectedness (sheer combinatoriality) of names and objects. And it is this principle which ordinary language makes use of in depicting things and situations.

The critical point here is that, even though we can designate things by names, (4.243) we cannot designate things by names in such a way as to *mean* them *as things*, but only in such a way as to *mean* them *as objects*. There is, of course, no difficulty in naming things, even in naming such complex things as solar systems and galaxies, but such names do not mean that what they refer to *is* complex, for *this* cannot be meant. It is, in other words, impossible to designate complexity *as complexity* or to designate it in such a way as to *mean* complexity. (A propositional element, Wittgenstein says, can show by a certain indeterminacy in the proposition in which it occurs that it designates a complex, (3.24) but it cannot *mean* this.)

The consequence is that names are of such a character that they mean objects, no matter what they designate. But what then about the apparent designation by ordinary words of properties and relations? Wittgenstein's view is that *what* is designated in these cases has to be distinguished from what is designated being a property or what is designated being a relation. We do not, in other words, designate "propertyness," but rather the way in which we designate shows that what we designate is a property. Properties and relations, therefore, are objects in so far as they are meanings (actually "objects of a thought") and they are "ways of designating" in so far as they are "properties" and "relations." Analysis (through the "description of expressions") reveals that the property-ness and relation-ness belong to the *way* in which such words are placed in relation to other words and not to the *what* it is which is designated. When the "ways of designating" are identified as residing in the syntax, then we are left with just what is referred to by the property-word or the relation-word which is now named as an "object of a thought" just as things are named. All the words in a completely analyzed proposition then become names, all on a par and all naming objects. (3.2, 3.201)

We find in this way that it is possible to name things, properties and relations all as objects because the "way of designating," shown by the syntax, takes care of the differences between things, properties and relations in so far as this is more than simple differences between designated contents. (In the sentence "Green is green" (3.323) where the first word designates a person and the last one a color, it is the placement of the last word which shows that it designates as a property-word, while *what* it designates is quite independent of its being in this sentence a property; and the word with the very same designation could figure as the subject of some other sentence, such as "Green is a pretty color.")

It is apparent that we could not distinguish "property-words" and "relation-words" from each other or from "thing-words" unless we were able to designate things independently of properties and relations. Words, this means, do not acquire thing-designating status syntactically. Things, as it were, have a status prior to the appearance of "property-words" or "relation-words" in propositions. And this is to be expected since we do not *picture* properties and relations, for the elements of a picture are not "correlated to" properties and relations, but to "entities." (2.1514) What is pictured are the possible relations of entities and of things. (2.15, 2.151) Hence it may be said that we encounter things before we have words designating properties or relations or before we have names which can (when a proposition has been completely analyzed) name the properties and relations, as well as the things, as objects.

iii

This brings us to the question of what are *entities (Sachen)* as distinct from both *objects* and *things?* Why is Wittgenstein compelled to introduce still a third term here? For, although the distinction is central between *things* and *objects* and between *things-in-situations* and *objects-in-states-of-affairs*, the epistemology of the book also requires *entities*.[2]

The word *thing (Ding)* means in the first instance the everyday particulars which we speak about all the time, the word *object (Gegenstand)* the simple things with only one form each required by logic, and the word *entity (Sache)* what any kind of picture can picture. Entities are what are generally called *sense data* or *sense phenomena*, whether visual, auditory, tactile, etc. Entities are the specific lines, shapes, durations, colors, tones, etc., to which the elements of some kind of a picture can be correlated, (2.1514) and which are related to each other in the same ways in which the elements of a picture can be related. (2.15) Pictures can, of course, represent entities or sense phenomena without representing any things (a picture for example as simply a design), or they may represent both sense phenomena and things (e.g. a landscape).[3]

What *objects, things* and *entities* all have in common is that they can all enter into structural relations, objects with objects, things with things, and entities with entities. (2.01) They are, in effect, three kinds of "units"—formal, physical and phenomenal—which are represented structurally when they are pictured, thought-of or named. Of the three, however, it is only objects which can stand alone structurally, having only pure combinatorial structure (which means that it is only in the case of objects that we deal with *all* units).

How *objects, things* and *entities* differ from each other and yet are involved with each other is brought out in what Wittgenstein has to say about pictures. The elements of a picture, he tells us, "correspond to" *objects*, while they are "correlated to" *entities*; (2.13, 2.1514) and it is through these two circumstances that a picture represents directly the structural relations of entities or sense phenomena to each other. (2.15) On the other hand, the elements of a picture neither "correspond to" nor are "correlated to" *things*, and so a picture is not able to represent the relation of things directly, but only to represent the *possible* relations of things. (2.151) There is, in other words, a determinateness about the way in which we picture entities or sense phe-

---

[2] The Pears-McGuinness translation, as has already been indicated, is in error where it fails to preserve the three separate terms at 2.01, 2.15, 2.1514 and 4.1272.

[3] Entities or sense phenomena are real or imaginary, and it is of no consequence which, since as represented they are real.

nomena which is lacking in the way in which we picture things. The most we can do with things is to show their possible relations.

Because in the *Tractatus* entities or sense phenomena are pictured by elements which "correspond to" objects, a picture for Wittgenstein is both a representation of phenomena (in Mach's sense) and a representation of logical possibility (in Hertz's sense). What is not pictured is the actual content; phenomena enter structurally and not as content, and such a structural character is involved in both pictorial form and logical form, without which there is no representation. What is actually experienced as ineffable content is of no concern to the "logic of depiction" and has nothing to do with what makes representation possible. In this sense phenomena are not involved.

iv

The *Tractatus* epistemology becomes clearer if we contrast Wittgenstein's distinction between *objects, things* and *entities* with Whitehead's distinctions between *scientific objects, perceptual objects* and *sense objects,* as these terms appear in Whitehead's earlier writings.[4] While Wittgenstein's *things* roughly correspond to Whitehead's *perceptual objects,* a fundamental difference becomes apparent between Wittgenstein's *objects* and Whitehead's *scientific objects.*

Whitehead's *scientific objects,* like Hertz's *invisible masses* or Russell's *zero quanta,* are what Wittgenstein calls in his *Notebooks* "pseudo-objects." (p. 36) An electron, which Whitehead cites as an example of a *scientific object,* would be for Wittgenstein a "postulated thing" introduced as part of a "form of description." Wittgenstein's objects, on the other hand, are in no way "material" or "hypothetical." They are "logical simples" (not in the sense of objects of logic for there are none of these, but in the sense of the simplest conceivable objects, which means objects with only one form each).

When Whitehead describes what he calls "objects in general," he comes closer to what Wittgenstein means by an object.[5] Such "objects in general," Whitehead says, have to be "recognizable," have no parts (where parts means spatial or temporal parts) and can be in more than

---

[4] *An Enquiry Concerning the Principles of Natural Knowledge,* (Cambridge University Press, 1919), Chpt. 7.
   [5] *Ibid.,* Chpt. 4.

one place at once. In Wittgenstein's language this means that objects (1) have external properties, (2) are simple and (3) the same ones can be in different repeatable structures.[6]

Objects, *things* and *entities* in the *Tractatus* are also not to be thought of as "types of objects," each having as it were equal ontological claims. For Wittgenstein only objects are substance, and things and entities, in so far as they are changing and alterable, manifest the external properties of the changing configuration of objects. Although, in the first instance, we *picture entities, describe things* and *name objects*, the objects alone are substantial because they are what *make possible* the picturing of the entities and the describing of the things.

Wittgenstein accepts a certain relativity of simplicity and complexity and hence of naming and describing. Simplicity and complexity, like naming and describing, emerge together, and the one is only conceivable along with the other. Objects do not appear apart from states of affairs or names apart from propositions, but what is to count as an object and what as a name depends on the manner of representation. Chairs, tables and books, used as a propositional sign, for example, can be called "spatial objects" when only their spatial arrangement is in question and all their other properties are taken only as "external (identifying) properties." But, on the other hand, they can also be called "things" in so far as they are complex and can be further described in terms of still other objects. (3.1431)

While we can only represent in terms of *objects* it is sense phenomena or *entities* which we picture and empirical *things* which we picture and speak about. The *Tractatus* consequently cannot dispense with either *entities* or *things*, even though what chiefly characterizes its point of view is the notion that both are "substantially" and "essentially" *objects*.

---

[6] Where Wittgenstein and Whitehead decisively part company is in the latter's distinction between *objects* and *events*. Events in the *Tractatus* are described in terms of objects and do not constitute a separate metaphysical category. This derives from Wittgenstein's conception of time as a form of objects and the impossibility of representing with sense anything like Whitehead's ultimate category of becoming or creativity. In the *Tractatus*, change cannot be described as such, and various conceptions of evolution, such as Whitehead's, have to qualify, not as metaphysical presuppositions of all descriptions, but as particular scientific (and in this case biological) "forms of description." (cf. 4.1122 where Wittgenstein goes out of his way to say that "Darwin's theory has no more to do with philosophy than any other hypothesis in natural science.")

V

Objects play the most fundamental role in the *Tractatus* because they are responsible not only for the "internal" or structural nature of the world, but also for its "external" or material properties. Wittgenstein tells us that the configuration of objects "produces" (*bildet*) states of affairs and also material properties. (2.0272, 2.0231) And it is the same configuration of objects (though this expression is entirely without meaning and cannot be used) which produces both.

The *Tractatus* underwrites and provides an ontological justification for the common scientific procedure of describing material properties, at empirically increasingly simple levels, in terms of further structures of objects, which themselves then still retain further material properties. The justification is that the world is of such a character that material properties *can* only be represented as structures of objects. A state of affairs, or structure of objects, is the "internal" nature of a material property, at whatever level it appears. We might also say that the specific particular occurrences of shapes, durations and colors in the world are the changing configuration of objects whose external properties are the properties by which we identify these shapes, durations and colors and whose internal properties are the structures of coordinates in terms of which they may be described. (The "configuration of objects" is the closest we get to what might be called "sheer particularity" or the "uniqueness" of each single occurrence. This, of course, cannot be described and is not even identifiable.)

This is Wittgenstein's early answer to the perennial "problem of universals": a material property as a universal is a structural possibility of a certain kind, indefinitely repeatable and indefinitely "representable." But the reason why material properties can be represented as structures of objects is because such structures are the internal properties of the same objects which have those material properties as their external properties. (It should be noted that this is a particularly offensive way of speaking since there is no way of talking about the "same objects" except in terms of the same structures.)

The simplest approach to the ontology of the *Tractatus* is in terms of what is required for an "object language," and specifically for what the *Tractatus* regards as the three primary dimensions of such a language—*reference, sense* and *truth or falsity*. In order to have exact reference we must have *names* and *objects;* in order to have fixed sense we must have these, and we must also have *form* and *structure;* and in order to have truth or falsity we must have all of the foregoing, and in addition we must have *reality* (existence and non-existence) and *logical form.*

The nature of language and its essential relation to the world requires then three factors:

1—what can only be *named* (objects or substance)
2—what can only be *shown* (logical form and sense)
3—what can only be *said* (existence or non-existence)

Ontologically the three levels are:

1—*substance*—which provides *all possible structures*
2—*reality*—which provides the *polarity of existence and non-existence*
3—*world*—which provides the *totality of existence*

To make this outline intelligible it is important not to confuse the forms which have to do with objects and logical form. In the *Tractatus* there are two basic kinds of forms at the level of substance—forms of objects and forms of states of affairs—and, *in addition,* there is the form of reality or logical form. The "substantial forms" give all the possible structures of the world, while the "logical forms" give all the possibilities of existence and non-existence of these structures. (*Essence,* on the other hand, applies only to the existing and refers to the possible structures which happen to exist, or the "internal" structural side of what actually exists.)

vi

The way by which the three basic levels fit together can perhaps be more clearly seen by comparing what Wittgenstein says with the three criteria by which Heinrich Hertz evaluated "pictures of things" in the Introduction to his *Principles of Mechanics,* a book which seems to have exerted a considerable influence on Wittgenstein.[7] It may be said that Wittgenstein takes Hertz's notion of *pictures* and gives it a much wider metaphysical and logical significance. Certain broad similarities, however, remain.

Hertz in this book describes scientific concepts as *pictures* and then characterizes such pictures in terms of three criteria: their "appro-

---

[7] *The Principles of Mechanics Presented in a New Form* (original English edition 1900, reprinted N.Y., 1956).

priateness," "permissibility" and "correctness." Although he describes these aspects of pictures in terms very different from Wittgenstein's, the three criteria correspond very closely to Wittgenstein's conceptions of what in language (1) is a matter of *arbitrary choice*, (2) is a matter of *logical necessity* and (3) is a matter of *accident*. In short, they correspond to what the *Tractatus* describes as (1) what can be *named*, (2) what can be *shown* and (3) what can be *said*.

Of the three *naming* occupies the fundamental place. For it is the assignment of names, a matter of our own choice, which involves us in formal commitments beyond our choice; and it is also the assignment of names which makes what we say coincide or fail to coincide with what accidentally happens to be the case. For after the formation of a thought as a logical picture (3.) and the expression of the thought as a proposition with a sense, (4.) the names in the proposition may still come to represent *what is not the case*.

All that is a matter of arbitrary choice in the *Tractatus* is the assignment of names. Wittgenstein speaks of "giving" a name a meaning and of "choosing" meanings. (5.4733, 4.5A) And he says: "For the sign of course is arbitrary." (3.322) (In the *symbol*, or the sign in use, on the other hand, he says that there is much that is arbitrary and much that is not arbitrary. (6.124)) Since we can name any *thing* at all, or make any sign stand for anything we want, a purely arbitrary element enters into every notation. We are free as to what we choose to name and, to a certain, more limited extent, as to *how* we choose to name it.

Hertz gives as the ways of evaluating the "appropriateness" of a representation the two further criteria of "distinctness" and "simplicity."[8] It should be noted that these two criteria might apply to the naming of *things*, but cannot apply to the naming of *objects*, since objects for Wittgenstein are already completely distinct and completely simple. While, in one sense, we are always naming things as objects, in another sense, we do not have the names of any objects at all, since we do not

---

[8] Hertz says:
> Of two images of the same object that is the more appropriate which pictures more of the essential relations of the object—the one which we may call the more distinct. Of two images of equal distinctness the more appropriate is the one which contains, in addition to the essential characteristics, the smaller number of superfluous or empty relations—the simpler of the two. (*ibid.*, p. 2)

Hertz, of course, is talking about scientific conceptions and not about the logical and metaphysical basis of *all* description.

know what the ultimate coordinates of description are, or the "number of names with different meanings." (5.55)

Once we have made an arbitrary choice of names, "something else is necessarily the case," and we find ourselves in the realm of logical possibility and logical necessity. (3.342) Here there is *nothing arbitrary at all.* Just as we can pick out two spatial objects at random, but once we have picked them out, there are only a limited number of ways in which they can be arranged in relation to each other in space (disregarding distance and considering only their "possible coordinations"), so, given two names selected at random, there are only two ways in which they can be arranged in spoken language or linear script. After the arbitrary choices, "all possibility" takes over, completely circumscribing what can be done with the choices which have been made.

In regard to Hertz's second criterion of "permissibility" it is a crucial point in the *Tractatus* that Wittgenstein does not distinguish between what is *permissible* and what is *possible.* The combinatorial conception of structural possibility enables him to hold that *everything that is possible is permissible.* Logic, he says, deals with *every* possibility, and there is no further possibility to dictate to it or from which a selection of the "permissible" might be made. Hence "whatever is possible in logic is also permitted." (5.473C) Or, as he put it in a letter to Russell: "You cannot prescribe to a symbol what it *may* be used to express. All that a symbol *can* express it *may* express." (*Notebooks.* pp. 129-130)

One of the results of this conception of logic is that logical syntax becomes a *description* of how it is possible for us to be doing what we are doing in representing the world, rather than any kind of a *prescription* about what would be the *best* way to represent it. For there is no best way; there are simply all the possible ways. We are not called upon to prescribe to language what can be done with it; we *find out* what *can* be done with it. (6.124) And everything that we find out tells us something about the essence of the world. (3.3421) The rules of logical syntax are not imposed upon language, but emerge once we find out *how* individual signs designate. (3.334) The only "requirement" or "postulate" is that of "definiteness of sense" (*Bestimmtheit des Sinnes*)—the same as the "requirement" that simple signs be possible. (3.23) Once given the possibility of simple signs and the arbitrary choice of meanings, then what we can do with them is fully determined by the nature of the signs and of the world.

While logical syntax is determined by how signs can designate, logical necessity proceeds from the one fundamental condition that if we have all possible structures, then only one of these can exist in any one logical place. What is logically impossible (e.g. the simultaneous presence of two colors at the same place and time in the visual field) is expressed by the law of non-contradiction. (6.3751) The assertion of what is the case, embedded in a proposition, involves the only logical constant, arising from this logical nature of the world. (5.47) Because it arises from the nature of the world this may be said to be the synthetic *a priori* aspect of logic. (cf. 6.33)[9]

Wittgenstein points to this synthetic *a priori* aspect of logic when he says:

> . . . logic is not a field in which we express what we wish with the help of signs, but rather one in which the nature of the natural and inevitable (or "essentially necessary") signs speaks for itself. (6.124)

The final aspect of language, *correctness* or *incorrectness*, as it is called by both Hertz and Wittgenstein, depends neither upon arbitrary choice, nor upon logical necessity, but simply upon sheer accident or what just happens to be the case in the world. There is no necessity about what happens to be the case. Anything that exists (or anything that could be described, experienced or said) could just as well not exist as exist. In regard to existence *vis a vis* non-existence sheer contingency reigns. (5.634)

In speaking of *correctness* or *incorrectness* of pictures Hertz says:

> We shall denote as incorrect any permissible images, if their essential relations contradict the relations of external things, i.e. if they do not satisfy our first fundamental requirement.

By "our first fundamental requirement" he means "the requirement that the consequents of the images must be the images of the conse-

---

[9] The success of this way of putting it depends upon being able to distinguish a logical place from what occupies it, since otherwise the statement would simply say that "one logical place cannot be two logical places." Wittgenstein says that the *existence* of a logical place (and here the word is *Existenz* and not *Bestehen*) "is guaranteed by the mere existence (also *Existenz*) of the constituents—by the existence (*Existenz*) of the proposition with a sense." (3.4) The logical nature of the world here hangs upon the difference between the terms *Existenz* and *Bestehen*.

quents." This "conformity between nature and thought" he understands as the conformity which permits the "anticipation of future
events," a conformity which "experience teaches us . . . does in fact
exist."[10]

Wittgenstein's conception of *correctness* or *incorrectness* differs
widely from this because it does not involve picturing relations between
present and future. It rests entirely upon the identity or lack of identity
between structures of logical pictures and structures of objects in the
world. Since time itself is a form of objects, correctness or incorrectness is divorced from any temporal succession. Hertz remains here the
physicist, standing upon the "fundamental requirement" of correct
prediction, while Wittgenstein, on the other hand, speaks of "pictures"
as a logician concerned with timeless possibility.

While Hertz says that he is concerned with "the images themselves" and not with "a scientific representation of the images," Wittgenstein's point of view suggests that, in fact, Hertz confuses the two.
(And this further comes out in Hertz's calling *appropriateness, permissibility* and *correctness* "postulates.") Wittgenstein wishes to separate what is required for *any* kind of a description from the "forms of
description" actually employed in science (which aim, for example,
at bringing the description of the world into a "unified form"). The
nature of language and world presupposed by description must not be
confused with the actual ways in which science goes about describing
the world (which include, for example, causality, not as a "necessity
of events," but as the "form of a law"). The "forms of description"
used by science already presuppose or make use of the logical forms
involved in being able to say anything about the world with sense.
Before we can formulate theories or laws about the material aspect of
the world or garner and report information about facts, we have to be
able to have thoughts and expressions of these thoughts which make
sense and which may turn out to be true or false. Hence the logico-
ontological character of the world precedes any theories or scientific
formulations about facts.

The *Tractatus* disentangles the logical from the scientific by showing that, just as it is perfectly possible to represent spatially what contradicts the laws of physics, but not what contradicts the laws of ge-

---

[10] Hertz, *op. cit.*, pp. 1-2.

ometry, (3.0321)[11] so it is possible in general to represent what contradicts the laws of any science, but not what contradicts the laws of logic. (cf. 6.342)

The *Tractatus* conception of language is, in some ways, a kind of "logical generalization" of Hertz's idea of scientific conceptions as "pictures of things." It widens Hertz's three criteria for evaluating pictures into three universal aspects of all language and the world. In place of Hertz's three "postulates" we have a fundamental ontology embracing irreducibly: (1) *substance* or finally simple and distinct objects; (2) *reality* as the single logical aspect of the world and (3) the *world* as what is the case or what accidentally—and yet nevertheless essentially—exists.

---

[11] Since it is impossible to give the geometrical coordinates of illusions *qua* illusions, the existence of "geometrical illusions" does not refute this. Figures that can be seen in two or more ways, for example, are to be regarded as involving two or more different facts. (5.5423) Something like this would also seem to apply to drawings of "geometrical impossibilities" such as those found in the work of M. C. Escher.

Objects and Things

. . . what lies behind this coat of many names.

L. C. BECKETT

For me there is a domain of what is objective, which is distinct from that of what is actual, whereas the psychological logicians take what is not actual to be subjective.

GOTTLOB FREGE

. . . all reality belongs only to unities. . . . Substantial unities are not parts but foundations of phenomena.

GOTTFRIED LEIBNIZ

That which is one is one, and that which is not-one is likewise one.

CHUANG-TZU

Identities or Things are Neither Cause nor Effect. They are Eternal.

WILLIAM BLAKE

CHAPTER 2

Objects and Things

i

The two principal aspects of language around which the *Tractatus* centers are *names* and *propositions,* with their equivalents in the world of *objects* and *states of affairs* and *things* and *situations.* Just what Wittgenstein meant by a *name* and how he was able to speak both of *names of objects* and *names of things* is best understood by first looking at the views of his teachers Frege and Russell especially on the subject of names.

In his *Principles of Mathematics* (1903) Russell distinguished between *things* and *concepts.* The former, he said, "are the terms indicated by proper names, the latter those indicated by all other words." He then gave as examples of *things:*

> Socrates is a thing because Socrates can never occur other-wise than as term in a proposition . . . Points, instants, bits of matter, particular states of mind, and particular existents generally, are things in the above sense, and so are many terms which do not exist, for example, the points in a non-Euclidean space and the pseudo-existents of a novel. All classes, it would seem, as numbers, men, spaces, etc., when taken as single terms, are things . . . (p. 45)

At first sight this distinction between *things* and *concepts* seems to parallel Frege's distinction between *objects* and *concepts,* which Frege expressed thus:

> A concept is the reference of a predicate; an object is something that can never be the whole reference of a predicate, but can be the reference of a subject. (*Philosophical Writings.* pp. 47-8)

The examples of names given by Frege are similar to Russell's examples: *Aristotle, Berlin* and

21

> Places, instants, stretches of time are, logically considered, ob-
> jects; hence the linguistic designation of a definite place, a
> definite instant, or a stretch of time is to be regarded as a proper
> name. (*ibid.*, p. 71)

Despite the apparent similarity, however, there was a difference
which amounted to a wide gulf between what Russell meant by a
proper name and what Frege meant. In Russell's philosophy it was, in
the end, sheer reference to a particular as such which for him made a
word a proper name. For Frege, on the other hand, a name had to
have more than a reference; it had to have a *sense* also, which meant
that there had to go along with it some way of *identifying* what it
referred to.

When Russell, therefore, spoke of naming Socrates as a *thing* and
Frege of naming the Moon as an *object*, the similarity was only superficial. Russell was thinking of Socrates as a sheer particularity, all of
whose attributes had to be attached by predicates and propositions.
Frege was thinking of the Moon as always having sufficient attributes to
be *identified and referred to in different ways*. Russell's paradigm was
the act of pointing at a particular *thereness*, and Frege's the act of
identifying what could be *commonly* thought of and spoken of.

This difference provides a convenient background for understanding Wittgenstein's treatment of names in the *Tractatus*. It may be said
that he found room for both Russell's and Frege's views, but in vastly
changed ways. Russell's original *things* became any "complexes" to
which we refer in ordinary language, but which can never be simple
referents, while Frege's objects became the internally related simples
which names *really mean*.

Russell's and Frege's difference on the subject of names focuses the
widely different orientations of their philosophies. On the one side,
Russell saw names as the way in which we indicate what we directly
experience, while, on the other, Frege saw them as the way in which
we think about the world. Behind this difference were long familiar
issues between empiricism and rationalism and nominalism and concep-
tualism.

Frege's way of dealing with names was an integral part of his view
that language and thought are objective in a way which sheer experience, with its element of "psychological privacy," is not. What was
important for him was whether names stood for a *common currency*,

and whether such objects were *actual* or not was altogether secondary. (He was prepared in the end to speak not only of numbers and logical functions as objects, but also of the True and the False as objects which could be named by sentences.) It was language and thought, and not the intuitions of sense experience, which had access to what was objective.

> I distinguish what I call objective from what is handleable or spatial or real. The axis of the earth is objective, so is the centre of gravity of the solar system, but I should not call them real in the way the earth itself is real. . . . What is objective (in space) is what is subject to laws, what can be conceived and judged, what is expressible in words. What is purely intuitable is not communicable. . . . I understand objective to mean what is independent of our sensation, intuition and imagination, and of all construction of mental pictures out of memories of earlier sensations, but not what is independent of the reason; for to undertake to say what things are like independent of the reason, would be as much as to judge without judging, or to wash the fur without wetting it. (*The Foundations of Arithmetic.* pp. 35-36)

In contrast with this, Russell's way of dealing with names was equally an integral part of his view that "All thinking has to start from acquaintance" (*Logic and Knowledge.* p. 42) and that "all cognitive relations . . . presuppose acquaintance." (p. 127) Names have to stand, in the first instance, for what we directly experience or meet, for otherwise language would make no contact with the world and would not refer to the world.

> What distinguishes the objects to which I can give names from other things is the fact that these objects are within my experience, that I am acquainted with them. (*ibid.*, p. 167)

> A name, in the narrow logical sense of the word whose meaning is a particular, can only be applied to a particular with which the speaker is acquainted, because you cannot name anything you are not acquainted with. (*ibid.*, p. 201)

The tendency of Russell's philosophy was to shrink names to the point where they all but disappeared, making what they referred to as minimal as possible until finally it is questionable whether they referred to anything at all.[1] The tendency of Frege's philosophy, on the other hand, was to expand names, until finally not only definite descriptions, but numbers and even whole sentences could be regarded as names. Russell's *things* became contentless points, and his names shrank to *this* and *that*. (*ibid.*, p. 201) Frege's *objects* became anything, however abstract or complex, which was not a concept.

In Russell's article *On Denoting* (1905) definite descriptions were ruled out as names. Five years later names of instants and points were ruled out as genuine names under the influence of Whitehead. In the article *On the Nature of Acquaintance* (1911) acquaintance with objects of an abstract logical character was still accepted. But by the time of *The Philosophy of Logical Atomism* (1918), which shows the influence of Wittgenstein, although not at this point, aquaintance had narrowed to direct sense experience and even ordinary names were ruled out as names.

> We are not acquainted with Socrates, and therefore cannot name him. When we use the word "Socrates," we are really using a description. (*ibid.*, p. 201)

The analysis of complexes, like tables, chairs and Socrates, Russell now said, brings them down to

> systems or series or classes of particulars, and the particulars are the real things, the particulars being sense data when they happen to be given to you. (*ibid.*, p. 274)

One consequence of this development was the idea that the "pure reference" of a name was something private. A "logically perfect language," Russell said, would be "largely private" because it would be a language in which "all the names that it would use would be private to that speaker and could not enter into the language of another speaker." (*ibid.*, p. 198) On this view what the word *red*, for example, means is what the speaker experiences when he experiences red, and this is something known only to him. Such a "name" was no name at all for Frege because it provided no way of recognizing what it was supposed to stand for, other than the private inexpressible experience of the user, and hence it lacked the publically identifiable reference neces-

---

[1] "The doctrine of Russell amounts very nearly to a rejection of proper names . . . " Alonzo Church: *Introduction to Mathematical Logic*. vol. 1, p. 4. "Names, in fact, can be dispensed with altogether in favor of unnaming general terms . . ." W. V. Quine: *The Ways of Paradox*. p. 128.

sary for a genuine name. Russell's prime name, the word *this* (used "to stand for a particular with which one is acquainted at the moment," (*ibid.*, p. 201)) cannot qualify for Frege because sheer particularity or givenness cannot be designated.

The essential point of difference, already spelled out in Russell's 1905 article, was Frege's contention that a name must have a *sense*, as well as a reference, and that it can even have a sense without having a reference (although then the proposition it belongs to has no truth value). (A sense is something like a thought which goes with a name to enable it to have a reference and so that it can be used again with the *same* reference.[2])

When we turn to the *Tractatus*, the impression is inescapable that what we have is something like Russell's notion of *names* applied to Frege's *objects*. Names, Wittgenstein tells us, are like points, (3.144) and by themselves they do *not* have sense, but only reference, for only propositions have sense. (3.3) But what they refer to or what they point at, is not what Russell said they apply to, bare particulars of sense experience, but rather identifiable objects having properties, and in this respect like Frege's objects. It is as if the Russellian arbitrariness of the name relation *per se* has been transferred from an empirical to a logico-linguistic context. But at the same time this purely referential conception of names rules out definite descriptions as names, as well as names of logical objects and propositions as names. We are left, as it were, with *what remains of Frege's objects if they are to be named by Russell's kind of names.*

Just how Wittgenstein arrived at this can be traced to a certain extent in his *Notes on Logic*, (dated September, 1913), and his *Notebooks* of 1914 and 1915. The *Notes on Logic* are concerned almost entirely with propositions and show that this side of Wittgenstein's philosophy was worked out first, while the ontology and specific ideas about names developed later. All that the *Notes on Logic* tell us about names is that they are "points;" that they are "not things but classes" and that "An indefinable symbol can only be a name." (*Notebooks*. pp. 97, 104, 105)

---

[2] To illustrate this: If I say, for example, "Socrates is dead," it is perfectly possible that I am talking about my cat, which bears the same name as the illustrious philosopher. The expression "my cat" gives a sense for the reference of the name in this case. I might have referred to, or thought of, the same object as "the cat which lives at my house" in which case the name "Socrates" would have had a different sense, though the same reference.

It is in the *Notebooks* that we see Wittgenstein struggling with the question of what kind of ontology is presupposed by his conception of propositions. It is evident that he is looking for *what it is that names really stand for*, and that the terms *things* and *objects* are distinguished, but are used in various over-lapping ways. At the outset he has in mind both *simple objects* and *things*, and we find the question: "Is a point in our visual field a simple object, a thing?" (*ibid.*, p. 2) A half year later comes this entry:

> We can even conceive a body apprehended as in movement, *and together with its movement*, as a thing. So the moon circling round the earth moves round the sun. . . . When I say " 'x' has reference" do I have the feeling: it is impossible that "x" should stand for, say, this knife or this letter? Not at all. On the contrary. (*ibid.*, p. 49)

And the following day he concludes:

> A complex just is a thing!

And a few days later:

> And why should we not say: "There are complexes; one can use names to name them, or propositions to portray them."?

Here is one movement in the *Notebooks*—toward recognizing *things* as *any kind of complexes which can be both named and described*.

At the same time there is another movement—toward recognizing *all objects as simple objects*. We find him saying that "complex objects do not exist" (*ibid.*, p. 63) and that it is "as if all objects were in a certain sense simple objects." (*ibid.*, p. 61) This is because the simplicity of objects is seen as relative to the specific senses of propositions:

> If the complexity of an object is definitive of the sense of the proposition, then it must be portrayed in the proposition to the extent that it does determine the sense. And to the extent that its composition is *not* definitive of *this* sense, to this extent the objects of this proposition are *simple*. (*ibid.*, p. 63)

The *Notebooks* distinguish at first between *complex objects* and *simple objects*:

> Even though we have no acquaintance with simple objects we *do* know complex objects by acquaintance, we know by acquaintance that they are complex. (*ibid.*, p. 50)

These complex objects finally appear as things:

> the matter is not settled by getting rid of names by means of
> definitions: complex spatial objects, for example, seem to me
> in some sense to be essentially things—I as it were see them
> as things—and the designation of them by means of names
> seems to be more than a mere trick of language. (*ibid.*, p. 47)

Things and *objects* here begin to diverge, the former to become what
we are acquainted with and name and describe in ordinary language,
and the latter to become what we are not acquainted with, but what is
needed for definiteness of sense and what is named by "real names."
Two conclusions are beginning to appear: (1) that we can name and
describe any complexes and (2) that simples can only be named. The
expressions *simple things* and *complex objects* are on the way to drop-
ping out; all *things* will become at least implicitly complex while all
objects become simple.

What is not decided in the *Notebooks* is whether there are, in addition to "relative simple objects" required for the specific senses of
propositions, also "absolute simple objects." It is left to the *Tractatus*
to speak of space, time and color as forms of objects and also to present
in many ways the differences between objects and things and the ways
in which objects and pictures are represented in pictures and in different kinds of propositions. These are the subjects to which we now
turn.

ii

What are *objects* or logical simples in the *Tractatus?* They must at
the outset be distinguished, on the one hand, from any material particles or hypothetical material particles like the elementary particles of
modern physics, and, on the other, from geometrical points. The *Tractatus's* objects constitute the basic "systems of sameness and difference"
which make up the internal structural nature of the world. They are
simple in having only one form each, but diverse enough in forms to
establish all possible structures and in external properties to provide all
content. In being both non-material and non-mathematical they resemble, perhaps more than anything else, Leibniz's monads (although,
unlike the monads, there is nothing "psychical" about them).

Like the elementary particles of physics Wittgenstein's objects are
indivisible and *have no parts but only properties.* But the particles of

physics can change into each other or disappear altogether, while Wittgenstein's objects are fixed and unchanging. (2.0271) Unlike both elementary particles and geometrical points they have forms, which means
specific ranges of possible combinations with other objects. All structure in the *Tractatus* ultimately rests, not upon the serial form of numbers or upon the properties of different classes or sets, but upon the
forms or combinatorial possibilities of names and what is named.

We can best understand these objects by thinking of them, not as
geometrical points, but as what would correspond to the *coordinates*
of such points. This is not quite accurate, however, because they are
the ontological equivalents, not of geometrical coordinates, but of what
Wittgenstein calls *logical coordinates,* of which spatial coordinates are
only one kind. (3.41) Logical coordinates permit the representation, not
only of spatial, but also of temporal, color and other phenomena. They
are the ontological equivalents of the "dimensional parameters" necessary to mark different possible places in different "property spaces."
Material properties in general are to be understood, (as Riemann, for
example, understood color), as the external appearances of "multiply-
extended manifolds," any possible place in such a manifold being given
by a structure of such "dimensional parameters." "All that is required
is that we should construct a system of signs with a particular number
of dimensions—with a particular mathematical multiplicity." (5.475)

As the *Tractatus* sees it, the smallest material particle that we can
imagine is still complex in the sense that it can be further described by
propositions of different forms (for example, spatial and temporal
forms). What *cannot* be further described are the dimensional coordinates needed for these descriptions. And what correspond to these
dimensional coordinates are ultimate substantial objects.

A combination of objects is ultimately thus (at the level of elementary propositions) the "internal" structural equivalent of a material
property. But it must not be supposed that such objects are "hypothetical" or "constructed." They make up the substance of the world,
and substance is both form and content, for we need the content or
external properties of the objects in order to recognize the different
structures. The forms and internal properties of objects constitute
structures and internal relations between structures, while the content
or external properties of objects are the material properties which we
use to identify objects and structures of objects.

Objects are not, therefore, merely conveniences for the structural descriptions of properties. For it is the configuration of objects which produces ("internally") structures and ("externally") material properties. (2.0272, 2.0231) Wittgenstein says that, just as we describe objects by their external properties, (and this applies, as will be seen, to the objects of a picture and the objects of a thought), so we describe reality by its internal properties. (4.023) The internal properties of reality are the internal properties of objects (which include not only their possibilities of combination, but the internal relations between their combinations), with the addition of the logical form of reality, which must, as will also be seen, be taken into account as an additional factor.

Objects are intrinsically structural. They cannot be known apart from their possible occurrences in structures, (2.0123) and they do not combine except structurally. (2.03, 2.031) (We use the term *structures* here instead of *states of affairs* because the essential aspect of a state of affairs is that it is a structure of objects.) The *form of an object* is all its possible occurrences in structures, possible occurrences which are known when an object is known. (2.0123) (When we know an object, we know, for example, whether it is spatial, temporal or colored.) The *form of a state of affairs* is all the possible combinations of any "all objects" which are given. (2.0124) (If, for example, we are given three objects, then there are just six possible linear combinations of all of them.) Objects, it may be said, *define possibility*. They establish the complete range of structural possibility for the world.

Now it must be recognized that *none of this applies to things*. Things as things have no forms and hence do not define possible structures. They do not, as it were, belong to the realm of possibility. What Wittgenstein tells us about things is that "It is essential to a thing that it should be a possible constituent (*Bestandteil*) of a state of affairs." (2.011) This being a "possible constituent" of a state of affairs is to be contrasted with objects which "hang together" (*zusammenhängen*) in states of affairs (2.032) or "fit into one another like the links of a chain." (2.03) Things *as things* do not hang together or are not structurally related to each other, although they must be able to enter into states of affairs and (as later parts of the *Tractatus* bring out) function structurally as objects when they correspond to the objects of a picture (2.13, 2.151) or to the objects of a thought. (3.2, 3.221)

This is perhaps the most basic of all the differences between *things* and *objects*: that things *as things* are not structurally related to each

other, while it is the very nature of objects that they are *always* structurally related to other objects. Wittgenstein expresses this by saying
that it is *essential* to things that they can enter into states of affairs,
(2.011) while it is the very *form* of objects that they are structurally
related in states of affairs. (2.0141, 2.031) (Here is the first indication
of the basic difference between *essence* and *form*, understandable in
general this way: the *essence* of the world is *its existing structure*, while
the *form* of the world is *all its possible structures*.)

Structure is *the* central factor in the *Tractatus* because it is only
through possible inner identities of structure that sense-experience (as
representable, though not as *content*, which is "private" and inexpressible), thought, language and world are related. The forms which these
have in common provide the framework for the possible structural
identities which permit the world to be represented. The difference
between the external relations between things and the internal relations
which they acquire when they are pictured, thought of or named as
objects is the crucial difference between *things* and *objects*. What establishes internal relations is that we deal with *all* objects and hence with
all possible structures of these objects. We never, on the other hand,
have in the same sense *all things*, (if only because we can always at any
time alter what it is we are going to name as a *thing*).

It may be said that *objects* define or constitute possible structures,
while *things* have their possible relations "written into them." (2.012)
Thus while things, from one point of view, are more or less accidental
combinations of properties, from another they share in the structural
possibilities of the world, and their occurrences are subject to these
possibilities. This is the measure of their independence and dependence
in this "form of connexion with states of affairs." (2.0122) They are
neither completely divorced from objects nor completely identical
with them.

An illustration will make this clearer. The following three propositions represent three different situations:

> A is west of B
> A is older than B
> A is darker than B

In each of these propositions *A* and *B* might be the names of the same
two different *things* (e.g. tables, men, cities, galaxies). (Certain pos-

sibilities are, nevertheless, excluded; they could not be the names of, for example, days, colors, sounds, feelings. These propositions do not represent possible situations for *those* things.) On the other hand, *A* and *B* could not be the names of the same two different *objects* in all three propositions, because we have here three different forms—spatial, temporal and colored. The propositions require, therefore, three different pairs of *objects*. (When we are able to regard the three propositions this way, we will also regard the specific namable natures of the three relations also as objects, treating the relationality *per se* as purely syntactical, a point to be discussed further below.)

Any common name or proper name that we might fill in for *A* and *B* even in any one of the above propositions would always be the name of a thing. And this shows that we are not acquainted with any objects —or any phenomena which are simply spatial, or simply temporal or simply colored. (A colored patch, for example, always has a spatial shape as well as a temporal duration; a musical sound always has a duration and a pitch, etc.) At this level objects are "formal things," which is to say that they are ordinary things stripped down to one form and content each. (At the still further reduced level where we get rid of relational terms altogether, the proposition itself asserts the existence of one property, and its names stand for the coordinates in logical space of this property; this is an elementary proposition.)

Structure in the *Tractatus* means "combinatoriality," involving always a closed field of possible combinations of given objects, even if this field may change as a whole, (as, for example, we get to know more objects). To have any structure we have to have identifiable units, and we have to be given some "all" of such units and hence some "all possible combinations." Only then may we speak of a structure. Ordinary things do not meet the requirements for establishing such structures because they have too many "parts" and can be taken in too many ways. But objects, each of which has only one form, do meet the requirements. Space, time and color may then be regarded as irreducible kinds of structural possibilities, any particular structure of which may exist or not exist in a given case in accordance with the logical form of reality.

iii

Almost throughout the *Tractatus* Wittgenstein is comparing and contrasting *objects* and *things*, sometimes in adjacent sentences. It is useful in order to get an over-all view to summarize some of the main contrasts in parallel columns before discussing some of them further.

Objects	*Things*
(1) "outside" space and time (2.0251)	"within" space and time (3.1431B)
(2) determine possibility (2.0231)	possibility "in" them (2.012)
(3) hang together in states of affairs (2.032)	possible constituents of states of affairs (2.011)
(4) contain possibility of all situations (2.014)	can occur in all possible situations (2.0122)
(5) known and given (2.0123, 2.0124)	pictured (2.151)
(6) always simple (2.02)	neither simple nor complex (3.24)
(7) internal and external properties (2.01231, 2.0233)	merely properties (2.02331)
(8) internally related (4.123)	externally related (4.122)
(9) can only be named (3.221)	named and described (2.02331)
(10) names designate and mean (3.203)	names only designate (4.243)
(11) distinguished only by names (2.0233)	distinguished by descriptions (2.02331)
(12) totality limits empirical reality (5.5561)	no totality (1.1)

One of the most instructive of these contrasts is the first which is illustrated at 3.1431 where Wittgenstein speaks of tables, chairs and books used as a propositional sign and calls them first *spatial objects* (*räumliche Gegenständen*) and then in the next sentence speaks of *the spatial arrangement of these things (gegenseitige räumliche Lage dieser Dinge)*. This juxtaposition of the two terms *objects* and *things* in adjacent sentences is calculated to bring out a crucial difference between them. The difference is that spatiality is "internal" to the objects (as indicated by the expression "spatial objects") while it is "external" to the things (as indicated by the expression "spatial arrangement of these things"). The things do not tell us that they are to be taken as spatial (instead of, for example, as colored); this stipulation has to be added. But if we have *spatial objects*, only the single form of space is to count, and everything else may be disregarded.

There is a contrast here between space, logically considered as a certain kind of possible relations, and space, empirically considered as a "container" for things. We often think of things as occupying space and as themselves spatially extended. But when we imagine the things as having no extension and no parts, and in addition no other possibilities of combination except spatial ones, then *all* the possible positions of such objects in relation to each other may be taken as defining what *we mean by space*. It was this latter conception which led Leibniz to say: "Space, just like time, is a certain order . . . which embraces not only actuals, but possibles also."[3] and Russell to say: "Space . . . is nothing but relations."[4]

Looked at in terms of *objects*, space is a certain kind of "relationality" inherent in objects themselves; looked at in terms of *things*, it is a prior possibility for arranging things. This is the *Tractatus's* version of the contrast between "relative space" (associated with Leibniz) and "absolute space" (associated with Newton). Einstein, who adopted the former view, described the two alternatives thus:

> These two concepts of space may be contrasted as follows: (a) space as positional quality of the world of material objects; (b) space as container of all material objects. In case (a), space without a material object is inconceivable. In case (b), a material object can only be conceived as existing in space; space then appears as a reality which in a certain sense is superior to the material world.[5]

Einstein then added:

> It required a severe struggle to arrive at the concept of independent and absolute space, indispensable for the development of theory. It has required no less strenuous effort sub-

---

[3] Quoted by Bertrand Russell in *A Critical Exposition of the Philosophy of Leibniz.* p. 245.

[4] Bertrand Russell—*Foundations of Geometry.* p. 128.

[5] Foreword to Max Jammer — *Concepts of Space*, (Harvard Univ. Press, 1957), p. xiv.

sequently to overcome this concept—a process which is probably by no means as yet completed.[6]

In the *Tractatus* not only space, but time and color also are, logically
considered, systems of different kinds of possible relations. Wittgenstein calls them "forms of objects,"[7] (2.0251) which means ways in
which different kinds of objects are able to combine. The objects themselves must be thought of as spaceless, timeless and colorless (2.0232),
only their configuration producing specific shapes, durations and colors.
(2.0231) In his *Foundations of Geometry* (1897) Russell had objected
to Riemann's conception of color as a multiply-extended manifold like
space, on the grounds that color points would have to be qualitatively
different, whereas space points are all the same. (p. 66) For Wittgenstein, however, both kinds of objects are not homogeneous, but *dimen-
sionally* different. It is evident that he had in mind the three color dimensions of hue, brightness and saturation, paralleling the three dimensions of space.[8] Such three-dimensional color space provides logical
places for all possible colors.[9]

A second contrast between *objects* and *things* occurs at 3.221 where
Wittgenstein writes:

> Objects can only be *named*. Signs are their representatives.
> I can speak *about* them. I cannot *put them into words*. Proposi-
> tions can only say *how* things are, not *what* they are.

Here the shift from *objects* to *things* is instructive because there is no
possibility of saying *what objects are* (since, because they are simple,
they can only be named). We might, however, be tempted to suppose
that we can say what things are since they can not only be named, but

---

[6] *Ibid.*, p. xv. In the *Tractatus* only infinity belongs to "absolute space";
(2.0131A) everything else belongs to relative, "knowable" space.

[7] Something like this idea as regards space goes back at least to medieval
thought. We are told that "The Moslem theologians think that matter is composed
of ultimate particles indivisible and altogether spaceless by themselves, forming
space by their combinations." Israel Isaac Efros—*The Problem of Space in Jewish
Medieval Philosophy.* p. 48.

[8] See Wittgenstein—*Zettel.* p. 49 where he raises the possibility of four-dimensional color. What Wittgenstein seems to overlook is that color is a characteristic
of light and not merely a property of objects.

[9] See Alphonse Chapanis—*Color Names for Color Space* in Wallace R. Brode
(edt.)—*Science in Progress. Sixteenth Series.* pp. 105-132. Also see Appendix 2 of
the present book on *Multiply-Extended Manifolds,* which discusses the Russell-
Riemann disagreement.

can also be described. (2.02331) It is Wittgenstein's point, however, that even in describing things we simply go on saying more about *how* they are and do not even in this case get to any *what*. The *what* always *turns into the how* because the *content* of the world does not in any circumstances get into propositions (since a proposition contains only the form and not the content of its sense (3.13)). Names are the closest we get to the content of the world, but they are always "formal," and content as such remains inexpressible.

Still a third example of the terms *objects* and *things* in juxtaposition occurs at 4.0311-4.0312, where, speaking of propositions representing situations, Wittgenstein says: "One name stands for one thing, another for another thing, and they are combined with one another." In the next entry he adds: "The possibility of propositions is based on the principle that objects have signs as their representatives." And this is followed by the important sentence: "My fundamental idea is that the 'logical constants' are not representatives; that there can be no representatives of the *logic* of facts."

These three sentences, appearing virtually in sequence, make three critical and closely inter-related points. They tell us: (1) that we *do* name things, (2) that when we name things, we do it on the principle of naming objects (*meaning* them as objects), and (3) but that we must not think that we can name anything that belongs to the "logical articulation" of the world, such as relations *qua* relations, or predicates *qua* predicates. It will be seen that we do name relations and predicates, not *as* relations and predicates, but only in their particularity as "objects of thought." (3.2)

To see the inter-relatedness of the three sentences quoted the term "logical constants" must be extended to cover the structural or syntactical aspects of ordinary propositions. And the prohibition against "logical constants" being "representatives" (or "standing for" anything) can then be seen as a prohibition against supposing that we can name "relationality" or "predicability," both of which are features of logical structure shown by syntactical *ways of designating*. *What* we name when we name relations, for example, is *not* their relationality (that is shown by where the name appears in the proposition (3.1432) or some other syntactical device), but the particularity of the relation, its thing-like or object-like character.

The cases where *objects* and *things* are juxtaposed are test cases for understanding the differences between them. The fundamental difference, however, is implicit throughout the whole text and lies in the consideration that objects *determine* possibility, while things have possibility "prejudged" (*präjudiziert*) in them (or "written into them") (2.012) The key sentence introducing objects and telling us why we need them is "Logic deals with every possibility, and all possibilities are its facts." (2.0121C) It is *objects* which provide all these possibilities, and they do it because they always come as *all* objects (5.524), which is far from being the case with things.

Wittgenstein's "finite combinatorial ontology" would appear to be an extension of what is involved in truth functional logic, where a set of initial elementary propositions must be considered as a "totality" in constructing truth possibilities. To have truth functions, in other words, we have to have all elementary propositions taken as a whole, the truth functions necessarily being set up for *all* of them at once. Since each elementary proposition in turn involves a finite number of names, for any set of elementary propositions we have at the same time what will count as *all objects*. This is spelled out at 5.524 where Wittgenstein says:

> If objects are given, then at the same time we are given *all* objects.
> If elementary propositions are given, then at the same time *all* elementary propositions are given.

Without these two *all*'s there is no logic in the *Tractatus's* sense. The ontology is, in effect, a natural concomitant of the logic.

This much of the contrast between *objects* and *things* may be summed up by saying that *objects* are always internally or structurally related and never anything but internally or structurally related, while *things*, on the other hand, are externally related in situations and only become internally related when they are objects in terms of pictures or thoughts. Just how this comes about, or how things become objects is what must now be examined.

iv

There are three different contexts in which *objects* appear in the *Tractatus*: (1) as what elements of pictures correspond to; (2.13) (2) as what elements of completely analyzed propositions correspond to; (3.2) and (3) as what elementary propositions name. The central thrust of the book lies in its descriptions of these three contexts and the ways in which they are related. And the success or failure of the *Tractatus as a system* probably depends more than anything else upon how plausible the attempts to relate them are.[10]

The three contexts are those of (1) sense experience (pictures), (2) ordinary language and (3) the essence of language or completely structural language. Objects are shown to be involved in all three, for Wittgenstein's main thesis is that *it is the structures which objects alone provide which make it possible for sense experience, thought and language to represent the world.*

The differences between the three contexts are shown by the circumstances that (1) in the case of pictures we have to deal with possible structures of *entities* and *things;* (2.15, 2.151) (2) in the case of ordinary language we have to deal with possible structures of *things* (including properties and relations as objects); (4.0311) and (3) in the case of elementary propositions we have to deal with possible structures of *objects.* The third case is the essential core of the other two.

With this in mind we can look at the three "kinds of objects" (which are, of course, all simply *objects*):

(1) *objects of a picture.* These are what the elements of a picture "correspond to" or "stand for." (2.13, 2.131) They are "correlated to" *entities* or occurrences of "sense phenomena" such as lines, shapes, colors, tones, etc. (2.1514) The "pictorial relationship," Wittgenstein tells us, consists of the correlations of the picture's elements (corresponding to *objects*) with *entities.* This is the way by which sense phenomena are represented structurally, whether this takes place in sense experience or in the actual physical creation of pictures. To visualize it we may imagine a picture hanging on the wall which contains nothing but, let us suppose, two black lines. These lines may be "correlated to" entities, such as, for example, two edges of a table if it happened to be possible to do this.[11] There are, of course, many ways in which the correlations can be made. Any picture has three forms, or "kinds of

---

[10] This is the Wittgenstein version of the old Platonic question of how the changing world of things (as pictured and referred to in ordinary language) is related to the unchanging world of objects (forms). See Appendix 3 for a discussion of this.

[11] If we had only one line, the "entities" would involve the *ends* of the line, and the picture of the line would be laid against the line in the world as one might lay a ruler against it, only the end points actually touching the object to be measured. (2.1512, 2.15121) It should be noted that we *measure objects* while we *picture entities,* and Wittgenstein is only giving an analogy here.

possibility," two of which (pictorial form and logical form) it has in common with reality (2.17, 2.18) and a third (representational form) which it does not have in common with reality, but which places it "outside" its subject. It is the third form which accounts for the possibility of different *kinds* of correlations, while the first two account for the possibility of any correlations at all.

(2) *objects of thought.* These are what the elements of a propositional sign "correspond to" when a proposition has been "completely analyzed." (3.2, 3.201) They are what simple signs or names in such a proposition *mean.* (3.202, 3.203) It will be seen that they are things, properties and relations when the complete analysis of a proposition has made it possible for us to *name* them and hence *mean* them as objects. It is the analysis of propositions which enable us to separate the semantic or "meaning" factor (the object meant) from the syntactical or "use" factor, which is the *way* in which the object is meant (i.e. as a thing, a property or a relation). We are so accustomed to regarding "propertyness" or "relationality" as parts of the "meaning-content" of property terms or relational terms that it is difficult at first to grasp Wittgenstein's view that the specific "content" of a property or a relation must be separated from the question of whether it *is* a property or a relation. But the point is that "propertyness" and "relationality" are not *parts* of what is designated, but belong entirely to the *way* in which something is designated. And this is shown by the consideration that any property or relation can appear as a thing to which further properties or relations can be ascribed. (e.g. *Green is cool. Fencing is harder than wrestling.*) Whether or not something is being named *as* a property or *as* a relation or *as* a thing is a matter of syntax. We do not *designate* it as that. We can only *designate* properties and relations as, in effect, things, while in a completely analyzed proposition we name them and mean them as objects.[12]

(3) *substantial objects* (or the objects named by elementary propositions). While the elements of a picture and the elements of a completely analyzed proposition "correspond to" objects, the elements of an elementary proposition do not "correspond to" objects, but are the names of objects. It is only elementary propositions which are un-

---

[12] This point is discussed at greater length below, especially in Chpt. 3, sect. vi, (topic (3)) and Chpt. 4, sects. ii, iii, iv.

equivocally confronted with the ultimate objects of the world. Substantial objects are, therefore, neither entities, things, properties or relations, but the final combinatorial units of all structure, presupposed by every other "kind of unit," but only directly named when we do not need to qualify any name syntactically any more and only "combinatorial syntax" is required to convey all sense.

All three "kinds of objects"—objects of pictures, objects of thought and substantial objects—behave in the same way: all are identifiable (although substantial objects have a "reduced" identity, a matter discussed below in section vi); all have forms or ranges of possible combinations with each other; and all are depicted in ways which may be correct or incorrect, true or false.

There is what might be called a *strict analogy* between pictures, completely analyzed propositions and elementary propositions. A picture represents possible structures of *entities* (and also of *things*) *in the same way* that a completely analyzed proposition represents possible structures of *things* (now including also properties and relations) and both of these do it *in the same way* that an elementary proposition represents possible structures of *objects*. Objects with forms are involved in all three cases.

The *differences* between the three "kinds of objects" may be summed up as follows:

(1) in the case of *pictorial objects* (correlated to entities) particular *pictorial forms* (space, time, color) prescribe the ways the objects may be combined and so may be said to be "external" to the objects themselves;

(2) in the case of *objects of thought* pictorial forms are, as it were, "included in" *logical forms* (which is to say that thoughts themselves are not spatial, temporal or colored), but the logical forms are now in the same way "external" to the objects, requiring in completely analyzed propositions syntactical devices to supply logical articulation;

(3) in the case of *substantial objects* both pictorial forms and logical forms are intrinsic to the objects and are conveyed entirely by combinatorial possibilities: (1) pictorial forms are incorporated as the forms of objects and (2) logical forms are incorporated as the forms of states of affairs arranged in terms of their possibilities of existence and non-existence.

We would expect these three cases to be paralleled by similar differences in ways of showing forms, and they are, for

(1) a picture "displays" (*aufweisen*) its pictorial form (2.172);

(2) a completely analyzed proposition "corresponds to" (*entspricht*) a logical form (3.315) and

(3) an elementary proposition has or shows a logical form. (5.555)

The distinction which is often overlooked is that between *completely analyzed propositions* and *elementary propositions*. Both contain names (and "It is only in the nexus of an elementary proposition that a name occurs in a proposition" (4.23)), but, strictly speaking, it is only elementary propositions which may be said to be "functions of names" (4.24) and only in elementary propositions that we have "names in immediate combination" (4.221) not requiring any additional logical articulation. The names in completely analyzed propositions still require syntactical devices to indicate the ways in which some of the names designate (whether as subject terms, predicate terms or relational terms), but this is no longer the case with elementary propositions where all the syntax is "internal" and given only by the combinations themselves.

In connection with various discussions about nominalism and realism it should be noted that properties remain as ultimate features of the world in the *Tractatus*, though not as "separate entities." Properties do not disappear in the transition from completely analyzed propositions to elementary propositions. The ultimate objects of the world have properties —both internal and external, the internal properties being shown by the way the objects combine and by internal similarities between the combinations, and the external properties appearing as what is available to identify the objects, either singly or in their combinations.

v

The difference between *objects* and *things* may also be looked at from the point of view of language. It is convenient then to recognize, not two, but three levels of language:

(1) *ordinary language* in which *words* are the simple signs (4.026, 3.14) and in which we have *expressions* which mark (*kennzeichnen*) a form and content (3.31D).

(2) *completely analyzed language* in which *names* are the simple signs (3.201) and these names *designate (bezeichnen)* things (4.243, 4.0311) and *mean objects of thought;* (3.203) and

(3) *essential language* (or elementary propositional language) in which *logically simple names* are the simple signs (3.202) and simple symbols (4.24) standing in immediate combination (*unmittelbarer Verbindung*) with each other; (4.221)

The principle of "all possible structures" (or what might be called in grammar "all possible word orders for a finite vocabulary") may be said to operate as the fundamental and essential one in all these cases. What is done in the analysis of language is to strip away conventional aspects (conventional grammatical forms) to arrive at essential aspects (corresponding to logical form). This "complete analysis," however, is still not final because it still leaves us with the necessity of distinguishing between subjects and predicates and between both of these and relational terms. The *Tractatus*, therefore, takes the further step of replacing even these distinctions with "immediate combinations of names," allowing a combination as a whole to represent a single property.

We are left with the essence of language as *structural representations of single properties.* Since such structural representations must also be capable of being true or false, they are in *logical form* (or the *form of reality*), which is the form which permits only one structure of all the possible structures of the names in a given proposition to exist in one logical place.

As the *Tractatus* looks at language, ordinary language with its conventional grammar conceals structure because, although it operates on the principle of "naming objects," the objects which it purports to name are *things,* which are far from simple. We have to have "real names," designating genuinely simple objects, before the structural skeleton is exposed; then we can see how ordinary language manages to do so much on the basis of "constructed simplicity" utilizing in a literally inconceivable variety of ways the principle of naming objects.

Something of the difference between naming things and naming objects comes out in the distinction between *designating (bezeichnen)* and *meaning (bedeuten).* Wittgenstein speaks of names designating things (4.243) and also of names designating objects (3.322, 3.3411, 4.126, 4.127). And he also speaks of names meaning objects. (3.203) But it is important that he never speaks of names meaning things. We *cannot* mean a thing *as a thing* because a thing is not a determinate referent. It is not a form and a content, (but, as it were, an assemblage of various properties of different forms). We can only name a thing by disregarding its complexity, which does not even come into question unless there is "an indeterminateness in the proposition in which it (a propositional element) occurs." (3.24D)

Wittgenstein speaks of designating and designation in cases where meaning is not in question (for example, designation of generality (4.0411, 5.522, 6.1203); designating formal concepts (4.127) and designating propositions (4.442)). It might appear that we have to be able to designate in order to mean, but not the reverse, and that meaning is something like exact and determinate designation. Wittgenstein's other uses of the term *meaning*, however, show that this is not the case. He speaks, for example, of philosophy as "meaning" what cannot be said (4.115), of truth possibilities of elementary propositions which "mean possibilities of existence and non-existence of states of affairs" (4.3) and of the limits of my language which "mean the limits of my world." (5.6) In these cases it would be more accurate to say that meaning is just what we *cannot* exactly designate. Objects are distinctive in that they *can* be both designated and meant. Here the two coincide.

The distinction between *objects* and *things* in relation to names is brought out at 4.243 where Wittgenstein asks:

> Can we understand two names without knowing whether they signify (*bezeichnen*) the same thing or two different things? Can we understand a proposition in which two names occur without knowing whether their meaning (*bedeuten*) is the same or different?

The wordings of these two questions indicate that names which signify or *designate things* can be understood apart from propositions, but names which *mean objects* cannot be understood apart from propositions. In the second case it is propositions which we understand.

This should be linked with the statement that "It is only in the nexus (*Zussamenhange*) of an elementary proposition that a name occurs in a proposition." (4.23) This tells us that when a name occurs in a proposition, even if the name designates a thing, it still *means the thing as an object*, because in *any* proposition a name stands in internal structural relations with the other names in the proposition, and this is the general condition for names occurring in any propositions at all. As the above quotation indicates, names may *designate* apart from propositions, but they cannot *mean* apart from propositions. And this parallels the partial independence of *things* which, within the limits of their possibilities, can be in many different situations, as against objects which "hang together" structurally in states of affairs. (2.0122)

In addition to the terms *designate* (*bezeichnen*) and *mean* (*bedeuten*) Wittgenstein uses, with regard to the expressions in ordinary propositions, the term *mark* or *characterize* (*kennzeichnen*). Any part of a proposition which is essential to the sense of a proposition and which propositions can have in common is called an *expression* (*Ausdruck*). Such an expression is said to *mark* (*kennzeichnen*) a form and content and in so doing to *characterize* (*characterisieren*) the sense of a proposition. (3.31)

Ordinary language compels us to start with expressions, rather than with single words (or even with signs and symbols), because ordinary language makes use of descriptive phrases which have the same references as single words. Expressions have meanings, (3.314) but they are not said to designate because expressions include descriptive phrases, and there is an ambiguity resulting from the condition that the individual words in a descriptive phrase have different designations from the phrase as a whole. This and various other ambiguities have to be removed before we can talk about names.

In a broad sense and speaking very roughly, we have to move in the *Tractatus* from expressions *marking* things to names *designating* things and finally to names *meaning* things as objects. And unless the final step is somehow implicit at the beginning the transitions cannot be made. What has to be uncovered in the end is the complete arbitrariness of a name together with its completely terminal reference and its inevitable syntax. And at this point we have simple meanings. Wittgenstein sums this up in the *Blue Book* (p. 34):

> What one wishes to say is: "Every sign is capable of interpretation; but the meaning mustn't be capable of interpretation. It is the last interpretation."

vi

The point at which the *Tractatus* is likely to strike most philosophical readers as most traditional and yet at the same time most divergent from tradition is in its conception of *substance*. The notion of sub-

stance as "what subsists independently of what is the case" (2.024)
and as "what is fixed, subsistent" *(das Feste, Bestehende)* in contrast
to "what is changing and unstable" *(das Wechseldne, Unbeständige)*
(2.0271) has a familiar Parmenidean ring. And familiar echoes are also
evoked by the notions that substance is the form of any world (2.022)
and that objects to make up the substance of the world must be simple.
(2.021)

What is not so familiar, and is harder to find any precedent for, is
the uniting of "atomism" and "formalism," and particularly the idea
that what exists is *combinations* of "atoms" and not "atoms" by themselves. It is the conception that a single ultimate object is not "self-con-
tained," but is necessarily linked to other objects. The ultimate units
of the world are not "in-themselves," but, as it were, "in-their-com-
binations." Reality belongs to structures, and not to the components
of structures in isolation.

This "structuralist" conception of substance reflects the shift from
traditional term logic to the propositional logic of Frege and of Whitehead and Russell. The metaphysics of the *Tractatus* is the metaphysics
of propositional, rather than term, logic. Just as propositional logic does
not permit us to take terms in isolation from each other, but only in
their propositional relations, so substance, as the *Tractatus* conceives it,
is no longer objects in isolation, but only objects in combination with
each other.

This involves what may be called a "principle of duality," analogous
to the "principle of duality" in projective geometry, which states that
points and lines cannot be defined independently of each other, and
also analogous to the similar duality of arguments and functions in the
theory of functions. In a similar way objects in the *Tractatus* cannot
be separated from their possible combinations. They are "identifiable,"
but ultimately, as will be seen, only "identifiable" in combinations.
(Such objects are not for that reason any less simple, since their simplicity consists in their having no parts and only one form each.)

Wittgenstein's "principle of duality" applies to *objects* and *states
of affairs* (and, equivocally, and with reservations, to *things* and *situations*), and it also applies to *names* and *propositions*. In the latter case
he formulates it thus: "Only in the nexus *(Zussamenhange)* of a proposition does a name have meaning." (3.3) More generally, it is formulated: "An expression only has meaning in a proposition," (3.314)
and "Like Frege and Russell I construe a proposition as a function of

the expressions contained in it." (3.318) And, still more generally, he says that words do not have two separate roles—by themselves and in propositions—but their role is the same in both cases. (2.0122)

Another way of stating the *Tractatus's* "principle of duality" is to say that the *meanings of names* cannot be divorced from the *senses of propositions*. When we try to represent either expressions or names by variables, these variables have to be understood as taking *propositions* as their values. (3.313, 3.314) The meaning of an expression may be said to be a function of all the senses of the propositions which the expression actually "characterizes." (3.31) (The "propositional bond" in the case of expressions is this "characterizing of a sense" while in the case of names it is also the "nexus" of a structure.)

When in ordinary life we mention a word in isolation and say that we know what it "means," we are in effect saying that we know all the ways in which it is used in propositions. This is in part a conventional matter, and we can classify the propositions which have the same expressions in common and in this way describe an expression as "the common characteristic mark of a class of propositions." (3.311) (A name, on the other hand, occurs in the nexus of a proposition, and its meaning is a function of all the *possible* ways in which it *can* occur.)

vii

It is the "principle of duality" which results in what is in many ways the most radical step in the *Tractatus*: the rejection of identity for objects and things and particularly the rejection of Leibniz's principle of the "identity of indiscernibles" (a rejection, however, which involves an acceptance, and even an extension, of Leibniz's related idea that there are no two identical things in the universe).

The basis for what the *Tractatus* has to say about this lies in the distintion between *identity* and *sameness*. No two objects or two things can be *identical* (for otherwise they would not be *two*), (5.5301, 5.5303) but they can be the *same*, since they *can be indistinguishable from each other while being just different*. Sameness and difference-in-some-respect are here made to depend upon difference-as-such, or mere numerical difference, with no difference of properties to mark this difference. *Two* things, in other words, must be *just* different *before* they can be said to be the same or different-in-some-particular-respect.

Two point are made here: (1) that "identity is not a relation between objects" (5.5301) while "to say of two things that they are identical is nonsense" (5.5303) (i.e. merely having *two* objects or *two* things prevents them from being identical) and (2) that objects or things *can* be different without being different in any respect. (2.0233, 2.02331) In the case where things are different without being different in any respect we can say that they are the *same* although we cannot say that they are *identical*, since they are still two.

Another distinction between *things* and *objects* appears here. Wittgenstein says that if a *thing* can be distinguished at all, it can be distinguished by a *description*, (that is, by describing the properties which it has which nothing else has). (2.02331) Objects having the same logical form, on the other hand, are not distinguished by descriptions, but only by external properties (that is, by being named differently). (2.0233) This means that we cannot identify a thing unless it has unique properties which could be described. But objects can get their "identities" structurally, provided that we have some way in which different structures can be identified. (When we depart from simply naming an object and describe it by its external properties, (4.023) then what we are dealing with is no longer an object, but a thing, which will have to be described in terms of some other objects, which in turn will be just simply named.) Mere naming of objects differently can mark them as different, while naming them with the same sign can mark them as the same.

One of several versions of his principle of the "identity of indiscernibles" which Leibniz gave appears in the *Monadology* (section 9): "For there are never two things in nature which are perfectly alike and in which it is impossible to find a difference that is internal or founded on an intrinsic discrimination."[13] The first part of this (which he phrases elsewhere as "There is no perfect similarity anywhere")[14] Wittgenstein accepts. But the second part (which Leibniz elsewhere phrases as "there are no two individual things in nature which differ only numerically. For surely it must be possible to give a reason why they are different, and this must be sought in some difference within themselves."[15])—this Wittgenstein does not accept.

Leibniz's view is that in nature differences between individual

---

[13] Liebniz—*Philosophical Papers and Letters*, (Leroy Loemker edt.), vol. 2, p. 1045.

[14] *Ibid.*, vol. 2, p. 822.

[15] *Ibid.*, vol. 1, p. 413.

things must be differences of properties, so that each thing must have at least one intrinsic property which no other thing has. In opposition to this, Wittgenstein says that there may be "several things that have the whole set of their properties in common" and in this case we cannot distinguish (*hervorheben*) one from the other, (2.02331) although, in his view, they may still be numerically different. That there may be other properties distinguishing them which we do not know about does not come into account, since the analysis of things leads to finite totalities of objects and structures of objects and not to infinite sets of properties—in the manner of Leibniz. This is why Wittgenstein speaks of "the whole set of their properties," implying that in dealing with things we are always dealing with limited sets of available properties. It is because we must talk about things as objects and in terms of objects (and hence in terms of "all possibilities") that we cannot recognize further intrinsic properties which cannot be so described. Intrinsic or internal properties are *all* exposed in objects and their structures, and differences which we cannot show that way cannot be shown.

An objection that is sometimes raised to this takes the form: How can two things have all their properties in common, for would they not at least be in two different places and so at least not have that property in common? The difficulty with this is that we have no way of determining the spatial places except by reference to the things considered as objects (which must, therefore, already be identifiable in some other way) or by reference to some other objects. If there were no way of distinguishing two things apart from their "places," there would be no way of telling one spatial relation from the same spatial relation with the terms reversed. (We can only say that "a being to the left of b" differs from "b being to the left of a" if a and b are already distinguishable from each other in some other way which guarantees that the two signs *a* and *b* are being used "consistently.")[16]

If (as Leibniz and Wittgenstein both maintain) space is an order of possible relations, (or a manifold of possible places), we need, as it were, already identifiable objects (or things considered as objects) to distinguish one relation or one place from another. We cannot,

---

[16] The objection that two things could always be distinguished because at least a would always have the property of "being different from b" and b the property of "being different from a" begs the question because it supposes that *these two properties are different*, which in turn supposes that we can already distinguish a and b in some other way.

therefore, use space to distinguish the objects. (And the same will apply to other "orders of possibility"—such as time and color. Although such "leap-frogging" is possible with regard to *things*, we cannot finally use colors to distinguish *objects*, if we need *objects* to distinguish colors.)

It will serve no purpose to "name" a group of things which are all the same differently if there is no way to tell which was named which when the things turn up again. And this is why things must be describably different to be significantly named differently. But we can still recognize the case where we cannot do this and where the things are just different without being able to be distinguished in this way. And this is the point where the disagreement with Leibniz comes. Sheer multiplicity or difference-as-such is possible in the case of *things even though it does not provide the possibility of genuine names.*

The case remains different, however, with *objects*. We must recall that it is objects in configuration which *produce* material properties (2.0231) and objects in states of affairs which are the structural equivalents of such properties. The question arises how we are able to name objects separately if we do not have access to them separately, but only in their combinations. The answer seems to be that if we can at least distinguish each of the possible structures of the objects, we can, *on that basis*, name the objects in such a way as to account for the different structures in terms of the different possible arrangements. It is just the material properties of the world which provide the ways of identifying the different structures and hence of naming the objects. (To illustrate this: If we had three eggs which were indistinguishable from each other, they *could* be distinguished if we could at least distinguish each of the six possible linear arrangements of the eggs. Each arrangement might be marked by a different color. We could then arrange the names so that each color would correspond to a different arrangement of the names and of the eggs.) This is the kind of "reduced identity" which objects have. In the *Tractatus*, in the case of elementary propositions, it is material properties which seem to permit us to identify different structures of objects and hence to name objects "individually" even when we have no access to them "individually."

Propositions and Pictures

A proposition may well be an incomplete picture of a certain situation, but it is always a *complete* picture.

WITTGENSTEIN 5.156

Completeness without completion is useful.

LAOTZU

The existence and non-existence of states of affairs is reality.

WITTGENSTEIN 2.06

We have the benefit of existence when we make use of non-existence.

LAOTZU

There is a perfection of a dream, an echo, a reflected image, a mirage or an illusion because it is informed about non-production.

Astasahasrika

There are primarily two schools of thought on the nature of the proposition. Of these two one believes in the indivisibility of the proposition, while the other admits its divisibility.

GAURINATH SASTRI

CHAPTER 3

Propositions and Pictures

i

One answer to the question "What is the subject of the *Tractatus?*" is *Propositions—the nature and kinds of propositions.*[1] And perhaps the best way to see the organization of the book is to see it in terms of this subject matter. Wittgenstein's numbering of the main sections then follows this scheme:[2]

1 and 2 — world and pictures as what is expressed in propositions
3 — analysis of propositions
4 — nature of propositions
5 — internal relations between propositions
6 — the general form of a proposition
       6.1 — logical propositions
       6.2 — mathematical propositions
       6.3 — scientific propositions
       6.4 — ethical propositions (there are none)
       6.5 — the unsayable and "my propositions"
7 — silence

In his *Notebooks* Wittgenstein says: "My *whole* task consists in explaining (*erklaren*) the nature of the proposition." (p. 39) (And he adds: "That is to say, in giving the nature of all facts whose picture the proposition *is*. In giving the nature of all being. And here being does not stand for existence—in that case it would be nonsensical.") Earlier he had written: "The point for us is simply to complete logic." (p. 4)

---

[1] No special term appears more often in the book than the term *Satz* (meaning either *sentence* or *proposition*). It is used more than 200 times in the 75 pages of the German text and another 75 times in various compounds such as *Elementarsatz* and *Satzzeichen.*

[2] See Appendix 1 for a discussion of the numbering and organization of the book.

These two tasks—*giving the nature of the proposition* and *completing logic*—are one and the same, because in his view if a proposition is possible at all, it is already "logical" and already involves the whole of logical space. (4.023E) The logic takes care of itself when a sense has been supplied to a proposition by giving meaning to certain of its parts. (*Notebooks*. p. 2) There cannot, in other words, be a proposition with sense without its already having logical form. The *Notebooks* put this very clearly by saying that a proposition "represents a possibility and itself *conspicuously* forms one part of a whole, whose features it bears—and from which it stands out." (p. 56)

A proposition contains the *possibility* of its truth, (p. 16) or the *possibility* of an existence, (p. 27) but no more than this. In order to contain just this much and no more it must meet two conditions: (1) it must express *one sense* or represent one possibility out of a range of all possibilities and (2) it must represent, not the *world*, (what exists), but *reality* (what exists and does not exist).

What is meant by these terms *sense, logical form, world* and *reality* comprises the brunt of what the *Tractatus* has to say about propositions.

ii

If we want to understand the *essence* of a propositional sign, Wittgenstein tells us, we should consider one composed of *spatial objects* (such as tables, chairs and books) or of the *spatial arrangement of such things*. (3.1431)

Before we discuss the question of how an arrangement of such objects *or* such an arrangement of things can function as a propositional sign we need to look more closely at these two arrangements and to add to them still one more which Wittgenstein calls *configuration (Konfiguration)*. For we have to do in the *Tractatus*, not merely with *objects*-(or things)-*in-states-of-affairs* and *things-in-situations*, but also with *objects-in-configuration* (2.0231, 2.0272) (also called *objects-in-the-situation*. (3.21))

These are, in effect, three different ways of looking at an arrangement, which in a certain sense remains the same arrangement. It can be seen as:

1 — *Configuration.* What is altogether changing and unstable. (2.0271) Objects entirely divorced from structure or possibil-

ity, or from any relations with each other. It should be noted that the word *configuration* has no plural in the *Tractatus*, and this is because there is no way of identifying *a* configuration, or telling one configuration from another. Wittgenstein says that the changing configuration of objects produces (*bilden*) both material properties and structures of objects. (2.0231, 2.0272)

2 — *Situations (Sachlagen)*. Arrangements of *things*, or of items which are complex and hence can be further described and stand in external relations to each other. Since things must be possible constituents of states of affairs, (2.011) but do not "hang together" in states of affairs until they are taken as "objects of a thought," (3.2) every situation is at the same time a possible state of affairs.

3 — *States of affairs (Sachverhalte)*. Structures of *objects*, or arrangements in which the relations between the objects are internal, since every state of affairs is one of "all possible states of affairs," or one structure is one of all possible structures of its objects. (2.03, 2.033) Since if any objects are given, we are given *all* objects (5.524A) and since if all objects are given, all possible states of affairs are also given, (2.0124) we are always dealing with finite combinatorial manifolds when we are dealing with states of affairs.

To distinguish these three we may say that when configuration involves external relations, or relations which in a completely analyzed proposition will themselves have to be "named," we have a *situation*. But when all the relations are internal, which means when all the objects involved have only one and the same form, then we have a state of affairs. (And this is the difference between a spatial arrangement of *things*, where it is necessary to specify the *kind of arrangement*, and an arrangement of spatial *objects*, where the *form of the objects* settles the structural possibilities.)

Wittgenstein tells us that objects, besides having determinate relations to each other in states of affairs, "contain the possibility of all situations." (2.014) This means that the inherent possibilities of combination of objects set limits to all the possible situations of things. (2.0122) Things have their possibilities of combination "written into"

them, (2.012) so that the varieties of possible external relations may be
said to be conditional upon the possibilities of internal relations. (To
illustrate this—we cannot with literal sense speak about a *day* as *colored;*
this is not a possible situation, and it is not a possible situation because
these properties cannot be conjoined in a fact.)

In order to take things as objects it is necessary to take them as
having just one form (for example, as being merely spatial) and lump
together all their other properties as "external properties," serving only
as a means of identifying them. (2.01, 2.0122, 3.1431B) Such an object
may be said to be described by giving its external properties, but such
a description does not make any assertion about it. (4.023)

From all this it can be seen that configuration as such cannot be
described. When we try to describe it, it becomes either a state of
affairs (*internally related objects*) or a possible situation (*externally
related things.*) The two kinds of propositional descriptions of *objects-
in-states-of-affairs* and *things-in-situations* are not, however, ultimately
independent of each other because the latter finally depends upon the
former and must make use of it. How this is done is part of the subse-
quent discussion.

iii

We turn to the questions: What has to happen to an arrangement
of tables, chairs and books to make it into a *picture?* And what has to
happen to it to make it into a *propositional sign?* And what is the difference between them?

In a museum we might see a room in which various items of furniture were arranged as a reproduction of another room (for example,
some historically important room). There might also be a doll house
version of this in which the same items appeared scaled down in size.
And, further, there might be a black and white drawing, an oil painting or a blue-print of the same room hanging on the wall. All these
would qualify as pictures under certain conditions. The question is:
What are the conditions which make them pictures?

The principal conditions are that they must *represent* (*darstellen*)
and themselves *present* (*vorstellen*) what they represent. (2.11, 2.15)
What makes them pictures is that in each case we can tell from what
they present the way something else is. Wittgenstein says that the elements of a picture are "correlated" to entities in such a way that the
picture "includes the pictorial relationship which makes it into a pic-

ture." (2.1513) This puzzling statement is sometimes taken to mean that a picture becomes a picture by being "correlated" to entities in the world. But such an interpretation leaves out a step. Wittgenstein's view seems rather to be that the "correlations" are *within* the picture itself and touch reality *within* the picture. The content of a picture itself is "correlated" to reality *before* it represents anything in the world, and it may *then* represent a fact or any reality whose form and logical form it has. (We can, for example, recognize a table in a picture without correlating it to any particular table because the elements of the picture are already correlated to entities in such a way as to picture that reality *within* the picture. We can *then* say that it is this table or that table in the world.)

In the pictures of the room mentioned above the elements will be different in each case, but they are all "correlated" to the same entities. And this will be the case *whether they actually represent something in the world or not*. The point is that they *could* represent something in the world, anything whose form and logical form they have. What has to happen first is that the picture as a picture represent reality by correlations of its elements with entities, even if these entities are only as we imagine them.

In a similar way (to mention some of Wittgenstein's other examples) a "stick drawing" may be recognized as "two men fencing;" tiny dolls and miniature automobiles may depict a street accident; or hieroglyphics may represent "a man prostrate before the sun." In all these cases possible situations are presented through "correlations" to reality *within the pictures,* and this is what makes it possible for the pictures to represent many different particular situations in the world, provided that they have the same form and logical form. And at the same time they may also be correct or incorrect in agreeing or disagreeing in any particular case with what they represent.

The question now arises: How do these same items of furniture become *propositional signs?* What must be done to them to turn them from a picture into a propositional sign?

Suppose, first, we let the chairs "stand for" men and the tables "stand for" automobiles. Then we can depict (up to a point) spatial relations between men and automobiles by the spatial relations between chairs and tables, and we will still have a picture (with the correlations, as it were, within the picture, so that we can "read off" the spatial situation of the men and automobiles from the spatial situation of the chairs and tables). But if we let the chairs and tables "stand for" musical notes, various structural relations may still be represented, but now finally the *form of picturing will be lost and absorbed completely into the logical form.*

In the third volume of his *Treatise of Formal Logic* (Copenhagen, 1931), Jorgen Jorgensen describes the way in which pictures go over into propositions thus:

> The more the properties of the symbols resemble those of the objects and the more the relations between the constituents of the objects exist also between the constituents of the symbols, the more the symbol approximates to an image, and the better we can do with pure object-symbols; and conversely: the less the symbols resemble their objects and the less the relations between the constituents of the objects are paralleled as between the constituents of the symbols, the more will the symbol approximate to a mere representation and the more we shall have to introduce special symbols for qualities and relations in addition to those for the objects themselves. (p. 266)

Jorgensen's statement suggests that there is a continuum between pictures and propositions. But for Wittgenstein there is a clear demarcation line between them, and this is indicated by what he says about *logical pictures* and about *thoughts*. For him it is impossible to get from pictures to propositional signs without thoughts, for *there is no propositional sign without a thought*. To see why this is so we have to look more closely at pictures.

In a picture it is necessary to distinguish between three forms: (1) a *form of picturing (Form der Abbildung)*, which is the possibility of the picture's particular kind of structure, a form which it has in common with reality—for example, being spatial or colored; (2.15, 2.17, 2.171) (2) a *form of representation (Form der Darstellung)*, which it does *not* have in common with reality, but which places it "outside" its subject; (2.173) and (3) *logical form or the form of reality (logische Form, Form der Wirklichkeit)*, which is the existence and non-existence of states of affairs and which, again, it has in common with reality. (2.18)

To give an example of this: A gramaphone record, it would seem, (4.014) might be described as a picture with a temporal form of picturing, (which it has in common with music), and a spatial form of representation, (which it does not have in common with it), while its logical form would be what it had in common with a musical score of the same piece. (2.181, 2.19) (Wittgenstein calls musical notation a "picture of music" and our phonetic notation—the alphabet—a "picture of our speech." (4.011))

A *form of picturing* is what makes possible a particular way of picturing, the form of picturing of a spatial picture, for example, permitting many different spatial representations. *Logical form*, on the other hand, is what makes possible picturing in *any way at all* and is the structural nature (together with the bi-polarity of reality) which underlies the particular forms of spatiality, temporality, color, etc. In every picture, whatever its particular pictorial form, such a bi-polar structural character will also be found, which however we will be able to distinguish from the other forms of the picture.

When this distinction cannot be made, and the pictorial form *is* the logical form, we have what Wittgenstein calls a *logical picture*. (2.181) This, which is still to be distinguished from a thought and from a propositional sign, describes the case where nothing in the picture itself depends on its being spatial or temporal or colored, etc. (It is possible that certain kinds of calendars, graphs and ideograms might qualify as logical pictures.)

Between any kinds of pictures and propositional signs stand *thoughts*, which are *logical pictures*, but logical pictures of *facts* (presumably both positive and negative). (3.) A thought is necessary for a proposition because a propositional sign can only be brought into a projective relation to the world by "thinking the sense of a proposition." (3.11) This is because a propositional sign does not present a situation as a picture does. (2.11) It can only be related to a situation by a thought. A thought also does not present a situation in order to represent it, but merely "contains the possibility of the situation of which it is the thought" (3.02) (as a picture "contains the possibility of the situation it represents").

Thoughts occupy a *pivotal* place in the *Tractatus* because they are two-sided. On the one hand, "A logical picture of facts is a thought" (3.) and, on the other, "A thought is a proposition with a sense." (4.) The numbering of these two key sentences should be noted and the switch of the word *thought (der Gedanke)* from the end of the first sentence to the beginning of the second. It seems clear that Wittgenstein is pointing to two aspects of a thought, (two aspects which, incidentally, seem to parallel in an interesting way Aristotle's distinction between the passive and active intellect, as discussed further below. See especially Chpt. 11, sect. ii, Chpt. 12, sect. iv; and Appendix 1).

As a "logical picture" a thought is "passive" and does not assert anything. As a "proposition with a sense," on the other hand, it is "active" and refers to the world to "say" something. As a logical picture, in other words, it is, like all pictures, something we "make to ourselves." (2.1) But as a proposition it is an *expression* or *projection*, as it were, making a claim. That this is what Wittgenstein had in mind is suggested by the passage immediately preceding the description of a thought as a "proposition with a sense" where he says: "The applied, thought (*gedachte*) propositional sign is the thought." (3.5) As a *logical picture* a thought, we might say, presents something "off its own bat," while as a *proposition* it relates itself to the world, or is applied or *thought* (now as a verb).

Another way of putting this might be to say that a picture has an intrinsic potential "referentiality." But it has no actual reference until we add in effect "*That* is how what it is a picture of is." The *that* has to be added to the *how*. A propositional sign, on the other hand, has no intrinsic "referentiality," and *its* relation to the world has to be thought if it is to have any application at all. "Thinking the sense of a proposition" *gives* a propositional sign its possible references.

We could use tables, chairs and books as propositional signs in an endless variety of ways. To set up an ordinary proposition we might, for example, allow the tables to stand for houses, the chairs for the color yellow and the books for the color red. Juxtaposing a table and a chair would then "say" "The house is yellow." But this would only be the case if we projected *that* possible situation into that sign by *thinking* that sense and thereby establishing the sign in a projective relation to any such possible situation.

It is important to observe exactly what a proposition includes and what it does not include because here is where we find the crucial distinction between *form* and *content*, which does not show up on the level of pictures.[3] Wittgenstein states this distinction in three ways (3.13) by saying that a proposition

1 — "includes all that the projection includes, but not what is projected;"

---

[3] See Chpt. 10, sect. ii below for a fuller discussion of this important distinction.

2 — "does not actually contain its sense, but does contain the possibility of expressing it;" and

3 — "contains the form, but not the content, of its sense."

What these statements say is that the experienced, qualitative content of a thought (or of a possible situation) does not get into a proposition, for a proposition contains only the *possibility* of expressing this. Sheer qualitative experience is part of the *sense* of a proposition (e.g. being able to recognize the color red), but *this* is not contained in the proposition. It, so to speak, remains in the thought and is only *expressed* in the proposition. Language does not, and cannot, contain the *content* of our experience of the world, the actual first-person immediate qualitative experience. All that can get into language is the form of this, which will come out as structure of words and of names.

A proposition, on this view, cannot contain a particularity in the sense of a particular content. Even if, for example, we have a proposition with proper names, such as "Socrates was the teacher of Plato," it is perfectly possible that these names refer in the thought of a speaker to two men, other than the famous philosophers. We appeal in any case to some commonly shared thought to establish the content of the sense. (And in this case we do not have to have directly experienced either of the two men, but only to have two particular men in mind.)

iv

We have been discussing propositions and pictures as structural representations of situations, setting to one side the specifically logical aspect of this. But Wittgenstein says that pictures present situations and represent possible situations, both in *logical* space. (2.11, 2.202) And all pictures have *logical* form, (2.182) while thoughts are *logical* pictures. (3.) And a proposition determines a locus in *logical* space (3.4) and mirrors *logical* form. (4.12)

It is time to ask what the force of the word "logical" in these and other contexts is. And this brings us to the second main aspect of propositions and pictures. If their first main aspect is their "structural" character, the second is their "logical" character. The first is provided by *objects*, or *substance* (or "all possibilities"); the second is provided by what Wittgenstein calls *reality (Wirklichkeit)*, or the bi-polarity of existence and non-existence for these possible structures. As the structural character of the world lies in objects and their possible combinations, the logical character lies in the bi-polarity of existence and non-existence which provides the form under which we represent these structures.

We turn now to this second main aspect of propositions and pictures—that they always represent, not the world, but *reality*. It is only because the world has substance or form and structure that we are able to represent it at all; but it is only because it is reality, having logical form, that we are able to represent truly or falsely. After the distinction between *things* and *objects*, there is no conception in the *Tractatus* that it is more important to understand clearly than this conception of *reality*. What does Wittgenstein mean by this term?

The *Tractatus* tells us the answer quite flatly:

> The existence and non-existence of states of affairs is reality. (2.06)

After a great deal of reflection we will return to the simplest explanation—that this means exactly what it says, and not one bit more or one bit less. For every state of affairs which exists there is the exactly equivalent non-existence of *this same state of affairs*, and the two together for all states of affairs constitute *reality*.

This must, however, be understood correctly. Wittgenstein tells us that

> The sum-total of reality is the world. (2.063)

In other words, *the sum-total of what exists and what does not exist is the same as the sum-total of what exists*. When we add up what exists and what does not exist, we get the same answer as when we add up what exists. How is this to be understood?

It is because what does not exist is not a different reality, but the *same reality* as what does exist. (To *p* and *not-p* correspond one and the same reality. (4.0621C)) Every case of what exists is matched by an exactly equivalent non-existence. There is, in other words, no difference between a state of affairs when it exists and when it does not exist except the uncharacterizable (and inconceivable) difference between sheer presence and sheer absence. (Not-red, for example, is not "everything-else-but-red;" nor is it "any-other-color-but-red;" it is just precisely not-red, or the sheer absence of something fully determinate.) Since the world consists of all the states of affairs which exist, reality, which is that plus the *very same* non-existence, adds up to no more than what exists.

We can see how Wittgenstein arrived at this distinction between *reality* and *world* by observing the progression of his thought from the *Notes on Logic* (written in 1913) through the *Notebooks* (written in 1914-16) to the *Tractatus* (written in 1917-20).

The *Notes on Logic* show the distinction originating in Frege's distinction between *sense* and *meaning* as applied to propositions. There Wittgenstein tells us that

> Thus a proposition has two poles (corresponding to case of its truth and case of its falsity). We call this the *sense* of a proposition. The meaning of a proposition is the fact which actually corresponds to it. The chief characteristic of my theory is: *p has the same meaning as not-p.* (*Notebooks.* p. 94)

As the distinction appears here, the *sense* of a proposition always involves two facts—a *positive fact* which corresponds to the proposition's being true and a *negative fact* which corresponds to its being false (and to understand the proposition we have to understand these two facts), while the *meaning* (or reference) is the *one* fact which actually does correspond to it and which we cannot know until we know whether the proposition *is* true *or* false. Whether a proposition is stated positively or negatively, it has the same meaning. Hence *sense* is two facts, and *meaning* is one fact.

In the *Notebooks* this distinction is linked with *pictures*. Here Wittgenstein says that the *sense* of a proposition is what it pictures (p. 19) and is a particular representing relation, (p. 22) while the *meaning* is settled by arbitrarily determined references (p. 17) and is the relation which actually holds or does not hold—that is, the truth relation. The sense must permit the possibility of both truth and falsity and we must be able to see how both possibilities can be represented by the same model. (p. 30)

Finally, in the *Tractatus* the ontology is introduced, including the distinction between *reality* and *world*. Wittgenstein now calls a proposition a "picture of reality." (4.01, 4.021) *Sense* becomes one possibility of true and false, (existence and non-existence), out of a range of all such possibilities provided by a *logical form*, and *fact* becomes the truth functional case of true or false (existence or non-existence) for such a particular sense.[4]

---

[4] Books and articles about the *Tractatus* are often careless about *and*'s and *or*'s in the text. The Plochman-Lawson *Index*, for example, copies 4.2 wrongly in three places, (pp. 8, 141, 164), substituting *or*'s for *and*'s (and also omitting a plural, an error also committed in several other places—e.g. pp. 38, 39, 69, 83, 140, 190).

The position of the *Tractatus* may be summarized as follows:

(1) the distinction between *reality* and *world* is introduced as the basis of the distinction between *sense* and *meaning;*

(2) it is not the truth or falsity of an elementary proposition, but *negation* as a truth functional operation which establishes the distinction between positive and negative facts;

(3) p has the same sense whether it is true or false, but p and not-p, as truth functions, do not have the same sense, but have opposite senses; (4.0621C)

(4) one and the same reality corresponds to p and not-p, but one and the same reality can be a positive fact or a negative fact *when we have negative propositions;* and

(5) we can either say then that one and the same reality (whatever it is) settles whether p is true or false, or we can say that whether there is a positive fact or a negative fact settles whether p or not-p is true.

While in the *Notebooks* a proposition is called "a measure of the world" (p. 41) in the *Tractatus* it is called "a model of reality as we imagine it." (4.01) We can now say that it is the very character of reality that one and the same reality permits two opposite senses, but what these two opposite senses are does not appear until the truth functional operation of negation establishes what corresponds to the falsity of an elementary proposition as a separate logical place. (4)

While the distinction between *sense* and *meaning* is finally grounded in that between *reality* and *world*, both *reality* and *world* are based upon *substance.* It is only because there are determinate structures which provided the possibilities or candidates for existence and non-existence that we can represent the world in terms of logical form and sense which settle everything except the yes *or* no of existence *or* non-existence. (4.023)[5]

v

Perhaps the most important difference between propositions and pictures which emerges is that *pictures have no meanings.* (The correspondence of their elements with objects is given at the start; the objects do not have to be meant. (2.13, 2.131)) It is significant that the words

---

[5] For further discussions of *reality* see Chpt. 5, sect. ii; Chpt. 6, sect. v; Chpt. 10, sect. iv; and Chpt. 13, sect. iii. Also immediately below—sect. vi. (topic (6)).

mean (bedeuten) and *meaning (Bedeutung)* do not occur for the first time until after the discussion of pictures is completed. (3.203) Consequently ordinary pictures cannot depict the world, but can only depict reality.

The case is different, however, with logical pictures, and Wittgenstein calls attention to this by saying "Logical pictures can depict the world." (2.19) (It should be noted, however, that they cannot be said to *describe* the world. It is propositions which describe the world (4.26) although they can only do it by first logically picturing reality. (4.06))

The determiner of the truth or falsity of a picture is reality, for a *picture* agrees with *reality* or fails to agree with it; *this* makes it true or false. (2.21) (Wittgenstein also says that the agreement or disagreement of the sense of a picture with reality constitutes its truth or falsity. (2.221, 2.222))

The question which brings out the difference between propositions and pictures is this: Although both pictures and propositions represent reality, does a *proposition* agree with or fail to agree with *reality*, or does it agree with or fail to agree with the *world?*

The question cannot be unambiguously answered because there are two alternative ways of speaking, each one of which is as justified or unjustified as the other. A proposition can agree or disagree with reality because a positive and negative proposition both correspond to one and the same reality. (4.0621C) And it can agree or disagree with the world because there is a single positive fact there in each case. Hence both reality and world can be completely described, the first by all true and false propositions and the second by all true propositions. (4.26) And both descriptions constitute the same totality.

What this means becomes clearer in the light of the two statements that "the totality of facts determine what is the case and also what is not the case" (1.12) and "The totality of existing states of affairs also determines which states of affairs do not exist." (2.05) The clue to the meaning of these statements is provided by the entry in the *Notebooks* reading:

> If all the positive statements about a thing are made, aren't all the negative ones already made too? And that is the whole point. (p. 33)

If we know everything that is, we also know everything that is not, for what-is-not differs in no way from what-is, since we can only describe what-is-not as exactly the same as what is (plus that-it-is-not, which is not in any way part of the description).

This sheds further light on the passage which tells us that "The sum-total of reality (the existence and non-existence of states of affairs) is the world (the totality of existing states of affairs)." (2.063, 2.06, 2.05) In the case of *reality* existence and non-existence *count for one* since everything which is there is balanced by an exactly equivalent absence. Whatever it is which falsifies any statement has its own equivalent negative. If we count up, therefore, all the states of affairs which exist, these cannot be any more than what count as the same— the same ones not existing.

This is simply the outcome of Wittgenstein's Fregean starting point that *one* meaning (in the *world*) corresponds to *two senses* (in *reality*). Every non-existing state of affairs has an existing one in its place (i.e. if the house is not-yellow, it is some other color). When we know the totality of what exists, every place is filled with an existence, and the same non-existent states of affairs are simply repeated over and over again in each appropriate case (and so cannot be "totalled" separately). *What reality gives in two ways, the world gives in one, but the two ways of reality do not count for any more than the one way of the world.*

As Wittgenstein already declared in the *Notes on Logic*, positive and negative facts are in a sense symmetrical since, once we have truth functional propositions, we can speak truly or falsely about either one. But the truth and falsity of elementary propositions are not in the same way symmetrical since we cannot make false statements take the place of true ones. Intending to describe the world falsely does not prevent these statements also from being true *or* false. We cannot, in other words, reverse the values "true" and "false" and wind up with a completely false description of the world since the intended false statements may just as well be true if things turn out to be that way. (4.062)

We cannot get away from "the way things are" even if we take the negative as positive, since they may be *that* way too.[6] But it is

---

6 This view, it may be pointed out, puts Wittgenstein in the Parmenidean tradition of the "priority of being" and separates him from philosophers (Heracleitean or Gnostic) who attribute to non-Being a status equal to Being. Of course Wittgenstein is talking about existence and non-existence, there is for him no non-Being since there are no non-objects.

finally, not pictures, but propositions, which give us access to the world, as distinct from reality. Pictures as such stop short at reality because they do not provide a single logical place. And the reason for this is that pictures, although they can be true or false, cannot be negated; all that can be negated is whether they hold or not. A picture cannot point to a single logical place, but always only to something externally bounded by what it is not.

Only an elementary proposition can assert the existence of a single state of affairs (as it were in sheer opposition to its non-existence). Such a proposition, in effect, transfers the negative "otherness" which "externally bounds" properties in reality into the mutually exclusive alternative of existence and non-existence for a single property. A totality of true pictures cannot therefore give us a picture of the world, but a totality of true elementary propositions in a certain sense can.

vi

There are six general aspects of propositions which Wittgenstein enumerates and discusses at the beginning of the second half of the *Tractatus*. These passages, (numbered in the 4.0's), give, in an informal and unsystematic way, something like a commentary on what is presented systematically in the rest of the book. And for this reason they provide an excellent introduction to the whole philosophy and are worth examining closely.

A proposition, he says:

(1) is a picture of reality or a model of reality as we imagine it; (4.01)
(2) has a sense which is understood without its being explained; (4.02)
(3) must use old expressions to communicate a new sense; (4.03)
(4) must have exactly as many distinguishable parts as in the situation which it represents; (4.04)
(5) has reality compared to it; (4.05)
(6) can be true or false only in virtue of being a picture of reality. (4.06)

We now consider these general aspects in the order in which they are taken up in the text.

(1) *Picture of reality*. (4.01) Wittgenstein here gives examples of sign languages, such as musical notation, phonetic notation, the sign *aRb*, gramaphone records, hieroglyphic script and alphabetic script.

The possibility of all these languages, and of all likeness (*Gleichnisse*) "is contained in the logic of depiction." (4.015) For example, there is a general rule connecting a symphony, its score and the grooves on a gramaphone record, which makes it possible to derive any one of the three from any other. This rule is the "law of projection" which projects the symphony into the score and the "rule for translating" which permits translating the score into the "language of gramaphone records." (4.0141)

The point is that there is something essential to the pictorial character in all these cases. All languages have a common logical plan which permits them to depict. And, Wittgenstein says, that this is "the same internal relation of depicting that holds between language and the world." (4.014) The difference is, of course, that we *make* the music, we *make* the musical score, and we *make* the gramaphone record; but, (apart from human artifacts), we do not make the *world*, (and we do not make *reality*). Nevertheless, that the internal relation between language and the world is the same as the internal relation between different languages is not for Wittgenstein a conclusion based on an analogy, but one based on *what is necessary for it to be possible* for language to be about the world.

(2) *Sense does not have to be clarified.* (4.02) This points to another basic difference between *sense* and *meaning*. The meanings of simple signs (words) have to be clarified in order to be understood, (4.026) but we understand the sense of a propositional sign "without its having been clarified to us." (4.02) In a contrast pregnant with implications Wittgenstein says that words have to be understood in terms of something else (hence the dictionary), but "with propositions we make ourselves understood." (4.026) The only way to understand the sense of a proposition is to understand its constituents (4.024C) and to know the situation that it represents. (4.021) But beyond this all we can do is to ask the speaker to make *himself* clearer.

It is in this discussion that the difference between *knowing (kennen)* and *understanding (verstehen)* appears. We both *know* and *understand* meanings, and understanding sometimes requires knowing (as when we cannot understand two names without knowing if they have the same or different meanings (4.243)). But we do not *know senses*; we only *understand* them. And we only understand them by *knowing* the situation they represent and by understanding the constituents of the propositions which express them. To know in the *Tractatus* (either *kennen* or *wissen*) has a finality denied to understanding. In a quite traditional way *knowing* applies to the world and reality, *understanding* to the sense of what we say about them.

It is important, however, that we do have to *know* something in order to understand a proposition—namely, the situation which it represents. The proposition must describe reality *completely* for this to be possible. Nothing must be left undetermined but the *yes* or *no* of truth or falsity. (4.023) In this way even if a proposition is an incomplete picture of a situation, it must always be (in its own terms) a complete picture. (5.156D) We have to know *everything* that a proposition says before we can know whether it is true or false.

(3) *Uses old expressions to communicate a new sense.* (4.03) "It belongs to the essence of a proposition that it can communicate a *new* sense to us." (4.027) The new sense is a situation which "is, as it were, constructed by way of experiment." (4.031) The passages which follow, laying down the principles for understanding how this is done, are possibly *the most important in the whole book.* They state the underlying principles upon which in Wittgenstein's view, all language rests.

Constructing (*zusammenstellen*) a situation involves three factors: (1) "the principle that objects have signs as their representatives," (4.0312A) (2) a proposition having to be "logically segmented," (4.032A) and (3) what provides the logical segmentation *per se* not being a representative, for "there can be no representatives of the *logic* of facts." (4.0312B)

All three factors are central to Wittgenstein's thought, but of the three it is the third one, drawing an absolute line between the first two, which is most fundamental and which he calls "my fundamental idea" (*mein Grundgedanke*) (4.0312B) The crucial point which this makes (and which can scarcely be over-stressed as a guiding theme in the book) is that the structure of language, whether of analyzed language or unanalyzed language, must be *wholly immanent in the names of objects.* There can be *no names for what supplies logical segmentation,* whether such logical segmentation is provided by the distinction between subject and predicate, or between thing-terms and relation-terms, or between, in the simplest possible case, the order of names.

The most important application of this is that although in ordinary language we appear to "name" properties and relations *as* properties and relations, we do *not* name them *as* properties and relations, but *as* objects and hence on the same principle that "objects have signs as their representatives." The "propertyness" and "relationality" of what is thereby named are carried entirely by conventions of grammatical structure.

Wittgenstein's "fundamental idea" means that *any* kind of structure, whether conventional or ontological, cannot be represented *per se* by signs. Structure can only be shown by an arrangement of names. And this principle has to hold even for the apparent "naming" of structural features *as* structural features in ordinary language (e.g. apparently "naming" a predicate *as* a predicate). What belongs to the *way* in which we name is not itself named. And in ordinary language predication and relationality belong to the *way* in which we name.

To say that propositions must be "logically segmented" is to say that they must have signs which function in different ways, but *not* to say that they must have signs which name something other than objects. All necessary structures can be carried by names alone once we permit the names to have the diversity of *meanings* which they have in ordinary language where the differences between properties and between relations emerge as different *meanings*, quite apart from the consideration that they are all properties in the one case or all relations in the other. What characterizes properties *as* properties or relations *as* relations is the *way* they are named and not some additional feature of *what* is named.

(4) *Exactly as much distinguishable in a proposition as in the situation it represents.* (4.04) This is a continuation of the previous section, for it is clear that Wittgenstein has in mind even ordinary propositions where the multiplicity includes even predicate and relational terms. We must be able to distinguish even in these cases just so many "meanings" in the situation as there are "meaning-terms" in the proposition, including predicate terms and relational terms. If this is not done, nonsense results, as in functional notation when we fail to specify just what is being generalized. (4.0411)

Wittgenstein uses the same argument here against the idealist's explanation that there is one form of spatial intuition which can account for the multiplicity of spatial relations. (4.0412) (Doubtless he is here thinking of Kant.)

(5) *Reality compared with propositions.* (4.05) There is no discussion of this point whatever; a single sentence merely announces it. And the reason seems clear, for any discussion would lead into a hope-

less regress. How can reality be "compared" to a proposition if we have no access to reality except through the thought which is already expressed in the proposition or through a picture (sense experience) which has the same logical form as the thought and the proposition? (If I can *only* see reality in a mirror, I cannot "compare" reality to what I see in the mirror.) We would have to suppose a gap between the reality imagined in the proposition and the "external" reality to which it is "compared." The only notion in the *Tractatus* which opens the door to this is the form of representation, (2.173) the only form which a picture does not have in common with reality. But the implications of this are nowhere discussed.

(6) *True or false only by being a picture of reality*. (4.06) This is what a logical picture or a picture of reality does: it permits propositions with opposite senses for one and the same reality. (4.0621) But how are we able to picture one and the same reality as existing and not-existing? How is this to be understood? The answer requires a step-by-step statement of Wittgenstein's view. Consider the assertion "Red."

First, some color is there because the form of the objects pictured is color.

Second, whatever color is pictured it is pictured logically—as red and not-red, yellow and not-yellow, blue and not-blue, etc. (The logical *form* is *all* colors so arranged.)

Third, one of these alternatives is singled out, and this is the *sense* of the proposition—for example, red.

Fourth, the sense is asserted or said as simply *red*, thereby making the claim that this state of affairs exists.

Fifth, this turns out to be true or false.

Sixth, if it turns out to be false, we can express this as a negative fact, or as the truth of a truth-functional negation affirming not-red.

Seventh, whatever makes the original proposition *red* true is the same reality as whatever makes it false.

It is the last point which, on the face of it, raises the most difficulties, for how can *red* and *not-red* "correspond to" one and the same reality? It is just the point about *reality*, however, that it does not distinguish between sheer *presence* and sheer *absence when in every other way these two conditions are exactly the same* (i.e. when *what* is present and *what* is absent are exactly the same). The point is unacceptable only if we suppose that if something is not-red, it is some other color, and this other color is certainly a different reality from red, and, therefore, red and not-red cannot be the same reality. But it is just the point of propositions as pictures of *reality* that they permit us to look at red and not-red, not in this way, but rather with not-red as simply the determinate absence of red (disregarding entirely whatever color might be there in its place). Looked at in this other way, red and not-red can be said to "correspond" to one and the same reality because there is no representable difference between them whatever.

We can say, therefore, that there "corresponds to" a single elementary proposition a "presence" and an "absence" which is the same "presence" and the same "absence," so that whether the elementary proposition is true or false depends upon no difference in the reality (although it does depend upon a difference in the world). Reality, in effect, "brackets" the unsayable difference between existence and non-existence, not recognizing it as anything that can be "pictured" (experienced) or thought or represented or described.

Wittgenstein supports this point by maintaining that it cannot be any difference in the reality which settles the truth or falsity of a proposition, or it would not be possible, as it is possible, to reverse the meanings of p and *not-p* and use p to mean what we now mean by *not-p* and *not-p* to mean what we now mean by p. (4.062)

Picturing reality enables propositions to be true or false by giving a determinate sense (just *not-red*), instead of an indeterminate one (any other color) to the falsity of an elementary proposition. And it is this which permits us to introduce truth functional negative propositions in symmetry with positive ones, thus permitting the truth of a positive proposition to guarantee the falsity of a negative one and vice versa. A logical picture of facts is just the kind of a picture which permits a sense which represents one possibility of existence *and* non-existence in such a way that *nothing* is left over except the non-representable alternative of existence *or* non-existence.

vii

Wittgenstein's conception of a proposition can now be summed up under seven main headings which tell us what a proposition does. He says that a proposition: (1) *expresses* a thought; (3.1) (2) *shows* its sense; (4.022) (3) *contains* the form of its sense; (3.13E) (4) *mirrors* its logical form; (4.121) (5) *represents* a situation; (4.021) (6) *describes* a state of affairs; (4.023) and (7) *says* how things are (3.221, 4.022)

The formula which brings together most of these is the proposition as a *picture of reality*. (4.01) The *thought expressed*, the *situation represented* and the *state of affairs described* are all equivalent to the *sense shown*, and all have the same *logical form* which is mirrored in the proposition. All this, however, is preliminary to the *essence* of a proposition, which is the last point listed above—namely, that a proposition *says what it shows*. The *essence* or *general form* of a proposition is a certain kind of description, which, when said, asserts that *This is how it is*. (*Es verhält sich so und so*.) (4.5) The description, which is purely structural, is simply "held up," and this is the assertion. In this way an elementary proposition contains, as it were, no verb at all. Its mere existence says that things are as it shows them to be.

Names, Signs and Symbols

Things are thinks, and thinks are words.

MAX MÜLLER

. . . The life of thought and science is the life inherent in symbols; so that it is wrong to say that a good language is *important* to good thought, merely; for it is of the essence of it.

CHARLES PEIRCE

Symbols are not what they seem to be.

WITTGENSTEIN

We cannot say that the common meaning of a word is its real meaning, because it does not give us a proper connection between things, and so we get no meaning at all.

Mimansa iv-ii

The difference between name and meaning which we experience on the empirical plane is a mere appearance, their identity being the only reality.

GAURINATH SASTRI

CHAPTER 4

Names, Signs and Symbols

i

Ever since Bertrand Russell's original Introduction to the *Tractatus* it has remained a common misunderstanding of the book to suppose that, as Russell said, "Mr. Wittgenstein is concerned with the conditions for a logically perfect language" and that Wittgenstein believed that "the whole function of language is to have meaning, and it only fulfills this function in proportion as it approaches to the ideal language which we postulate." (p. x)

A number of passages in the *Tractatus* should warn us against this interpretation. For example:

> In fact, all the propositions of our everyday language, just as they stand, are in perfect logical order. (5.5563)

Or again:

> It now seems possible to give the most general propositional form: that is, to give a description of the propositions of *any* sign-language *whatsoever* in such a way that every possible sense can be expressed by a symbol satisfying the description, . . . (4.5A)

And again:

> And I say that any possible proposition is legitimately constructed (*gebildet*), and if it has no sense, that can only be because we have failed to give a *meaning* to some of its constituents. (5.4733A)

If the *Tractatus* has anything to do with a logically perfect language, it is only because Wittgenstein believes that something like this already lies at the heart of all language. The language which we have is already logically perfect, but this is hidden by the "enormously complicated" "tacit conventions" which it employs. (4.002E) To reveal this hidden logic we do not have to "postulate" anything (unless it be the possibility of determinate sense); all we have to do is to uncover the logical forms of the propositions which we already have (3.317) Nothing has to be changed or improved; all there is to find is immanent in everyday speech.

Wittgenstein is in no way a language-reformer or language-unifier. He has no zeal to make language better (whatever that might mean). His concern is to elucidate how language is able to do what it does. The *Tractatus* deals with a "hidden core" of language, which is indeed in "perfect logical order." But it does this to show what *is* involved in language, not what *ought* to be involved.

In the *Tractatus* it is *man (der Mensch)*, and not the philosopher, who "possesses the ability to construct languages capable of expressing every sense." (4.002) Philosophers go wrong in failing to understand the logic of this common language, (4.003) which is the only language we have. How else could we understand how language works except from the example of our own language? And from where else would we draw notions of "improving" it ("improvements" which could do no more than in some way or other truncate it)? (Perhaps indeed it is the failure to understand the logic of our language which makes us suppose that language as a whole *could* be improved.)

Philosophy, as Wittgenstein understands it, does not seek to clarify language, but to clarify thoughts. (4.112D) Language misleads because it disguises thought, since it was designed for other purposes, (perhaps of equal importance), than to reveal thought. (4.002) What has to be done is not to "reconstruct" language, but to reveal the thought which language disguises, by clarifying propositions. (4.112) To try to make language a better vehicle for thought is to put the cart before the horse. Rather we have to make thoughts, so often confused in language, clear and sharp. (4.112E) Language, as it were, becomes a better vehicle by having something better to say. And we express ourselves more clearly by having something clearer to express.

Any language contains at its center the same essence as any other language, and this would apply equally well to any language which a "reforming philosopher" might construct. The *Tractatus* attempts to show what this essence or "hidden core," which is already operating full-blast in everyday language, is. This is why it is misleading, to say the least, to describe the *Tractatus* as concerned with an "ideal language," unless it is understood that this "ideal language" is the core of every language.[1]

ii

What lies at the center of any language, in Wittgenstein's view, is the capacity for "structural picturing." The analysis of any language will arrive at some kind of signs whose immediate combination will represent some kind of structure in reality. Such a combination Wittgenstein calls an elementary proposition, (4.22) and, he says, all other propositions can be regarded as "generalizations" of these elementary ones. (4.52)

While all propositions are functions of the expressions contained in them, (3.318) elementary propositions are functions of names. (4.24) To understand the relation between ordinary language and elementary propositions involves, among other things, understanding the relation between *expressions* and *names*. And this is a large part of the subject of the sections numbered 3 in the *Tractatus* which we discuss in this chapter.

The term "expression" covers not only words or the simple signs of ordinary language, (4.026) but also descriptive phrases. In getting from *expressions* to *names* Wittgenstein makes use of the notions of *signs* and *symbols*. An expression is called a *symbol*, but only parenthetically, (3.31) because from another point of view it may involve several symbols. Expressions have *meanings*, (3.314) but are not said to *designate*, since the individual words in a descriptive phrase have different designations.

Symbols and signs are related in this way: A symbol is a sign in use or "a sign used with a sense," (3.326) while a sign is "what can be perceived of a symbol," (3.32) but it is also a symbol considered apart from its "way of designation" or merely in terms of its designation. A sign, in other words, is not a totally meaningless mark on a piece of paper, but, as Wittgenstein says: "We cannot set out a sign form without knowing whether anything corresponds to it." (5.5542)

Both *signs* and *symbols* designate and have meanings, but a *sign* is arbitrary, (3.322) (although there are also "naturally necessary" signs, (6.124)), while in a *symbol* there is much that is arbitrary and much

---

[1] "The truth of the matter is that language is an essentially perfect means of expression and communication among every known people." Edward Sapir—*Language* in *Encyclopedia of Social Sciences.* 9:155.

that is not arbitrary. (6.124)) A *sign* that is not used is meaningless, (3.328) while there is no such thing as a *symbol* that is not used. A *sign* can be given a sense, though it cannot be given a wrong sense. (5.4732) And similarly *symbols* are not in themselves illegitimate, but can be made to work by arbitrary determinations. (5.473) *Symbols*, on the other hand, contain what is essential and what is not essential, the former being what is necessary for them to express their sense. (4.465)

Besides speaking of *expressions, signs* and *symbols* Wittgenstein also speaks of the *elements* of a propositional sign (3.2) or *propositional elements* (3.24C) and of a *constituent* of a proposition. (3.315, 4.024, 5.4733) In the *Notes on Logic* he tells us that a *constituent* is a particular, while a *component* is a particular, or relation, etc. (p. 94) The term *component* is not used in the *Tractatus*, while the term *constituent* is broadened to cover all words, or everything which may be translated from one language into another. (4.025) (The term *element* would seem to be broader still, covering signs which have no independent meanings and could not be translated separately apart from propositions.)

The critical term is, of course, *names*. A name is a certain kind of a sign (and hence also a certain kind of a symbol) used in propositions. It is what Wittgenstein calls a *simple sign* and a *simple symbol*. (3.202, 4.24) Elements of a propositional sign, he tells us, become simple signs only when a proposition has been "completely analyzed" so that elements may "correspond to the objects of the thought." (3.2, 3.201) When a thought, in other words, is expressed in a proposition in such a way that elements of the propositional sign "correspond to" objects of the thought, these elements become *names*.

What makes signs into names is their "corresponding to" or "meaning" or being "the representatives of" objects. And such objects are here, in the first instance, the "objects of the thought" or the simple references of a thought, *whatever they may be*. (They may, it will be seen, be things, properties or relations, when these appear as simple, indefinable referents without their "logical" features, these logical features being a matter of "ways of designation" and not of "meaning.")

Signs may be complex (5.515) or they may be signs *of* complexes, (3.3442) but in a thought which is expressed in a completely analyzed proposition the objects of the thought will be simple and may have as representatives names or simple signs, however complex these same references might turn out to be in a manner of speaking, *in some other proposition.* As Wittgenstein tells us in his *Notebooks,* all that is required is determinateness of reference for a particular sense. (p. 63) If the thought or the sense became "more determinate," it would no longer be *that* thought or *that* sense.

What appear as "the objects of the thought" which we name, therefore, are whatever objects are arrived at as necessary to establish a fully determinate sense for the proposition which expresses that particular thought, regardless of whether another proposition, *with another sense,* might represent the situation still more determinately, in a factual sense.

A completely analyzed proposition (representing a possible situation) is still not an elementary proposition (asserting the existence of a single state of affairs). It is simply an ordinary proposition when this ordinary proposition has been analyzed in such a way as to *separate its meanings from its syntactical features.* Such a completely analyzed proposition then illustrates the principle of *names meaning objects,* even though the objects in this case are "the objects of the thought" which include things, properties and relations *as meanings.* No more definiteness is required than is required to make clear a particular thought.

This point must be stressed: that a proposition is completely analyzed when *its* sense is made clear—not when we have reached "factual" absolutes, but when we have reached the simples that are necessary in order to make *that* particular sense determinate. Just as we do not require the exactness of atomic physics in ordinary language, so in every proposition we need just as much "determinateness of reference" as its sense needs. (We do not have to know anything about the inside of a watch in order to be able to speak with perfect clarity about the watch. (*Notebooks.* p. 70)) Just as we can apply *numbers* to all kinds of everyday things, treating them for the moment as mathematical units, so we can apply *names* to all kinds of everyday things, *treating them for the moment as logical units.* Hence it must be recognized that the terms *name* and *object* are in one sense relative, since what will count as a simple in one proposition will not necessarily count as a simple in another.

In an ordinary proposition we will find a name (1) meaning an object, (3.203) even when it stands for or designates a thing; (4.0311, 4.243) (2) meaning an object even when it stands for or designates a relation, for it is not the "relationality" which is designated (3.1432) (that is handled by the "way of designation"), but the particular "content" or "meaning" of the relation; and (3) meaning an object even when it designates a predicate, for, again, it is not the "predication" which is designated (3.323C) but only the nature or content of the particular predicate. The term "object" in all these cases means that what is designated, for the particular sense in question, is simple and has no parts.

Beyond this, Wittgenstein tells us that a name, besides being a *simple sign (einfaches Zeichen)* is also a *proto-sign (Urzeichen)* This means that the name cannot be analyzed *(zergliedern)* any further by means of a definition. (3.26) The word *green* used in an ordinary proposition as the name of a color, when the proposition is completely analyzed so as to separate the *way* of designating from *what* is designated, can be taken as an example. A further definition of *green* in terms, for example, of optics or electromagnetic theory, would go beyond the sense intended in the ordinary proposition. It is not that the names used in ordinary propositions *could* not be further defined, but that if they were further defined, they would no longer be *those* names contributing to *that* sense.

When Wittgenstein says that "A name cannot be analyzed any further by means of a definition" (3.23) this would, if taken in one way, exclude every empirical particular from being named, since there is no empirical particular which might not at some time be further defined. This kind of a name (referring to nothing empirical) does indeed describe the names in elementary propositions. But it is not what Wittgenstein has in mind when speaking of names in ordinary propositions when "completely analyzed" and when we name "the objects of the thought." *We do use names in ordinary propositions on the principle of having them function as representatives of objects.* This is one of the ways in which ordinary language utilizes ultimate logical principles which permit that "all the propositions of our everyday language, just as they stand, are in perfect logical order." (5.5563)

To see this more clearly, however, we must examine the logic of everyday language in more detail.

iii

In discussing the logic of everyday language we have to consider three basic factors: *meaning, sense* and *ways of designation (Bezeichnungsweisen, Art und Weise bezeichnen).* Roughly speaking, words and names have meanings, propositions have sense, and "ways of designation" involve a great deal of what is usually called grammar (parts of speech and rules for the uses of different kinds of words), and what becomes logical syntax.

Although these three factors enter into everyday language, the essence of language is seen as involving just two of them—*meaning* and *sense*. The third factor drops out and is replaced by logical forms, which makes no distinction between kinds of words, but only between arrangements of names. Hence in its essence language is two-directional—one direction being a pointing, referring, "semantic" direction toward the world, and the latter a lateral, connecting or "syntactic" direction toward other words. The first direction—what a word refers to—is an expression's meaning; and the second direction—what the words connected together in a proposition show—is the form and sense of the proposition.

The "hidden core" of every language resides in the structural possibilities of various multiplicities of "referring elements" with different ranges of possible "combinabilities." Through such structures, when we add the "logical" or "reality" feature of bi-polarity, the world may be pictured truly or falsely.

Everyday language, however, besides this core, contains a vast number of more or less arbitrary and conventional grammatical aspects. Consequently we find ways of classifying words, such as nouns, verbs, adjectives, etc., and by tense, case, gender, voice, modality, etc. These constitute an enormous variety of "ways of designating" based upon "tacit conventions" which make everyday language "a part of the human organism and no less complicated than it." (4.002) The problem in understanding language, as the *Tractatus* conceives it, is to see how the structural and logical core is embodied in, and operates through, this vast variety of conventional grammatical disguises.[2] To do this we have to consider the interrelations of *meanings, senses,* and *ways of designating.*

The crucial point with regard to *meaning*, first of all, is that meaning is *what* we designate, and in language we can designate anything

---

[2] Wittgenstein believed at this point that "distrust of grammar is the first requisite for philosophizing," (*Notebooks.* p. 93) a statement he would have continued to support in his later philosophy, when he had given up the idea of a "structural core" of language, but still believed that it is grammar which suggests "bad pictures" to us.

at all (from the motes in a sunbeam to the galaxies and from relations between the motes to properties of the galaxies).[3]

In naming an "object of thought" in a "completely analyzed proposition" we are meaning whatever we name as an object (that is, as a simple and indefinable) and recognizing as relegated to syntax anything having to do with the "way of designation." (3.2) The vast variety of predicates and relations can be designated in their particularity in this way, meant as objects, while the condition that they *are* properties and relations is handed over to be expressed entirely by syntax. In this way ordinary propositions make use of the principle that "objects have signs as their representatives" (4.0312A) for talking about the innumerable external and material relations and properties of the world. (That properties and relations may be taken as objects is shown by the possibility of their being subjects in subject-predicate sentences, or of entering into relations themselves, without change of meaning, although with change of syntax.)

What ties together the essential core of language with ordinary language is that the same combinatorial principles apply to both. Thus when Wittgenstein, instead of saying "Names only occur in elementary propositions," writes "It is only in the nexus (*Zusammenhange*) of the elementary proposition that the name occurs in a proposition," (4.23) this should be understood as meaning that names can occur in ordinary propositions, when completely analyzed, but only in the same kind of connectedness or structure as in elementary propositions.

Meanings are all on the same level, and there are no "kinds of meanings." Where there appear to be different "kinds of meanings" (substance, properties and relations) the differences really lie in the different ways of designating. In respect to what we choose to name designation is arbitrary. But it is not arbitrary in respect to what makes it possible to designate in a certain way. That things *can* be designated in a certain way tells us something about the world. What it tells us about, however, is *logical form*, and *not* that there are different *kinds of entities* corresponding, for example, to subjects, predicates and relations.

iv

The way in which ordinary language makes use of the "logic of

---

[3] Anything can be named. But it should be noted that *names* themselves cannot be named. Names *mean* objects, and we cannot mean a name as an object, for it will then cease to be a name.

depiction" in naming things (and properties and relations when they are "objects of the thought") can be brought out by considering a specific example.

Consider the proposition "Amos loves Sophia." A great deal has been written on the question of how Wittgenstein could have conceived that all the possible relations between Amos and Sophia could be represented merely by arrangements of names.[4] Whatever we take Amos and Sophia to be (persons, pets, trolls, etc.) there are an enormous variety of possible situations which they may be in (spatial, temporal, historical, biological, psychological, etc.) How, we ask ourselves, could all these relations possibly be represented merely by arranging the two names *Amos* and *Sophia?*

Conceivably, it has been suggested, the two names might be written at different distances from each other and in different directions in order to represent different relations. But the sheer mathematical complexity involved in handling all possible relations in this way staggers the imagination. And, in addition, this would no longer give us an account of how our ordinary speech and writing do it, but only a new substitute map-like kind of writing.

The difficulty begins to clear up once we recognize two fundamental points:

(1) The proposition "Amos loves Sophia" is *not an elementary proposition*. It is not an elementary proposition because (a) it contains a name for a relation, *loves*, while there are no names of relations in elementary propositions and (b) Amos and Sophia are not ontologically simple *objects*, but complex *things*, and elementary propositions name only ontologically simple objects.

(2) Although "Amos loves Sophia" is not an elementary proposition, when it is *completely analyzed* (that is, when the term *loves* is recognized as having a different "way of designating" from the other two terms), it may be regarded as naming three "objects of thought" (two things and a "relation"). And in this way it *presents* a state of affairs (one of six possible permutations of *these* objects) and by this represents a possible situation (or possible relation which Amos and Sophia can be in).

---

[4] See especially the articles by Ellis, Copi, O'Shaughnessy, and Keyt in *Essays on Wittgenstein's Tractatus*, edited by Irving M. Copi and Robert W. Beard. And also E. Daitz—*The Picture Theory of Meaning* in *Mind*, 62 (1953), pp. 184-201.

We can see here the fundamental difference between an elementary proposition and an ordinary proposition: an elementary proposition asserts the existence of a *state of affairs*, (4.21) and it does this by means of a structure of names. An ordinary proposition, on the other hand, represents a *situation*, (4.031) and it does this by naming *things-in-the-situation*. (4.0311) It is when such an ordinary proposition is "completely analyzed," (3.201, 3.202) (and it can only be completely analyzed in one way, (3.25)) that its words become names of "the objects of the thought," and *these* names are then in structural combinations, with the different "ways of designating" shown only by the syntax. It is only because we do name properties and relations in this way that "all the propositions of our ordinary language, just as they stand, are in perfect logical order." (5.5563)

At the very beginning of his *Notebooks* Wittgenstein states his program this way: "If syntactical rules for functions can be set up *at all*, then the whole theory of things, properties, etc., is superfluous." (p. 2) And on the next page he adds: "if *everything* that needs to be shown is shown by the existence of subject-predicate *sentences*, etc., the task of philosophy is different from what I originally supposed." (p. 3) These passages show Wittgenstein's awareness that syntax can handle all grammatical differences without resort to further justifications. The door is open for "propertyness," "predicateness" and "relationality" to be dealt with entirely syntactically, while the "natures" of specific properties, predicates, relations are "neutral" meanings of names, all on the same level.[5]

What has kept alive discussion of this question has been the impossibility of seeing how the mere arrangements of names of objects could possibly express the almost endless variety of relations described in ordinary language. But once we distinguish between *things* and *objects* (and *situations* and *states of affairs*) and once we recognize what is meant by *objects of a thought*, (3.2) then the difficulty disappears. For in a "completely analyzed proposition" properties and relations are

---

[5] "It is somewhat venturesome and yet not an altogether unreasonable speculation that sees in word order and stress the primary methods for the expression of all syntactic relations and looks upon the present relational value of specific words and elements as but a secondary condition due to a transfer of values." Edward Sapir—*Language—An Introduction to the Study of Speech*, (N.Y., 1949), pp. 113-4. Sapir is, of course, suggesting a genetic hypothesis, and not a logical analysis. (Wittgenstein's own use of italics, incidentally, might suggest that *stress* is more important than philosophers have recognized.)

named as "objects of a thought," even though in an elementary proposition even this is not necessary. Contrary to what some commentators have argued, Wittgenstein never abandoned the view which he expressed in the *Notebooks* that "Relations and properties, etc. are *objects too.*" (p. 61) What he did do was to distinguish between *completely analyzed propositions* in which relations and properties are *named*, and *elementary propositions*, each of which asserts only one state of affairs, in which they are not named.

In the case of the proposition "Amos loves Sophia," if we ask how many objects there are in the *configuration* which this proposition "corresponds to," (3.21) the answer must be that there are *three*. We can say that there are two *things* in the situation (Amos and Sophia), but three "objects of the thought" (Amos, Sophia, loves). Or we can say that the particular two-term contingent external relation between Amos and Sophia is handled by the proposition as a three-term description of a state of affairs, made possible by naming the "meaning" of the relation as a third term, and taking its position *between* the other two as showing that it *is* a relational term. (Cf. 4.012)

Such naming of "objects of the thought," in other words, will only work if there is some way to distinguish between the thing-terms and the relation-term. This cannot be done if we take them all as *signs*, but only if we take them as *symbols*, with in this case two different "ways of designating." That the term *loves* does have a different "way of designating" from the other two terms is shown by its position between the other two terms (although this could just as well be shown by some other convention such as writing the word backwards or upside down.)[6] The word's syntactical role (that it *is* a relational term) is thus distinguished from its meaning (*what* relation).

In ordinary propositions *word order* is used to indicate differences in "ways of designating" and even the difference between a proposition and a description (though here some languages also use the copula). "House (is) green" is a proposition, while "green house" is only a description. (4.023D) What makes "House (is) green" a proposition is that it is logically segmented by the last word designating differently from the first one. *This*, however, is only shown by its *being* the last

---

[6] In the iconography of old-fashioned Valentine cards a pink heart with an arrow through it, placed between two persons, symbolized mutual love (or hoped-for mutual love). Here there is a symbol for the relation, and it seems natural to place it *between* the two things. (cf. 4.012)

word, and in another proposition it might be the first word, while retaining the same meaning as it had when it was the last word. (E.g. "Green is a common color" has "green" referring to the same "object" as "House is green.") Altering the arrangement of the names does not alter the meanings, but only the logical articulation of the meanings.

Subject-predicate propositions cannot be elementary propositions because the difference between subject-words and predicate-words must be regarded as conventional and not belonging to what is essential to language.[7] We can have a language without this distinction, but then the logical articulation involved will have to be handled in some other way. The general principle will, however, remain the same —that a proposition *presents (vorstellen)* a state of affairs to *represent (darstellen)* a situation. (4.031, 4.0311) (And this by contrast with a picture which *presents (vorstellen)* a situation in logical space to *represent (darstellen)* a possible situation in logical space. (2.11, 2.202))

The sharp separation between meaning and syntax and between meaning and sense is perhaps the most characteristic feature of Wittgenstein's analysis of propositions. We turn now to examine how this is carried out in what he has to say about *signs* and *symbols*.

v

In analyzing propositions to arrive at their general forms (those involving symbols) and their logical forms (those involving only signs) we have to make use of variables, all of which can be considered as propositional variables. (3.314) The procedure will be to substitute variables for symbols in the one case and variables for signs in the other case, and in each case to make no further statements about meanings, but to substitute the variables solely on the basis of *description of propositions*.

The first analysis which leads to the *general form of the propositions* which can contain the same expression (or symbol) requires using a variable for all these propositions. And Wittgenstein tells us, in the longest italicized passage in the book, that in stipulating the values for such a variable "the only thing essential to the stipulation is *that it is*

---

[7] "So far as the act of thinking is concerned, subject and predicate are one and the same, and there are many languages in which they are so treated." A. H. Sayce—*The Science of Language.* v. 2, p. 329.

merely a description of symbols and states nothing about what is signified." (3.317D) There are good reasons for the emphasis here. The sentence is important because it rules out any attempt to base logical or grammatical distinctions on further assertions about meanings (*such as, for example, that meanings are of different ontological types, such as substances, properties or relations*).

Wittgenstein's view is that the different ways in which symbols contribute to the senses of the different propositions which they may be in must not be justified by further statements about the meanings of the symbols. We cannot, in other words, recognize *anything* about the *way* in which a symbol designates from the *meaning* of the symbol, but only from the way in which the symbol contributes to the senses of the different propositions which it can be in, which propositions these *are* being arbitrarily stipulated out of all those which they *can* be. A subject-term must be distinguished from a predicate-term, for example, on the basis of the complete sense of a proposition (since a subject in one proposition can serve as a predicate in another and vice versa) and not on the basis of further supposed differences between the nature of what the subject-term refers to and the nature of what the predicate-term refers to. Differences in *kinds* of meanings are not what make subjects subjects or predicates predicates.

What counts in a proposition is what terms (having the meanings which they do have) can go with what other terms. And this is determined by classifying propositions themselves and not by talking about ontological characteristics of what the terms signify. We do not have to distinguish things, properties and relations ontologically; all we have to do is to take account of the ways in which expressions actually occur in propositions. Symbols, in other words, already have their meanings, and *we have no further access to the meanings which would permit us to use the meanings for explaining differences between the symbols.* An analysis in terms of the *possible sense-characterizings of symbols* will be sufficient.

And what goes for symbols goes also for signs. In a similar way Wittgenstein says that the meaning of a sign must not play a role in logical syntax. "It must be possible to establish logical syntax without mentioning the meaning of a sign; only the description of expressions may be presupposed." (3.33) This does not mean that we deal with signs that have no meanings at all; it means that we have to take the meanings of the signs for granted without mentioning them again. (cf.

6.124) This illustrates a general principle of the *Tractatus*. Just as language has to take logic for granted, so logic has to take the meanings of language for granted and not attempt to make logical distinctions by further *ad hoc* appeals to these meanings.[8]

With this in mind we can think of a proposition as being determined in two ways—depending upon whether we think of its elements as expressions (or symbols) or as constituents (or signs). The first way of taking it involves the different possible "sense-characterizings" of the same expressions (i.e. the different propositions which the same expressions can be in.) (3.31) And the second way involves the different meanings possible in the same form of a proposition. (3.315)

In the first case, since *expressions* (or *symbols*) are what characterize the senses of propositions, (3.31A) each occurrence of an expression in a proposition can be thought of as one instance of all that expression's possible "sense-characterizings." So an expression belongs to a class of possible "sense-characterizings" and can be represented by the general form of the propositions with those senses (3.312) or by a variable whose values are those propositions. (3.313)

In the second case, since *constituents* (or *signs*) do not "characterize" sense, but only determine it by their designations, each sign can be thought of as an instance of what can be meant when the sense remains the same. So, in this case a proposition with variables replacing its signs can represent classes of propositions with those meanings and finally a single such class which "corresponds to" a logical form. (3.315)

Several things should be noted about these two analyses: (1) whether we are talking about *expressions (symbols)* or *constituents (signs)* they can be represented by variables; (2) since both expressions and constituents have meanings only in propositions, the variables in each case can be thought of as having *propositions* as their values; (3) the variables in each case, therefore, stand for *classes* of propositions; (4) the variables may also be said to designate *formal concepts* or represent constant forms; (4.127, 4.1271) (5) what propositions are to be in the

---

[8] Russell's "theory of types," Wittgenstein says, "must be wrong because he had to mention the meaning of signs when establishing the rules for them." (3.331) Parenthetically, it should be noted that the objection that relations are of a "higher type" than objects (and therefore cannot be "named" on a par with objects) has no force against Wittgenstein, who does not recognize "types" because he does not permit us to say anything further about meanings when analyzing propositions or establishing logical syntax. Immanent *forms* wholly replace *types* in the *Tractatus*.

classes is determined by *arbitrary stipulation* in the case of expressions (symbols) (3.317) and by *arbitrary conventions about meanings* in the case of constituents (signs); (3.315) and (6) we arrive in the first case at the *general form* of a number of propositions and in the second case at the *logical form* of a single proposition.

This last point requires further discussion. What propositions we start with in one sense is not arbitrary or conventional. It is given propositions of ordinary language, propositions which *already make sense*. What *is* arbitrary or conventional is the meaning which ordinary language has given to the signs in them and the propositions which we choose, or stipulate, to represent the possible "sense-characterizings" of the symbols in them. In effect, a proposition has two natures—one given by the *general forms representing its symbols,* and the other by the *logical form of its combination of signs.*

It is an important point, however, that Wittgenstein does not say that the analysis with signs leads to a logical form, but to a class of propositions which "corresponds to" a logical form. (3.315) The reason why he cannot say that it *is* a logical form is because we have been taking the words merely as signs, and the words in ordinary propositions *cannot* be taken merely as signs because they are in addition symbols, (i.e. retain different "ways of designating" as well as different designations). Hence he has to add that a sign only *determines* a logical form when it is taken *together with* its logico-syntactical employment. (3.327) The contrast then is that the sheer possible meanings of the signs "correspond to" a logical form, but only the signs with their "ways of designation" *determine* a logical form.

All this again makes clear that ordinary propositions, even when analyzed, do not bring us to elementary propositions, because syntax is still involved with the ordinary propositions and not merely structure and logical form. What has been shown is that the signs which carry the different "ways of designating" in ordinary propositions, if taken merely as signs, give us what "corresponds to" a logical form. And this is the way in which ordinary propositions have, as it were, concealed in them, the structural character of elementary propositions. So it can be said of *words* what Wittgenstein says of *things*—that their independence is a "form of connectedness" (*Zusammenhang*) with structures. (2.0122)

To illustrate this we take the proposition "The house is red." The symbol *house* can be represented by the general form of the propositions with senses which the word *house* characterizes. (We can write "The house is X.") Or it can be represented by a variable which takes propositions of this form as its values. (3.313) Similarly the symbol *red* can be represented by a variable which takes propositions of this form as its values. (We can write "Y is red.")

The proposition "The house is red" thus produces two propositional variables. The two variables represent, in effect, "things which can be said about houses" and "things which can be said to be red," (*red* being only one of the things which can be said about *houses* and *houses* being only one of the things which can be said to be *red*). This is as far as we can go. The sense of this particular proposition is something like the intersection of two arbitrarily chosen classes of propositions, selected from all those in which its symbols, taken separately, can occur.

If we now take the two terms *house* and *red* merely as *signs* with conventionally established meanings and substitute variables for them, we get something like: all the meanings which could substitute for the sign *house* in the proposition and all the meanings which could substitute for the sign *red*. The question of sense is here taken for granted, but when *all* the variables are substituted, the specific sense of the original proposition is lost and only what "corresponds to" its logical form remains.

What expressions occur in *what* propositions is, of course, not wholly arbitrary. It depends upon what expressions *can* occur in what propositions, which in turn depends upon what situations are *possible* and therefore *can* be represented. It is determined in the first instance by a logical form, or the possible structures of all the meanings of the expressions in a proposition. But it is also determined by the forms of the propositions in which the expressions can occur, for, as Wittgenstein says: "An expression presupposes the forms of all the propositions in which it can occur." (3.311) (We must bear in mind that it is *not* possible for certain expressions to occur with sense with certain other expressions—for example, we cannot put an *event* in a hole; watches cannot *fence* with each other; the color *green* cannot go to sleep, etc. These are impossible situations which cannot be expressed or represented by propositions with sense.)

The propositions which serve as the values for a propositional variable are propositions in which an expression *does* occur, and these are an arbitrarily selected group from those in which it *can* occur. Wittgenstein emphasizes that it is not essential how the propositions are selected "whose common mark the variable is." (3.317) The reason is that, *however they are selected*, they will be instances of the same general form, which is not arbitrary, but is based on the forms of all the propositions *presupposed* by an expression. What Wittgenstein says in another context may be applicable here: "the definition of classes itself guarantees the existence of the real functions." (*Notebooks.* p. 29)

Every ordinary proposition, it would seem, must have at least two expressions or symbols designating in different ways in it, since it must be logically segmented, and its analysis will produce at least two different kinds of propositional variables. This outcome, though more generally stated, is not so far removed from the traditional requirement of the subject-predicate form. What is distinctive is that no ontological considerations are permitted to justify this. Whatever is not conventional in it is accounted for in terms of structure and logical form.

vi

The analysis of propositions involves one further important distinction—that, involving form and essence, between the *forms* of propositions and what is *essential* to a proposition. (3.31, 3.341) The former is what is presupposed by the expressions in propositions and the latter what is in common between propositions with the same sense.

Thus Wittgenstein distinguishes between:

(1) propositions expressing *different* senses with the *same* expressions, and
(2) propositions expressing the *same* sense with *different* expressions.

In the first case we are concerned with the way in which we use the *same* words to say innumerable *different* things, and in the second case with the innumerable ways in which we can say the *same* thing.

In addition to the formal analysis which uncovers presupposed forms by the use of variables, we must also look, therefore, at what is *essential* in any one instance of such a form. (Here, as elsewhere in the *Tractatus*, the *essential* is a single, indefinitely repeatable structure, while the *formal* is all the possible structures, of which this is one. Formal analysis depends upon the distinction between what is "possible" and what is "impossible;" what is "essential" on the other hand is distinguished from what is "accidental.")

Wittgenstein puts this latter distinction this way:

> Accidental features are those that result from the particular
> way in which the propositional sign is produced. Essential
> features are those without which the proposition could not
> express its sense. (3.34)
> So what is essential in a proposition is what all propositions
> which can express the same sense have in common. (3.341A)

For example, it is accidental whether a proposition is spoken in German, English or Swahili, to the extent that a proposition in each of these languages can express the *same* sense.

The matter is not so simple, however, because accidental features, besides being the unavoidable results of custom and convention, also produce "the most fundamental confusions" in natural languages. (3.324) To bring out what is essential in language, therefore, we have to make use of "a sign-language that is governed by *logical* grammar— by logical syntax." (3.325) It is only of correct sign-languages that we can say that *translatability* into each other is what is essential in them or what they all have in common. (3.343)

A logical grammar or logical syntax, Wittgenstein says, must meet two requirements: (1) it must bring signs and symbols into harmony by not using the same sign for different symbols (e.g. not using the same sign for a noun and an adjective), and (2) it must not use "in a superficially similar way signs that have different modes of signification," (e.g. the word *is* used as a copula, sign for identity and expression of existence). (3.325, 3.323)

It might be thought that if we have a *logical syntax*, all will be well. But this is unfortunately not the case, as Wittgenstein's frequent criticisms of Frege and Russell bring out. He concedes that Frege and Russell made use of logical syntax, but he adds that this still "fails to exclude all mistakes." (3.325B) We need something *more* than a logical syntax; we need a correct logical point of view (4.1213) or correct conceptual notation. (5.534) But what is this?

Russell, for example, is said to have been in error in understanding signs themselves in such a way as to give rise to the paradoxical possibility-impossibility of a sign being able to be *contained in itself*, rather than understanding them in such a way as to bring out the *complete impossibility* of this. The "theory of types" then compounds the error by an extra-logical appeal to meanings to set the whole thing straight again. (3.331, 3.332, 3.333)

The word *correct (richtig)* plays an important, but often overlooked, role in the *Tractatus* (as something like a word for *"meta-true"*). Pictures, thoughts and propositions are said to be *true* or *false*. But pictures, (2.17, 2.173, 2.18, 2.21) sign languages, (3.343) a logical conception, (4.1213) logic, (5.45) conceptual notation, (5.534) explanation, (5.5422, 6.112) a method in philosophy, (6.53) and a way of seeing the world (6.54) are said to be *correct* (or occasionally *incorrect*). What makes these correct in most cases is that they enable us to think and express ourselves clearly. (4.116) And this is the goal of philosophy—the logical clarification of thoughts.

In the some twelve or so places where Wittgenstein *corrects* Frege and Russell it is because they are held to be, in most cases, guilty of "logical supererogation"—trying to say what cannot be said, introducing notations, definitions, laws where the symbolism itself should be sufficient. Wittgenstein sums up his objections in two fundamental remarks: "The precedent to which we are constantly inclined to appeal must reside in the symbol itself." (5.525C) and "Self-evidence, which Russell talked about so much, can become dispensable in logic only because language itself prevents every logical mistake." (5.4731)

Russell is criticized for not allowing signs themselves to show the formal properties of objects. (4.12721) We cannot designate such formal properties of objects directly, for we cannot use a sign to indicate a common characteristic of two different objects since signs are arbitrary. (3.322) Such formal properties are distinctive features, not of the objects themselves, but of the symbols which designate and mean the objects. (4.126F) And the sign for the characteristics or criteria of a formal concept must be chosen so as to show "a distinctive feature of all symbols whose meanings fall under the concept," (4.126G) (as is done in logic by using capital letters, small letters, letters from the beginning of the alphabet and the end of the alphabet, Greek letters, Latin letters, etc.) Hence we express formal properties of objects by signs standing for characteristics of formal concepts.

Russell's mistake in Wittgenstein's view was to suppose that it is possible "to introduce as primitive ideas objects belonging to a formal concept *and* the formal concept itself." (4.12721). And this is one of the errors leading into paradoxes and type theory. But why did Russell do this, and what is the fundamental issue between him and Wittgenstein at this point? It is evident that Russell's need to introduce formal concepts separately arose from his *rejection of internal relations* and especially of internal relations between propositions. If forms are not *immanent* in objects, in the world and in language so as to permit internal relations, (4.122) then formal concepts will *have* to be "introduced separately." Wittgenstein's point of view with regard to this was already indicated in the *Notes to Moore* when he wrote: "*Internal* relations are relations between types, which can't be expressed in propositions, but are all shown in the symbols themselves and can be exhibited systematically in tautologies." (*Notebooks.* p. 115)

Wittgenstein's whole approach here illustrates once again a cardinal principle of his method: instead of trying to separate the "hard" from the "soft" (or, we might add, to impose the "hard" on the "soft" in the manner of some "logistic philosophers") he tries to "see the hardness of the soft." (*Notebooks.* p. 44) Hence instead of trying to separate the logical from ordinary language, or to impose it on ordinary language, he tries to find the logical *in* ordinary language. And, similarly, instead of prescribing rules for symbolism, he tries to allow the symbolism to take care of its own rules and to "speak for itself."

As so often happens, Wittgenstein himself has given the best description of this. In his *Zettel* he wrote:

> Here we come up against a remarkable and characteristic phenomenon in philosophical investigations: the difficulty—I might say—is not that of finding the solution, but rather that of recognizing as the solution something that looks as if it were only a preliminary to it. "We have already said everything. Not anything that follows from this, no, *this* itself is the solution!"
> This is connected, I believe, with our wrongly expecting an explanation, whereas the solution of the difficulty is a description, if we give it the right place in our considerations. If we dwell upon it, and do not try to go beyond it.
> The difficulty here is: to stop. (sect. 314, p. 58)

Russell's mistake, in Wittgenstein's view, was in attempting to go beyond a description, for names themselves know how to prevent any mistakes, if we understand names correctly as *already having a formal character.*

Forms

All genuine philosophy moves entirely in the realm of possibilities.

MORITZ SCHLICK

The idea of form is more fundamental than the idea of class.

BERTRAND RUSSELL

Space, just like time, is a certain order . . . which embraces not only actuals but possibles also.

GOTTFRIED LEIBNIZ

Procul dubio non est mundus factus in tempore, sed cum tempore.
(Verily, the world was made not in time, but with time.)

ST. AUGUSTINE

Always stand by form against force.

JOHN RUSKIN

CHAPTER 5

Forms

i

Logic, as it is understood in the *Tractatus*, is something like the *science of possibility*. Wittgenstein says it deals with (*handeln*) *all possibilities* as its "facts." (2.0121C) Or it might be said that it presupposes "all possibilities" in somewhat the way that empirical science presupposes facts. Logic, as it were, stands in between the "all possibilities" which it presupposes and the facts which presuppose it. Hence what is necessary for any true description of the world is *logical form* (existence and non-existence), but what is necessary for logical form is *ontological form* (the "all possibilities" which individually exist and do not exist).

What logic "has to do with" are *forms*, or different kinds of "all possibilities." But it must not be supposed that logic has a special "subject-matter," (6.124, 6.111) for what it deals with are just the forms of the world. These appear under what Wittgenstein calls the *form of reality*, for it is *reality* which has the form which is logical form. (2.18) This is the framework, or logical scaffolding, determining logical space, (3.42C) which is necessary to make possible any representation of the world at all (correctly or incorrectly, by pictures or by propositions).

Logic is not "informative" (*gehaltvoll*), (6.111) but requires in order that it may have determinate sense to work with (3.23) the substance of the world or different "orders of possibilities" (i.e. what comes to the same thing, different "property spaces," conceived as discrete manifolds). These different "orders of possibilities," or different "manifolds of names" are distinguished from each other by their elements having different *forms* or different capacities for combination. The *Tractatus* thus understands *forms of objects* (possibilities of combinations) as underlying and determining *forms of states of affairs* (all possibilities of combinations of given objects), and the latter as supplying all the ranges of possible structures corresponding to the material properties of the world. (2.0251, 2.033, 2.0121)

95

What gives the *Tractatus* its apodictic and enunciatory tone is that it talks about different kinds of "all possibilities" and the ways in which they underlie the empirical world. These are, on Wittgenstein's own showing, just the kinds of statements which are, in an illuminating (*erläutern*) way, nonsensical (*unsinnig*) since they attempt to say something *about* what properly belongs only to the *way* in which we say anything. It does not make sense (and in addition is unilluminating) to ask what there must *be (sein)* in order that something may be the case. (5.5542) The *Tractatus's* special brand of "nonsense" (6.53, 6.54) is talking about how it is *possible* to represent the world logically. (Not what *we* must *make* so in order to be able to do this, but what about the *world* permits us to do it.)

The language of the book is the language of modality—of *can* and *cannot* (what *can* and *cannot* be or be said, what is or is not *possible*) and of *must* (what is necessary in order that something else may be possible). The underlying cadence is the cadence of modality. "It is possible . . . we can, I can, it can;" "It is impossible . . . we cannot, I cannot, it cannot;" "It determines . . . we must, I must, it must;" "In order to, must;" "Only if, can;" "If can, cannot;" "If can, must;" etc.

Necessity arises here because we are dealing with "all possibilities" as the world gives them (and often, implicitly or explicitly, in contrast to what is impossible). The core of the method is the movement between the empirically possible (*things-in-situations*) and the formally possible (*objects-in-states-of-affairs*). It is the formally possible which sets limits to the empirically possible (2.0122) as well as providing the possibility of representing it. (2.15, 3.2, 3.21)

Generally in philosophy, Wittgenstein says, the individual case "turns out to be unimportant," but it becomes important because it discloses something about what is possible. (3.3421) And what is possible is only possible in terms of "all possibility," which then in turn shows what is necessary. It is possibility which discloses the essential or structural character of propositions, description and world. (3.3421, 5.4711) And with this the empirical or accidental element drops out, and, in the case of language, we have sheer arbitrary designation bound up directly with syntactical necessity.

Complete arbitrariness of the individual item and complete structural inter-connectedness appear together. That these two "dimensions" of substance, language and description are wholly separate from each other and at the same time wholly contiguous, reflects the striking way in which arbitrariness and necessity unite. For the "essence of notation" is "that when we have determined something arbitrarily, something else is necessarily the case." (3.42)

All this helps to explain the enormous emphasis on *form* in the *Tractatus*. The book is a statement about the formal presuppositions of language or *what makes language possible*. Different kinds of possibility appear as different kinds of forms. In the *Notebooks* Wittgenstein says that the word *all* is the mark of form. (pp. 38-9) What makes possibility other than "mere possibility" (*nur-möglich*) is its being "all possibility," for "Nothing in the province of logic can be merely possible." (2.0121C)

It should be noted that variables can express form, but they can express it only because they presuppose it; they do not "create" it or "define" it in the sense of arbitrarily setting it up. (3.311, 3.315, 4.1272, 4.1273) Logic surrounds the world *as given* and presupposes that "names have meaning and elementary propositions sense." (6.124) Wittgenstein says that "every variable represents a constant form that all its values possess," (4.12721) but every variable (including variable names) can be understood as a propositional variable, (3.314) and hence as presupposing the forms of all the propositions in which its values can occur.

Forms, in Wittgenstein's view, give us different kinds of essential generality, which belong not merely to language and to human constructions, but to the very nature of the world, and to that which even any imagined world must have in common with the real one. (2.022)

How, once the meanings of names have been arbitrarily assigned, logical syntax then depends upon form and not upon further arbitrary choices and constructions can be seen by an examination of what Wittgenstein says about the forms of the world as mirrored in a logical way by pictures and propositions. Beyond the arbitrary act of naming, language depends upon immanent forms, and not upon further arbitrary choices, for, as he says, analysis does not "resolve the sign for a complex in an arbitrary way; for instance it would not have a different resolution every time it was incorporated in a different proposition." (3.3442)

Before discussing this further, however, it is desirable to have a general inventory of the various kinds of forms in the *Tractatus* in order to bring out a number of points about them all. They can be conveniently grouped under five main headings:

1 – *Forms pertaining to objects and states of affairs* (ontological forms)
    form of the world (2.022, 2.023, 2.026)
    form of an object (2.0141, 2.0251)
    form of a state of affairs (2.033)
    form of a fact (5.156)
    form of independence and form of dependence (2.0122)
    form of reality (2.18)
    logical form (2.18)
    logical form of an object (2.0233)
    logical form of reality (4.121)

2 – *Forms pertaining to pictures*
    form of picturing (*Form der Abbildung*) (2.15)
    form of representation (*Form der Darstellung*) (2.173)
    logical form of a picture (*logische Form*) (2.18)
    logical form of picturing (*logische Form der Abbildung*)
        (2.201)

3 – *Forms pertaining to propositions*
    form of a sign (5.5542)
    form of an expression (4.242)
    form of sense of a proposition (3.13)
    form of a proposition (3.311, 4.012, 5.131, 5.24, 5.5422)
    propositional form (5.1311, 5.156, 5.541)
    form of a function (3.333)
    forms of elementary propositions (5.556)
    general forms of propositions (3.312)
    general form of a proposition (4.5, 6.)
    general propositional form (4.53, 5.47, 5.471, 5.54)
    most general propositional form (4.5, 5.472)
    general form of an operation (6.002)
    logical form of expressions (6.23)
    logical form of a proposition (4.0031, 4.12, 4.121)
    logical form of elementary proposition (5.555)

4 – *Forms pertaining especially to logic and mathematics*
    form of a sign (5.501, 6.1203, 5.5542)
    form of the term of a series (5.2522B)
    form of a definition (4.241)
    form of a proof (6.1264)

general form of operation for producing series (4.1273)
general form of a truth function (6.)
general form of a number (6.022)
general form of a whole number (6.03)
most general form of combinations of logical signs (5.46)

5 — *Forms pertaining to science*
form of description (6.34, 6.341)
form of a law (6.32)
logical form of a law (6.33)

Four points may be made about forms in general as they appear on this list:

(1) Although it looks as if there is indeed a plethora of forms (virtually a form for everything!), it is very important to notice *what there are no* forms of. There is no form of *names;* and there is no form of *elementary propositions* as such, as distinct from other propositions. And this is important because it establishes the "openness" of language. "Old expressions" can be used "to communicate a new sense" (4.027) partly because there is no *a priori* limit to what can be named. As Wittgenstein says: "We are unable to give the number of names with different meanings." (5.55) There may be infinitely many names, (5.535) just as there may be infinitely many objects, (4.2211) but names are not *given* the way objects are. (2.0124) In addition it should be noted also that there is no form of *situations* and only a "weak" form of *things* (a form of independence is *their* form of dependence).

(2) Forms are arrived at in different ways. Ontological forms are "known" and "given"; (2.0123, 2.0124) forms of picturing and forms of propositions are "presupposed"; (2.15, 3.311) logical form is "in common" between pictures and reality and "mirrors itself" in propositions. (2.18, 4.121) Forms of elementary propositions, on the other hand, are *invented (erfinden)* within what is possible (5.555, cf. 4.221) and scientific forms of description are *optional* within what is possible. (6.33, 6.34, 6.341)

(3) Forms cannot be distinguished from one another by saying that one has this property and another that one. (4.1241) It is *operations* which are needed to express the *difference between forms.* (5.24, 5.241) Although we can speak in a certain way of the formal prop-

erties of objects and states of affairs, (4.122) the formal properties
of language and the world have to be *shown*. (6.12)

(4) The distinction between *forms, general forms* and *logical forms*
is of special interest because it involves the question of the relation
between *forms* and *classes*. It should be noted that there are *no
general ontological forms*. General forms are what forms of *propositions* have in common, and this can be expressed by propositional
variables with values from arbitrarily chosen *classes* of propositions.
The classes, however, do not determine the general forms, but
rather *presuppose them* for their *own* determination. (3.311) (Instead of the class we can give the formal law which governs the
forming of the propositions. (5.501F)) *Logical forms* are those
which involve *reality*, or existence and non-existence taken as one,
with only a "directional" difference of sense. Logical forms, in
a sense, "incorporate" other forms, giving them this "reality" status.
It should be noted that, not only are there *no general ontological
forms*, but there are also *no general logical forms*, for, as Wittgenstein says: "In logic there is no co-ordinate status, and there
can be no classification." (5.454) It becomes clear that there are
no ontological classes, no classes of pictures and *no logical classes*.
There are only classes of names (which cannot express sense) and
classes of propositions (which are general schemas of sense). (3.142,
3.311, 3.315) And, since classes of names are propositional variables
also, (3.314B) both of these classes do not determine forms, but
depend upon the forms of propositions. *Classes*, in short, everywhere yield to *forms*.

ii

The ontological forms provide the most direct entry into the formal
aspect of the *Tractatus*. There are four such basic ontological forms
which make up this core of Wittgenstein's system:

(1) *the form of the world,* which is objects or possible states of affairs;
(2.023, 2.0124)
(2) *the form of an object,* which is the possibility of an object's occurring in states of affairs; (2.0141)
(3) *the form of a state of affairs,* which is the possibility of the structure of a state of affairs (2.033) and
(4) *logical form,* which is the possibilities of the existence and non-

existence of states of affairs or a single possibility of the existence
and non-existence of a state of affairs. (2.06, 2.18)

All these forms are different kinds of "all possibilities." They all
illustrate the point that there is in the *Tractatus* no "mere possibility,"
but that every possibility is seen as one out of a determinately given
field of possibilities.[1]

With this in mind we can translate the four kinds of ontological
forms into four kinds of "all possibilities": (1) all possible states of
affairs; (2) all possible occurrences of an object in states of affairs; (3)
all possible kinds of states of affairs and (4) all possible existences and
non-existences of states of affairs.

That these are four different fields of "all possibilities" can be seen
from the following illustration (which, however, is somewhat misleading for reasons to be indicated). Suppose, for example, we imagine a
world with only three objects, all of which have the same form. Then
what possibilities does such a world provide? We have:

(1) all possible states of affairs or combinations of objects, which is
    twelve, (ab, ba, ac, ca, bc, cb, abc, acb, bac, bca, cab, cba);
(2) all possible occurrences of each separate object in these combina-
    tions which is *ten*, (a, for example, does not occur in *bc* or *cb*,
    etc.);
(3) all possible kinds of structures (combinations with the same ob-
    jects), which is *four*, (ab, ba), (ac, ca), (bc, cb), (abc, acb, bac,
    bca, cab, cba);
(4) all possible combinations of any one combination with all other
    combinations of the same kind which is again *twelve*, (ab (ba), ba
    (ab) . . . abc(acb, bac, bca, cab, cba), bac(abc, acb, bca, cab,
    cba) . . . .).

In Wittgenstein's terminology these illustrate in a world with three
objects of the same form: (1) the form of such a world, (2) the forms
of objects, (3) the forms of states of affairs and (4) the logical forms.
(This last should not be confused with the number of possibilities of
existence and non-existence of states of affairs, which is the same as

---

[1] What Hermann Weyl characterized as "the boldness perpetrated from the
beginning in mathematics, namely, of treating a field of constructive possibilities
as a closed aggregate of objects existing in themselves," (*Philosophy of Mathematics
and Natural Science*, p. 50), if transposed into a realist and structural key, would
come close to describing Wittgenstein's conception of *substance*.

the number of truth possibilities of elementary propositions: for one
state of affairs there are two of these, for two states of affairs four,
for three eight, and so on. (4.27) The number of possible truth functions is then determined by this according to the formula at 4.42. For
one state of affairs it is four, for two states of affairs sixty-four, and
so on.)

Some important reservations must now be made about this illustration if it is not to be misunderstood:

(1) The supposition of a universe with only three objects in it cannot
mean more than that three objects are *given* as *all* objects and we
do not *know* any more objects. (2.0124, 5.524) The world that we
talk about is only the world that we *do* talk about and not a world
unknown and "beyond all limits." (5.61) It is, therefore, in a manner
of speaking, always "merely possible" that new objects will show
up and even objects with new forms. But it does not make sense
to say this. We can only say that any world that we imagine will
have to have some form in common with the real one (i.e. will
have to have *some* structural possibilities). (2.022)

(2) A world with only three objects is, of course, impossible, since it
would not be possible to have pictures or propositional signs in
such a world because pictures and propositional signs are also facts
(2.141, 3.143) and hence also involve objects which will have to
be different objects from those represented. A picture of a world
with three objects will involve three more objects and a propositional sign at least still another three more.

(3) A world with three objects is impossible for still another, and even
more basic, reason: because it would be a world without facts (and
it is facts that we picture (2.1)). A single state of affairs, even if it
exists, is not a fact. A fact is a *conjunction* of existing states of
affairs. To have a fact we must have at least *two* existing states of
affairs. And this will also apply to pictures and propositional signs
as facts. (To give a specific example we do not encounter objects
which are only spatial or only temporal, but *facts* which are combinations of spatial structures and temporal structures.)

(4) It may be objected that we are here treating states of affairs as
linear combinatorialities, instead of, for example, making use of a
third (or perhaps still more) dimensions. But, of course, whenever
we form propositions about objects, we represent them in a "two

dimensional" script, and it is a contention of the *Tractatus* that *any* possible situation which can be experienced (i.e. pictured) can be *projected* into "the preceptible sign of a proposition (spoken or written, etc.)." (3.11) (Propositions may be three-dimensional if arbitrary "naming" is involved. (3.1431) Otherwise such representations are pictures with "correlations" to "entities" rather than "naming" of simples. (2.1514)) In his *Notebooks* Wittgenstein asks (p. 6): "What is the ground of our—certainly well-founded—confidence that we shall be able to express any sense we like in our two-dimensional script?" It is clear that by "two dimensional" is meant having the two "directions" of left and right (or, temporally, of before and after), which geometrically count as one dimension, and also having the recognizably different individual signs made possible by utilizing the "up and down" "directions" which geometrically count as a second dimension. The answer which he arrived at to the question is the conception of *projection*. He conceived that, just as a three-dimensional landscape can be "projected" onto a two-dimensional canvas, so a possible situation (a three-dimensional arrangement of things) can be "projected" into a "two-dimensional" written or spoken script. That we can represent "all possible positions" of a body in three-dimensional space by linear strings of coordinates gives a rough idea of how this can be done.

(5) Finally the question may be raised whether, if all objects are given, every possible structure of them must not include *all* of them (excluding, for example, in the case of three objects, structures with only two objects, such as *ab* and *ca*). This restriction is too stringent, however, since nothing forbids the absence of an object from a single possible structure, even when it is known that it has the same form as the other objects in the structure. Wittgenstein speaks of knowing a *single* object, even though we have to know at the same time all its possible occurrences. (2.0123)

More needs to be said about the meaning of the word *fact (Tatsache)*, especially in the attempt to understand what is meant by the expression *form of a fact*, (5.156C) as well as *structure of a fact*. (2.034)

One of the most common mistakes made by commentators on the *Tractatus* is to suppose that a *fact* is an existing state of affairs or the existence of a state of affairs. Wittgenstein's view is that "What is the case—a fact—is the existence of states of affairs," (2.) and the plural, so often overlooked, is necessary to distinguish between facts and states of affairs. In his letter to Russell of 19.8.19 Wittgenstein makes the distinction clear by saying that "*Sachverhalt* (state of affairs) is what corresponds to an *Elementarsatz* if it is true. *Tatsache (fact)* is what corresponds to the logical product of elementary propositions when this product is true." (*Notebooks*. p. 129) Facts, in other words, are what correspond in the world to truth-functional conjunctions of true elementary propositions.[2]

Because of this it is possible for Wittgenstein to say both that "The totality of existing states of affairs is the world" (2.04) and that "The world is the totality of facts." (1.1) These two totalities are the same because any given fact is just a conjunction of existing states of affairs. (He also says "The facts in logical space are the world." (1.13) Logical space is the space of logical form—the form of reality—which is what permits the operation which generates truth functions and makes it possible for Wittgenstein to say that "elementary propositions themselves contain all logical operations." (5.47))

Facts themselves, it should be noted, also have structures, and we are told that "The structure of a fact consists of the structures of states of affairs." (2.034) And Wittgenstein also speaks of the "structural properties" of facts (also called "internal properties") which are "features" of facts "(in the sense in which we speak of facial features, for example)." (4.122, 4.1221) These properties may also be regarded as internal relations between facts or between possible situations. (4.125) We see such relations by seeing that "The structures of propositions stand in internal relations to each other." (5.2)

Since the same states of affairs appear in many different facts and, in addition, states of affairs of the same forms appear in different facts, we can talk about both the structural properties of facts and the formal properties of objects and states of affairs. (4.122) The structural properties of facts, however, will be nothing but the structures of the states

---

[2] The word *Tatsache* has a definite meaning for Wittgenstein and the English word *fact* (used to translate it) should not be inserted in the text where *Tatsache* does not appear as the Pears-McGuinness translation does at 2.15, 4.5, 5.1363, 5.634, 6.12, 6.1201, 6.124, 6.342, and in a different way at 5.43, 5.5351, and 5.5563. The proper use of the word *Tatsache (fact)* is not only essential to understanding the *Tractatus*, but is itself one of the main usages which the *Tractatus* wishes to clarify. The English colloquial expression "in fact," is therefore better avoided.

of affairs which make them up and which are shared by different facts, or which are in certain internal relations to each other. (4.123)

The expression *form of a fact* suggests cases where the forms of the states of affairs which in conjunction make up a fact may be known without the specific states of affairs being known. Hence Wittgenstein speaks of using probability "if our knowledge of a fact is not indeed complete, but we do know *something* about its form." (5.156) (We might, for example, know that the balls in an urn *were* colored, some black and some white, without knowing which color would be drawn in a particular case.)

What is of great importance for the whole outlook of the *Tractatus* is the central position of *facts*. And it is essential to see why facts, and not objects or states of affairs, constitute the real center of gravity of the book.

It is Wittgenstein's view that the world consists of facts, (1.1) and it is facts which we picture (2.1) and speak about (4.122) by means of pictures and propositional signs which are themselves facts. (2.141, 3.14B) The reason for this way of putting it is that, just as we cannot "identify" individual objects as objects except in states of affairs, so we cannot "identify" particular states of affairs as states of affairs except in facts. What, for example, distinguishes one instance of blue from another instance of the same shade of blue can only be that they are in different facts (i.e. are conjoined with different other properties). If different facts did not have at least some different properties (e.g. some spatial or temporal difference) they would be indistinguishable.

It is because, in a sense, our relation to the world *begins with facts* and *ends with facts* that Wittgenstein opens the *Tractatus* by talking about facts. He does this even though facts are ontologically the *last* step in the progression from *objects*, to *states of affairs*, to *existing states of affairs* and finally to *conjunctions of existing states of affairs*, which are *facts*. All except the last are prior to what we actually encounter at the level of experience (pictures). The world which we encounter is the world which "divides into facts." (1.2) It is facts which surround us and which we picture and have thoughts of before they are recognized as conjunctions of properties or conjunctions of existing states of affairs.

Another way of putting this is to say that *any* object of a certain form may become *this* object, but only after there are *states of affairs* of which it is a part. And, analogously, *any* state of affairs of a certain form may become *this* state of affairs, but only after there is a *fact* of which *it* is a part. *Empirical particularity only emerges at the level of facts* (which is, in ordinary language, the level of *things*). In ordinary language *we name things as objects and picture and describe them as facts.* And it is the possibility of being able to do *both* which shows that things embody the forms of the world (i.e. are distinguishable as spatial, temporal, colored, etc.) and at the same time are conjunctions of specific (structurally constituted) properties of these forms.

iii

We turn now to the forms having to do with pictures and propositions. What pictures and propositions have in common is that they both represent, not the world, but what Wittgenstein calls *reality* *(Wirklichkeit).* Unlike the *world*, which is existing states of affairs, (2.04) *reality* is the *existence and non-existence of states of affairs.* (2.06) What is critical here is the notion of *one and the same reality* having always *two* opposite senses—a positive one and a negative one. (4.0621C) That there is only one reality in both cases is shown by the possibility of *p* and *not-p* saying the same thing, for we could, if we like, reverse them and use *not-p* the way we now use *p* and vice versa, (4.0621A) (a reversal which we could *not* make with true and false propositions. (4.062)).

How are we to think of existence and non-existence as two "senses" of one and the same reality? The clue to understanding this is the comparison which Wittgenstein makes between this and spatial objects, where one and the same spatial object always permits two different descriptions—one in terms of the space which constitutes the object and the other in terms of the space which surrounds the object. (*Notebooks.* p. 30) The very same object may be described either by describing the place where it is or the place where it is not. (Or we might think of the positive and negative of a photograph, where we have exactly the same scene with the light values reversed.)

But everything depends upon how the analogy is to be taken. Wittgenstein's answer is:

> The proposition, the picture, the model are—in the negative sense—like a solid body restricting the freedom of movement of others; in the positive sense, like the space bounded by solid substance, in which there is room for a body. (*Notebooks.* p. 30, cf. 4.463)

We might have expected this to be put the other way around—that the *positive* sense of a proposition is like a solid body, "restricting the freedom of movement of others," while the *negative* sense leaves "room for a body." But it is just Wittgenstein's point that it is the positive which permits *something* to be there, while the negative closes out the space and says nothing but exactly what-is-not-there. (Thus a proposition which says *Red* permits Red or something else to be there, while one which says *not-Red* leaves no door open but not-Red.)

In the *Tractatus* this same quotation from the *Notebooks* appears in connection with the discussion of tautology and contradiction. Negative sense is connected with *contradiction*, which "fills the whole of logical space leaving no point in it for reality," while positive sense is connected with *tautology*, which "leaves open to reality the whole— the infinite whole—of logical space." (4.463C)

While reality is the world in its polar character of existence and non-existence, the *form of reality*, or *logical form*, (2.18) is all the possibilities of this, or all the possibilities of existence and non-existence for structures of objects of each form. On the one hand we picture reality. And *also* such a picture has the *logical form* that this arrangement of existence and non-existence is one possibility out of all such possible arrangements involving all colors. (In an elementary proposition a single color is asserted to exist as distinguished from all the other colors which logically could have existed in its place.)

The entire analysis of forms leads up to the idea of *logical form*, or all possibilities of existence and non-existence for a certain form of states of affairs, (of which the *sense* of a proposition will be one such possibility). Ordinary language, Wittgenstein says in his *Aristotelian Society* article,[3] misleads us (at least in the case of Indo-European languages) by projecting all logical forms into the subject-predicate form and the relational form (and perhaps he might have added the noun-verb form), and this obscures the *much larger number of logical forms*. In the logical forms of ordinary propositions we have: all possible combinations of existence and non-existence of all the possible combinations of objects having the same multiplicity as the objects in a possible situation.

The "protopicture" of a proposition (which "corresponds to" a

---

[3] *Knowledge Experience and Realism*, Aristotelian Society, Supplementary Volume IX, (1929), pp. 162-171.

logical form) is the complete range of possible structures of a given form which the proposition *could* represent, when these structures are arranged "logically" or in accordance with their possibilities of exisence and non-existence. The logical form of an elementary proposition can be given in two ways, as either (1) the totality of possible elementary propositions with the same multiplicities of the same names or (2) a single general proposition containing variables in place of these names. The general proposition shows all the possible senses which a certain range of elementary propositions may have and from which each elementary proposition selects just one.

iv

Besides the ontological forms and the various forms having to do with pictures and propositions the *Tractatus* also speaks of *forms which appear in science—forms of description* and *forms of the laws of science*. These are not forms which are presupposed by the very possibility of any description at all, but forms chosen for the purposes of specific actual descriptions.

On the level of science we take for granted the conditions which make any description at all possible and proceed to describe facts and relations between facts. We are not, therefore, talking then about what makes it possible to talk with sense about the world, but are concerned with what actually exists. The word *form* no longer means "what makes possible any description," but "what we have chosen as one possible way of describing."

Mechanics, Wittgenstein says, is distinguished from logic because the particular *way* in which mechanics is able to describe the world tells us something about the world, while the possibility of being able to describe it in *any way at all* (which is all that logic provides) tells us nothing about the world, (6.342) (though "the possibility of each individual case discloses something about the essence of the world." (3.3421)) What logic "brackets out" is just the "disjunction" between existence and non-existence. Hence while mechanics attempts to describe the *world*, logic is concerned with the prior structure of *reality* which is what permits such descriptions. Logic gives us the possible arrangements of *true and false statements,* on the basis of possible sense, while mechanics is "an attempt to construct according to a single plan all the *true* propositions that we need for the description of the world." (6.343)

Forms in science are "optional" and are "imposed upon" the description of the world in order to bring it into a unified form. Hence *a form of description* puts the representation of facts into a particular system, and this system has a logical character which is shown when it is formulated in terms of axioms (6.341) or rules which prescribe the particular way in which the descriptions may be given. The facts then appear in this "unified form" because only this way of describing is being used.

To illustrate this, we can consider an analogy: if the rules for making a certain map stipulated that only towns with populations of over 2,000 are to be shown it might appear as a necessity of nature or a law of nature that there *are* no towns smaller than this. But this "necessity" arises only from the chosen form of description. On the other hand, that there *are* towns larger than this is shown by its being possible to use such a map. The map, in effect, "defines" what is to be represented, and then, if it can be used, we see that things are to that extent indeed that way. (It should be noted also that we can speak of the *possibility of using a form of description,* an expression that would be quite meaningless with regard to other forms.)

All necessity in the *Tractatus* is logical necessity, (6.37) and there is no possibility of inferring from the existence or non-existence of one state of affairs to the existence or non-existence of another one (2.062) or from the existence of one situation to the existence of another entirely different situation. (5.135) However we achieve a unity of description, seeming to require what must be or what must happen, it is always conceivable that it will not be or will not happen. (As it is logically possible that the sun will not rise tomorrow or that bodies in a Newtonian gravitational field will not fall, etc.) Other possibilities which have been excluded only by the particular form of description chosen may still occur.

Wittgenstein draws an analogy between describing a picture and describing the world. (6.342) We are able to describe a picture completely; and *that* a picture is able to be described completely by a particular description having a particular form, Wittgenstein says, "characterizes" the picture. On the other hand, we are not able to describe the *world completely*, but only more *simply* with one form of description than another, and that it can be described at all in the way that it can be and also more simply in one way than another, tells us something about the world. (6.342)

The only way in which the world could be described *completely* would be by listing all true elementary propositions. (4.26) But this would not give us the relations between facts, but something like a list of what exists. At the level of facts what takes the place of being able to describe the world *completely* is being able to describe it more or less *simply*. The preference for the simplest law that can be reconciled with our experiences has no logical justification, however, but only a psychological one. (6.363) The demand for simples in ontology is the demand that sense be determinate. (3.23) And arriving at the simplest propositions is an obvious (*offenbar*) consequence of analysis. (4.221) But the choice of the simpler form of description (6.342) and the simplest law has only a psychological justification. (6.3631)

V

The *Tractatus* also anticipates the question: How do we arrive at a form of description? Its answer is that we have "*a priori* insights about the forms in which the propositions of science can be cast." (6.34) Examples of such *a priori* insights are minimum principles in mechanics, laws of least action, the principle of sufficient reason, laws of continuity and of least effort, etc. These are all *forms of laws* (or something analogous to logical forms of forms of description).

Conservation laws, in particular, Wittgenstein says, do not involve some *a priori belief*, but rather express "*a priori knowledge* of the possibility of a logical form." (6.33) They express, in other words, our knowledge that there *can be* fixed ranges of possibilities, or that we can deal with such fixed ranges of possibility in regard to energy, momentum, the space-time field, etc. We know, as it were ahead of time, that specific laws can be cast into that form.

The most basic case is the so-called "law of causality," which Wittgenstein describes as "the form of a law." [4] It is not, however, the form of the laws of mechanics, since mechanics is capable of giving descriptions without invoking causes (simply by enlarging the system of facts being described). In physics, however, (and in mechanics in so far as it is a part of physics), we encounter "laws of the causal form."

What is meant by the assertion that causality is the "form of a law"? Simply that causality expresses what makes laws of nature possible

---

[4] The 1922 English edition of the *Tractatus* has a footnote here at 6.32 reading "*I.e.* not the form of one particular law, but of any law of a certain sort (B.R.)."

since it amounts to something like a universal requirement that in every case the difference between the occurrence of an event and the non-occurrence of an event must mean that some factor is present in the first case which is not present in the second case. This is, as it were, the presupposition of every law of nature.

Wittgenstein draws an analogy between this and the way in which we are compelled to represent the passage of time. (6.3611) For just as we have to distinguish between *occurrence* and *non-occurrence* in terms of *some* additional factor, so we can only distinguish between *earlier* and *later* by comparing the process involved to some other process "such as the working of a chronometer." There simply is no factual difference corresponding to the difference between occurrence and non-occurrence as such or to the difference between earlier and later as such, and so we are in effect compelled to find the needed asymmetries to make these distinctions elsewhere. The "law of causality" expresses this need for an asymmetry between two events which permits us to describe the *one* of the two which occurs when either of the two could just as well have occurred.

Here Wittgenstein introduces another parallel provided by Kant's problem of the right and left hands which cannot be made to coincide. (6.36111)[5] He points out that this same Kantian difficulty holds in one-dimensional space, since we cannot describe any difference between the two "directions" of a single line (or the two "ends" of a single line) merely in terms of the line itself. The issue, however, is not a matter of being unable to "make them coincide" since, given a second dimension, it is easy enough to swing one half of the line around to "make it coincide" with the other half, and, similarly, given a four-dimensional space, a right hand glove could be "turned around" so that it could be put on a left hand. (6.36111B)

What is the resemblance between this problem of left-right symmetry and the questions of causality and the passage of time with which it is linked in the *Tractatus*? The resemblance is that in this case too we deal with a "difference" which only shows up in a complete symmetry and where we can only describe *one* of the two symmetrical

[5] Kant—*Prolegomenon to Any Future Metaphysics*—sect. 13. Also *On the Primary Reason for Distinguishing Direction in Space* (1768), included in Gabriele Rabel—*Kant*, (Oxford, 1963), pp. 86-87. Cf. Norman Kemp Smith—*Commentary to Critique of Pure Reason*, (New York, 1962), pp. 161-166. The matter is discussed, most entertainingly, by Martin Gardner in *The Ambidextrous Universe*, (New York, 1964), esp. pp. 160-172.

factors apart from the other if some asymmetry can be found. Left and right are completely congruent and are only distinguishable in terms of each other. It is impossible, therefore, to describe the difference between them by describing *one* of them.

This question is completely separated by Wittgenstein from the question of whether the symmetrical figures can be superimposed or "made to coincide." The impossibility of such "coinciding" is what Kant took as showing their (otherwise indescribable) difference. For Wittgenstein, however, such "coinciding" is not a logical impossibility since it could be overcome by introducing higher dimensions. Yet the problem remains, nevertheless, not as based upon the "impossibility of coinciding," but upon the impossibility of *describing one* of a completely symmetrical pair.[6]

In an analogous way what the "law of causality" expresses is that if two events are completely "congruent" and yet one happens and the other does not, there will be no way of describing *this* difference and such a situation will be unthinkable. All that can be described is the case where there *is* some additional factor which distinguishes the two. For Wittgenstein's point is that nothing can mark the difference between occurrence and non-occurrence except our being able to find some factor present in the one case and not in the other. What the "law of causality" "is meant to exclude" cannot be described, (6.362) for it would be a situation in which no reason whatsoever could be given for the difference between an event being merely possible and having actually occurred.

It is evident from this that causality belongs to the way in which we describe the world and not to the world itself. Wittgenstein says that there is no causal nexus in the world, and belief in such a nexus is a superstition. (5.136, 5.1361) We can see, therefore, what causality is *not*:

(1) it is not an inner connection between events—like the inner con-

---

6 Speaking of Euclid's *Elements*, Schopenhauer wrote: "It surprises me that the eighth axiom, 'Figures that coincide with one another are equal to one another,' is not rather attacked (rather than the eleventh or parallel postulate). For '*coinciding with one another*' is either a mere tautology, or something quite empirical, belonging not to pure intuition or perception, but to external sensuous experience. Thus it presupposes mobility of the figures, but matter alone is movable in space. Consequently this reference to coincidence with one another forsakes pure space, the sole element of geometry, in order to pass over to the material and empirical." *The World as Will and Representation*, trans. E. J. Payne, vol. II, p. 131. Schopenhauer here anticipates Hilbert and other twentieth-century geometers.

nection between objects in a state of affairs, or like the inner connection between propositions in logical inference, where one sense is contained in another sense, or like the inner identity between knowledge and what is known;

(2) neither is it a factual matter, an assertion about the world or about what happens to be the case, so that it could be expressed in a proposition which might turn out to be true or false;

(3) nor, finally, is it a law of nature or a form of description which might be applied in some cases, but not in others, and which describes the world in a particular way and might turn out to be more or less simple than some other way of describing it.

What is it then? Wittgenstein's answer is that it is a general rule for giving descriptions of the world in such a way as to permit the formulation of laws of nature. It is the formal element in the description of facts corresponding to the requirement that description shall be possible in every case. It is what guarantees the possibility of laws of nature.[7]

What distinguishes the descriptions of science in Wittgenstein's view is that they have a formal aspect. We choose descriptions which involve a certain lawfulness or regularity and hence a logical character. (6.3) The possibility of being able to describe the world in these ways does not, he says, then tell us anything about the world. But the *results* of such descriptions, the possibility of being able to describe it *in the precise ways* in which we do, *does* tell us something about the world. (6.342B) It tells us about the essence of the world, (3.3421) or its repeatable, representable structure. For we must remember that "any description of the world by means of mechanics will be of the completely general kind. For example, it will never mention *particular* point-masses: it will only talk about *any point-masses whatsoever*." (6.3432) And this is an example of Wittgenstein's more general point that

> We can describe the world completely by means of fully generalized propositions, i.e. without first correlating any name with a particular object. (5.526).

---

[7] The seeming conflict between this and current views in quantum mechanics may be more apparent than real since what is involved in the latter may be rather "limits of description" than "non-causal laws."

Negation and Operations

Great Negative, how vainly would the wise
Inquire, define, distinguish, teach, devise
Didst thou not stand to point their blind philosophies.

JOHN WILMOT — *Earl of Rochester*

Non-existence enters into even the impenetrable.

LAOTZU

Whatever can be said in words is able to say something only
by dint of saying nothing at all.

Visesha-cinta Brahma-pariprccha

That existents are without own-being is because their alter-
being is seen; an existent without own-being does not occur;
hence the emptiness of existents. If own-being does not occur,
to whom might alter-being belong? If own-being does occur,
to whom might alter-being belong?

NAGARJUNA

Nothing comes out of the sack but what was in it.

Persian proverb

CHAPTER 6

Negation and Operations

i

There are three aspects of negation in the *Tractatus* which have to be kept clearly separate:

(1) the *ontological basis*—which is the positive-negative character of *reality* (2.06) which permits elementary propositions to be true and false and permits one and the same reality to correspond to two opposite senses when a proposition is negated; (4.0621)
(2) the *operation of Negation (Negation)* (5.5, 5.502)—which is an operation peculiar to the *Tractatus* and is "the one and only general primitive sign in logic" (5.472) and which expresses the rule common to all truth operations; (5.476) and
(3) the *operation of negation (Verneinung*—sometimes translated *denial)*—which is the familiar operation which reverses the sense of a single proposition (5.2341C, 4.0641) or of an elementary proposition. (5.3)

These three aspects of negation are closely inter-related. The "general" operation of Negation (which Wittgenstein calls *Negation* and which will here be spelt with a capital letter to distinguish it) is based on the truth and falsity of elementary propositions as permitted by *reality*, (5.5) while the "specific" operation of negation, which he calls *Verneinung*, is the application of this "general" operation to a single proposition. (5.51) Logically speaking, we require the truth and falsity of elementary propositions before we can have any truth operations, (5.233) and we then also require the rule for constructing truth functions (5.476) (or the most general form for the combinations of logical signs (5.46)) before we can have specific logical operations.

Ultimately all negation depends upon the *polar character of reality* and *the nature of a proposition as a logical picture of reality*. For it is Wittgenstein's view that the entire logical scaffolding of the world is

needed before even one proposition can make sense. (4.023E) Here
again, as everywhere in the *Tractatus*, it must be emphasized that *we
do not prescribe logical properties to a proposition*, but rather a proposition must have all its logical properties just in order to be a proposition at all. This is a consequence of Wittgenstein's view that *we cannot
give signs logical properties in addition to using them as signs*, but rather
the very use of them as signs inevitably involves and shows all the logical properties which they can have (and which the world must have
if they are to represent the world). (cf. *Notebooks*. p. 11)

This view is stated in different ways in the *Notebooks*:

> in order for a proposition to be *capable* of making *sense*, the
> world must already have just the logical structure that it has.
> (p. 14)
> Although the proposition must only point to a region of logical
> space, still the whole of logical space must *already* be given
> by it. (p. 31)
> Even the unanalyzed proposition mirrors logical properties
> of its meaning. (p. 10)

In the *Notebooks* Wittgenstein also puts it this way: "Roughly
speaking, before any proposition can make sense at all the logical
constants must have reference." (p. 15) In the *Tractatus* he does not
speak this way and expressly repudiates this way of speaking, (4.0312)
but the same thought is expressed in the view that *all the logical constants must be implicit in the very nature of a proposition*. (For example, he says that "elementary propositions themselves contain all
logical operations." (5.47))

While the *Notebooks* speak of logical constants having meaning or
reference, all such "logical reference" in the *Tractatus* boils down to
the polar character of reality, which, *even before there are any logical
operations*, is represented by the mere act of picturing itself. (2.12)
And logical constants are reduced to the "sole logical constant" of Negation (*Negation*). The *Tractatus* in fact denies that there *are* any logical constants in Frege's or Russell's sense at all. (5.4) It speaks of *apparent* logical constants, (5.441) *apparent* primitive signs in logic
(5.461) and *apparent* relations in logic. (5.461) *The whole Frege-Russell
logical apparatus for propositional logic is shown indeed to depend
upon the polar character of reality and the one fundamental operation
called Negation.*

The most basic distinction in the *Tractatus* is between, on the one hand, both *reality* (which gives "reference" for both truth and falsity) and the *operation of Negation (Negation)* (which "constructs" every "joint falsity" into a different logical place), and, on the other hand, *world* (which settles truth *or* falsity) and elementary propositions (as *either* true or false).

The reason why Wittgenstein can say that there are no "logical constants" in the Frege-Russell sense is because all such "logical constants" are interdefinable and hence must depend on something else. The clinching argument is that "All results of truth operations on truth functions are identical when these results are one and the same truth function of elementary propositions." (5.41) This means that all logical operations leading to one and the same truth function are interchangeable and therefore not independent of each other. Such interdefinability shows we have to do with only conventionally primitive signs, (5.42B) and this, as will be seen, applies to Sheffer's stroke function as well as to the other logical connectives. (Negation in its fundamental aspect, is the exception, since "every proposition has only one negative, since there is only one proposition that lies completely outside it." (5.513))

What we take as the number of fundamental operations that are necessary, Wittgenstein says, depends solely on notation, (5.474) for there is only one general primitive sign which defines whatever fundamental signs a notation calls for. (5.472, 5.5, 5.502) Whatever primitive signs we use, we must "show clearly how they are placed relatively to one another and justify their existence" (5.45) for the primitive *concepts* of logic must be independent of each other. (5.451)

What takes the place of logical constants in the *Tractatus* are *operations*, and specifically *truth operations*. The sections numbered in the 5's deal with this topic. Particularly important are (1) the equivalence between a *formal series* (or the internal relation which orders such a series) and an *operation*, as what produces one term from another, (5.232) and (2) the conception of *successive applications of an operation*, which describes a peculiarity of operations—that, unlike functions, they can be applied repeatedly to their own results. (5.2521)

But before discussing operations Wittgenstein discusses *truth functions*. (5.1) Here, as elsewhere, he starts with what is "given," what is "given" being understood formally and structurally from the very start. As "given," propositions are internally related to one another, and one proposition can "contain the sense of" another.

(5.122) That the truth of one proposition *follows from* the truth of another "finds expression in the relations in which the forms of propositions stand to one another." (5.131) Representing a proposition as the result of an operation is then a *manner of expression (Ausdrucksweise)* to *emphasize (hervorheben)* the internal relations between structures of propositions. (5.21)

What is an *operation?* Wittgenstein tells us two principal things about it: (1) that it expresses a relation between the structures of propositions (5.22) which depends upon the "internal similarity of their forms" (5.231) and (2) that at the same time, as a variable, it "gives expression to difference between the forms" and is "a mark of the difference between the forms." (5.24, 5.241) (These two aspects foreshadow the difference between *tautologies* and *contradictions*.)

It is because propositions are internally related to each other (4.125) that truth functions are not mere mechanical and empty expedients, but can bring out the internal relations between possible situations. (4.125) Representing propositions as truth functions of elementary propositions is a way of seeing how the truth of one proposition "follows from" the truth of another. While one elementary proposition cannot follow from another, (5.134) they may nevertheless be internally related, and it is truth functions which enable us to recognize this.

Three fundamental questions arise concerning negation which have to be examined more fully:

(1) What is the operation called by Wittgenstein *Negation* and *how* does it give rise to all the other logical operations?
(2) How does this operation relate to what is ordinarily called negation, which he calls *Verneinung?*
(3) How do both of these operations get a foothold in the world?

ii

The operation which Wittgenstein calls *Negation* occupies a central place in the *Tractatus*—indeed perhaps *the* central place because it not only expresses the common rule for all logical operations, (5.476, 5.5) but also serves as the basis for the *general form of a truth function*, (6.A) the *general form of an operation* (6.01) and even the *general form of a proposition.* (6.B) Wittgenstein's understanding of the world in terms of immanent forms comes to a kind of climax in these "general

forms," which in turn all involve the possibility of this universal operation of *Negation*.

The most important point to bear in mind about *Negation* is that
it is an operation which is peculiar to the *Tractatus* and is *not to be
confused with* ordinary negation or with Sheffer's stroke function, with
both of which it has, however, a great deal in common. Wittgenstein's
operation expresses the rule which is common to all logical operations,
including ordinary negation and Sheffer's operation. It is not itself
one of these operations, but what they all have in common. (5.46)

It is also important to see why it cannot be called the "general"
operation, though it has the appearance of this. Wittgenstein tells us
that "In logic there cannot be a more general and a more special."
(5.454B) (This Ogden translation is closer to the German than the
Pears and McGuinness: "no distinction between the general and the
specific.") For in logic there can be no "side-by-sideness" (*Nebe-
neinander*) and no classification. (5.454A) The proper expression for
an operation is a *formal series*, (5.232) and in terms of such a series we
can speak of the *general form of an operation*. (6.01) But there is no
"general operation" because an operation is a transition *between* propositions which shows itself in a variable, but cannot be represented
without showing *what* it is a transition between. "The occurrence of
an *operation* cannot, *of course*, have any import by itself." (*Notebooks*.
p. 44) (We might say that "forms of internal relations between forms"
could only appear as *forms of series*.)

Even if there is no classification in logic, we can still speak of the
common rule for different uses of the negation sign (5.512C) and "the
real general primitive signs" in logic (5.46) which express a rule. (5.476)
The basis for the former is that it "mirrors negation" (5.512C) while
the latter can be expressed as a formal series. (5.5)

Everything which is common to the different signs of negation,
Wittgenstein says in the *Notebooks*, "must obviously proceed from the
meaning of negation itself. And so in this way the sign of negation must
surely mirror its own reference." (p. 34) In the *Notebooks* he can still
say that "The sign 'not' is the class of all negating signs," (p. 42) and
still speak of "the class of all negating operations." (p. 43) (This would
suggest a "general form of negation" or a "general operation of negation.")

In the *Tractatus* this way of speaking in terms of "classification" in
logic is replaced by: (1) the reference to the common *rule* for the

use of the negation sign, (5.512C) (2) the operation of *Negation* which expresses the rule, not merely for negation, but for *all* truth operations (5.5) and (3) the *general form of an operation* which represents, not merely truth operations, but all transition from one proposition to another. (6.01)

Speaking of the "common rule" which governs the use of the negation sign, (prescribing, for example, that a double negation, a quadruple negation, or any "even-numbered" negations give us again the original affirmation, while a triple negation, a quintuple negation or any "odd-numbered" negations all supply the original single negation), Wittgenstein still says in the *Tractatus* that what is common to all these uses "mirrors negation." (5.512C) It would appear that negation must still, in some sense, have a "reference," even if no other logical operations do.

With this in mind we can distinguish two aspects of ordinary negation: (1) the aspect which puts it *on a par with other logical operations,* so that the rule governing it appears "once a notation has been established," as is the case with logical addition and logical multiplication; (5.513) and (2) the aspect which gives it a *unique status* and which is what it shares with the rule underlying all truth operations and even with the general form of an operation. The specific rule for the use of the negation sign could vary with the choice of notation; but the *essential character of negation* (or what is "mirrored" by any specific rule) cannot vary.

What is *essential* to negation is that negation produces a proposition which has nothing in common with another proposition. It alone establishes two propositions as "opposed" to each other (5.513B) or as having "opposed" senses. (4.0621) There is no other operation or combination of operations which can produce this result, for there is only one proposition which lies completely "outside of" another proposition. (5.513B) Negation in this sense is not "interdefinable." (5.42)

On the other hand, negation, like other operations can be "cancelled out" and can "vanish." (5.253, 5.254) And this is what happens when we "negate a negation," for this is not an operation by which we "deal with" negation as if it were an object. (5.44C) Wittgenstein says that "It is a property of affirmation that it can be conceived as double negation." (6.231A) Ordinary negation becomes "interdefinable" when the rule common to it and all other operations is formulated as the operation which Wittgenstein calls *Negation* as distinct from *Verneinung*.

What distinguishes *Negation* from *Verneinung* is that

(1) *Negation* is applied to any number of elementary propositions and not merely to one;

(2) *Negation* involves the "successive application" of an operation (or an operation "applied repeatedly to its own results" (5.2521)) and

(3) *Negation* produces all possible truth functions for any number of elementary propositions and not merely opposite senses for each elementary proposition separately.

Negation is something like the "logical expansion" of the "dual reference" (for truth and falsity) which is contained in *reality*, establishing separate logical places for the cases of the falsity of elementary propositions (as well as their possible *joint falsities*) so that it *becomes possible to assert truly the negation of any false statement*. In this way a complete symmetry is established for language on the basis of the original (ontologically guaranteed) true-and-false-possibilities of elementary propositions. In this process we generate all logical operations. But how is this actually done?

iii

A number of objections have been raised to Wittgenstein's operation of Negation, objections which are not effective because they fail to take into account that this is a unique operation defined by Wittgenstein in a unique way. The operation is performed on elementary propositions and on its own results, accepting as true only cases of *joint falsity*, in accordance with the formula (. . . T). Since Wittgenstein *defines* this operation by saying that for two propositions it gives $-p. - q$ (neither p nor q), (5.51) it is not relevant to object that "When we negate p, q we do not arrive at $-p. -q$ but at $-p, -q$."[1] Wittgenstein is at liberty to define the operation in any way he chooses, even if it involves negating propositions separately *and then adding a conjunction in place of a comma*.

Similarly the objection that a second Negation of the first Negation

---

[1] David Favrholdt—*An Interpretation and Critique of Wittgenstein's "Tractatus,"* (Copenhagen, 1965), p. 132.

should restore the truth values which we started with is not convincing if the operation does not behave that way. And, as it is, the Negation of $-p\,.-q$ does not restore p,q, (which has no single truth value, but two separate truth values), but applying FFFT to FFFT gives instead the truth values TTTF, which are the truth values for $p\,v\,q$. It is, therefore, not correct to say that Wittgenstein "overlooked that $N(N(p))$ must always be equivalent to p."[2] There is no reason why what holds for ordinary negation (*Verneinung*) has to hold for this special operation. (Wittgenstein says that "It is a property of affirmation that it can be construed as double negation (*Verneinung*)." (6.231) But he does not say that it *has* to be construed this way, nor that it *has* to be construed this way in the "basic" operation of Negation (*Negation*).)

We can now proceed to see how the truth functions are actually arrived at. With two elementary propositions p,q the *first* application of the operation produces a truth function $-p\,.-q$, which has the truth values of the stroke function (FFFT). (It should be noted that we do not negate the two *propositions* separately, as having the truth values TF and TF, but rather we take the truth values of the two propositions when they are "taken together"—namely, TFTF and TTFF—and negate *these* separately and then conjoin the results, arriving at FFFT. And also we do not negate the *conjunction* $p\,.\,q$, but the two "truth-valuely" related propositions p,q.)

The *second* application of the operation may then be the Negation of this first result, which gives $-(-p\,.-q)$, which has the truth values TTTF, (FFFT applied to FFFT), which are the truth values of $p\,v\,q$.

The *third* application of the operation may then be to the results of the first and second applications taken together, giving $-((-p\,.-q)\,.\,(p\,v\,q))$ which has the truth values FFFF (FFFT applied to FFFT and TTTF).

For the fourth application we can return to p, taken as a truth function of itself, and negate p (TFTF) together with the result of the first application (FFFT), getting the truth values FTFF, (which are the truth values of $q\,.-p$). For the *fifth* application we can then take p (TFTF) together with the result of the third application (FFFF), which gives FTFT (or the truth values of $-p$).

Proceeding in this way by selecting only truth functions to Negate

---

[2] *Ibid.*, p. 196.

which produce new truth functions, we find that eleven further applications of the operation will supply the remaining columns of the truth table for two elementary propositions. The same results can be reached in many different ways. But we need not be disturbed by the arbitrariness of the way in which the selections of what to negate are made, since Wittgenstein indicates that it is not essential how this is done, (cf. 5.501E) and the point is only that it can be done. The reason Wittgenstein "did not examine the procedure of selection involved in the operation of negation"[3] is because which of many ways in which this is done is a matter of no consequence.

It may be noted that we only need the elementary propositions for the first application of the operation, and after this we can apply it to truth functional propositions (including among these elementary propositions taken as truth functions of themselves).

Wittgenstein's operation of Negation can produce all the familiar truth functional operations on the condition that we can distinguish p , q from p . q. *We must begin with propositions which are only "taken together"* and not *"taken in conjunction."* Successive applications of the operation then do not "cancel" each other, but, if properly chosen, (and it does not matter just how), lead to further truth functions. The Negation of a Negation here does not restore what we started with. But neither does it introduce new sense. Instead it unfolds the different logical places implicit in elementary propositions. Nothing essentially new at the level of sense and meaning is added by any logical operation. This is a hallmark of Wittgenstein's "extensionalist" view of propositions, and it is what sets his philosophy in sharp opposition to many other philosophies.[4]

iv

It is essential to Wittgenstein's philosophy that negation (whether as *Verneinung* or *Negation*) should not arise as the action of a subject, but should have an "objective" character. Negation cannot even be in the *Tractatus* something like a presupposition of logical description,

---

[3] *Ibid.*, p. 196.

[4] In Hegel's philosophy, for example, it has been pointed out to me by Professor Gotthard Günther, that *negation of a negation* gives rise to a *new sense.* Thus we have *Being* and *not-Being,* and the negation of *not-Being* does not give us *Being* again, but rather *Becoming.* Wittgenstein's Negation of a Negation unfolds purely logical operations without altering sense.

unless such a presupposition is grounded "objectively" and not merely in a subject (whether, for example, in an individual subject in the manner of Kant or in a universal subject in the manner of Hegel). This raises the question of what this "objective" character is.

The negation sign, of course, like every other logical constant, corresponds to nothing in reality. (4.0621) Negation is not an expression which "characterizes" the sense of a proposition (and consequently there is no *form of negation*). Negation is a logical operation. But, more than this, when defined in a certain way and expressed as a formal series, it is the general form of *any* operation, (6.01) "the most general form of transition from one proposition to another." (6.01B)

Looked at in this way, the significance of negation (or any operation) is that it "gives expression to the difference between the forms;" it "characterizes (*kennzeichnen*) the difference between the forms." (5.241) Different logical operations characterize such difference in different ways (or, as it were, "punctuate" differently (5.4611)), while what is common to all of them, the operation of Negation, *marks sheer difference as such*.

This gives us a clue as to what negation (of any sort) "refers" to, or what it "mirrors." It "mirrors" *formal difference* as such, and this is its foothold in the world. Any operation is a kind of "differencing," a way of establishing a different logical place. What is common to all operations is simply "differencing."

Such an operation of establishing a different proposition depends upon (or in a way "mirrors") the *logical form of reality*. And this is the same form which "mirrors itself" in any proposition. (4.121) Hence the *general form of an operation is the same as the general form of a proposition*. (6.) Propositions and operations may both be said to "mirror" reality or have reality "mirrored" in them. Thus (1) an elementary proposition "mirrors" reality through its capacity for being true and false; (2) the "specific" operation of negation (*Verneinung*) "mirrors" it by reversing sense and establishing true-false possibilities for a contradictory assertion and (3) the "common" operation of negation (*Negation*) "mirrors" it by establishing true-false values for *every* possibility of a "joint falsity."

The *difference* between propositions is, of course, not part of their sense. All difference is, as it were, just difference (all, in effect, the "same difference"). This can be understood by considering descriptions of states of affairs or situations. When these are described, the differences between them do not have to involve further descriptions. If, for example, we have described two things fully, and someone then says: "Now tell us in what ways the two things are different," it would be sufficient to reply: "This has already been done; the ways in which they are different are given with the descriptions; all that can be added is that they *are* different. If we were naming the things, different names would do; since we are describing them, different propositions will do."

Operations on elementary propositions mark *difference as such*. In the first instance this is the difference between two contradictory senses "prejudged" in an elementary proposition. The number of possible additional "differences" (or different logical places) then depends upon the number of elementary propositions available. The elementary propositions have to be taken together, and the number of possibilities of agreement and disagreement with their truth values reckoned up. The true-false character of the propositions when they are taken together initially completely determines all the further possible ways of their being "taken together." The elementary proposition comes carrying all of this determinate logical space with it.

Two "limiting cases" turn up in this "expansion," where the resulting truth functional propositions lose their "representative" or "sense-bearing" characters and no longer have *any possible* reference or *say* anything. These are the cases of *tautology* and *contradiction*. Although both "lack sense" (*sinnlos*), (4.461) they are not nonsensical (*unsinnig*), (4.4611) since at least they are opposite poles and play quite different roles. The difference between a *tautology* and a *contradiction* is indeed of the greatest importance, and needs to be carefully scrutinized.

A contradiction (such as *p and not-p*) says "everything." It says *too much—more* than *can* be said. (It is the limiting case of *how much* can be said, and every proposition follows from it.) A tautology, on the other hand, says "nothing"—*less* than *has* to be said. (Hence it is the limiting case of *how little* can be said, and *no* proposition follows from it.) Contradictions, as it were, settle everything and leave nothing open, while tautologies settle nothing and leave everything open. (4.463) Neither can determine reality, for the one "over-determines" it, and the other "under-determines" it.

In the *Notebooks* Wittgenstein calls *contradiction* "the class of *all propositions*" and *tautology* "what is common to any classes of propositions that have nothing in common." (p. 54) In the *Tractatus* the former becomes "the common factor of propositions which *no* proposition has in common with another," while the latter becomes "the common factor of all propositions that have nothing in common with one another." (5.143A) The first may be said to be its form as marking a particular *yes* and *no*, and the second its form as marking a particular possibility. Wittgenstein also says that if two propositions contradict one another, this is shown by their *structure*. (4.1211) But *that* a tautology is yielded by a certain way of combining propositions shows that the propositions possess the necessary *structural properties* to permit this. (6.12)

These passages suggest that contradiction shows something like the "*boundary between possibility and impossibility,*" while tautology shows something like "*forms of possibility.*" It is as if *saying* and *showing* are opposite to each other in a contradiction and, in effect, there cancel each other out, while *saying* and *showing* are in agreement in a tautology and hence something may be shown. (*Notebooks.* p. 12) As will be seen, it *could* be the other way around: we *could* use contradictions instead of tautologies to show structural possibilities. (6.1202)

Wittgenstein says that a *decisive point* lies in the consideration "that certain combinations of symbols—whose essence involves the possession of a determinate character—are tautologies." (6.124) This *decisive point* is that "Logic is not a field in which *we* express what we want with the help of signs, but rather one in which the nature of the natural and inevitable signs speaks for itself." (6.124)

This passage sums up the *Tractatus's* conception of logic. It tells us that it is tautologies which reveal that logic is *not* an arbitrary human creation, but rather "natural and inevitable" (*naturnotwendig*) signs speaking for themselves. The possibilities, in other words, for the "zeroing out" of sense by bringing propositions into combinations which say nothing, (6.121) shows, not only that the world *has* a logical structure, but *what* that logical structure is.

That contradiction and tautology *could* change places and we could use contradiction the way we now use tautology (6.1202) illustrates once again Wittgenstein's important distinction between the initial "symmetry" between positive and negative and the initial "asymmetry" of true and false. (4.062, 4.0621) We could mean the negative as we now mean the positive and vice versa, but we *could not* mean the false as we now mean the true and vice versa. It is the *pure contingency* of the *world* which determines true *or* false, while it is the *pure necessity* of *reality* which determines true *and* false. Contradictions *show* propositions confronting the world; tautologies show them confronting reality. But every contradition has a corresponding tautology (e.g. *p and not-p* is matched by *not (p and not-p)*) and everything we want to show by the one we *could* show by the other. (6.1201)

v

To the question how negation gets a foothold in the world the answer is because the world is always *represented as reality*. The "shadow" which language, thought and pictures cast on the world is that they represent it, not as what-is-the-case, (for that is not known), but as *both* what-is-the-case and what-is-not-the-case (for that can be "meant").

This answer requires that what-is-not-the-case have no additional "meaning" beyond what-is-the-case. The actual "content" of reality and world must be the same. We cannot "add up" what-is-not and arrive at something different from what we get by "adding up" what-is. (2.063) What-is-not must have its full nature not only determined by what-is, but in some way identical with what-is. The question then becomes: How does the *Tractatus* conceive of what-is-not?

What-is-not must be understood as what-it-is-(that-is-not). The "difference" between existence and non-existence must, for representation, count as *no difference at all*. When something does not exist, it must be exactly the same something as it would be if it did exist.

This means that in representing the world we always have to do with two opposite senses which have no distinguishably different "natures." (4.0621) As Wittgenstein put it in the *Philosophical Investigations:*

> The agreement, the harmony, of thought and reality consists in this: If I say falsely that something is *red*, then, for all that, it isn't *red*. (#429)

(i.e. we have said exactly *what* it is not.)

Non-existence, as the *Tractatus* understands it, is always "determinate non-existence." This can be distinguished from "indeterminate non-existence," on the one hand, and from "what is there instead" on the other. "Determinate non-existence" involves the complete nature of what-is-not-there. And in knowing *what*-is-not in this case, we know a great deal indeed, and actually as much as we know if we know *what*-is.[5]

The *Tractatus* proceeds on the view that all representation gives equally what-may-be-there and what-may-not-be-there so that everything is settled both ways, except for a *yes* or *no*. (4.023) True-or-false has no more "content" than exist-or-not-exist which is, as it were, no "content" at all. (It is not until negation appears that a *separate sense* can be given to what-is-not, and this has to be understood in terms of truth possibilities.)

As regards the second distinction, it is the *world* which supplies for a "determinate absence" "what is there instead," even if it is only empty space. ("Can we regard a part of space as a thing? In a certain sense we obviously always do this when we talk of spatial things." (*Notebooks*. p. 47)) Reality supplies determinate existence and nonexistence, but never "what may be there instead." The "what is there instead" fills out the "what is the case" to make it equal to "what is the case and what is not the case."

Wittgenstein uses a striking analogy in his *Notes on Logic* to show the place of negation (though the way it is put would undoubtedly have been different if the same analogy had appeared in the *Tractatus*). He says:

> The comparison of language and reality is like that of a retinal image and visual image: to the blind spot nothing in the visual image seems to correspond, and thereby the boundaries of the blind spot determine the visual image—just as true negations of atomic (elementary) propositions determine reality. (*Notebooks*. p. 95)

The analogy seems to work out like this: the boundaries of what we cannot see (the blind place in the visual field) "determine" what we can see, in this way—that they establish the conditions for seeing, which are that *the field must be seen in such a way that the blind place is not seen.* (For example, binocular vision is required, and only so much detail can be seen, even if the given field itself is microscopic in detail.) What is analogous to the blind spot is *non-existence*, which appears in

---

[5] This distinction goes back at least to Plato, who distinguished between *me on* (determinate not) and *ouk on* (the absolute not). Compare also the medieval distinction between the *nihil negativum* (absolute nothing) and *nihil privativum* (relative nothing) derived from Aristotle.

such a way that it cannot be "seen" (or initially said), and this determines what *can* be said. Non-existence thus determines the conditions for representing the world because it determines something like the "fineness of the mesh of sense"—or *at what point sense is to be taken as determinate for the meanings in question.*[6] Even when the network of meaning is "infinitely fine" (5.511) the blind spot must still be there since sense must still be determinate.

Wittgenstein alludes to another analogy—the introduction of the sign "O" in order to make the decimal notation possible. (*Notebooks.* p. 31) Just as negation can "determine" any reality, so the sign "O" can determine, as a "place-holder," any counting number system. (And we *could* get on without "O" as we *could* get on without negative propositions.) The "blind spot" in language is perhaps even more like the minus sign, supplying for every existence an equivalent counter-existence or anti-existence which is just as likely to turn up as the corresponding existence.

The condition governing non-existence is that we cannot initially *say* it, though it must always be *shown*. (For if we try to say it, *this* may turn out to be the way things are and what we are saying will be true. (4.062)) All elementary propositions are necessarily affirmative, even if we use *not-p* to say what we normally say by *p*. What happens is that reality *allows* p as well as *not-p*, but it does not allow the *assertion* of p as well as *not-p*. (*Notebooks.* p. 56) What we picture in a proposition is a *possibility* of existence and non-existence allowed by reality.

The steps in this process may be outlined as follows:

(1) A proposition determines a logical place, which is a possibility of an existence. (3.411)

(2) When we are dealing with a single state of affairs, a possibility of an existence is the same as a possibility of non-existence.

(3) Reality thus permits two truth possibilities for every one logical place. (2.06)

---

[6] It is tempting to push the analogy one step further. Physiologically, the blind spot is the place where the optic nerve enters the eye and hence the place where the eye is incapacitated for its normal function by the condition which makes it possible for it to function at all (i.e. its connection with the brain). Analogously, it might be said that the world is "connected" to what makes it "world" (i.e. language) just by what is not world (i.e. reality). For, as Wittgenstein says, "certainly the methods of measurement by p and *not-p* have some special advantage over all others." (*Notebooks.* p. 33)

(4) The operation of negation (*Verneinung*) establishes the two pos-
    sibilities as two different logical places. (4.0641B)
(5) The "common" operation of Negation (*Negation*) establishes *all*
    logical places permitted by any number of elementary proposi-
    tions. (5.2521, 5.5)
(6) This gives us a system of signs with a particular number of dimen-
    sions, filling out the given logical space. (5.475)
(7) In this way logic "mirrors" the world. (6.13)

vi

This brings us to the question of *facts* and of *positive* and *negative* facts. It must be repeated again that a fact is not a single existing
state of affairs, but rather "the existence of states of affairs" (in the
plural). (2.) This, however, is ambiguous for it may mean *any* possible
combination of existing states of affairs, or it might mean *combinations*
which actually exist. In a letter to Russell Wittgenstein says that a
Tatsache (fact) is "what corresponds to the logical product of elementary propositions when this product is true." (*Notebooks*. p. 129)
This suggests the direction to look in.

A logical product of elementary propositions can be distinguished
from the truth funtional conjunction of these same elementary propositions, since we can arrive at the logical product without using the
operation of Negation or constructing the truth functions. And Wittgenstein seems to allow for this by preserving the distinction between
operations and *truth operations* (5.2341B) and continuing to speak of
logical products. (3.42, 6.3751) States of affairs exist in combinations,
and it is evident that we do not encounter all possible combinations of
existing states of affairs. The distinction between logical products and
truth functional conjunctions seems to provide a way out here, since we
must have some means of distinguishing those combinations of existing
states of affairs which exist from those combinations which do not
exist. And we must have some way of distinguishing positive and negative facts which does not require that *all* existing states of affairs be
involved in one and *all* non-existing ones in the other.

To illustrate how this might work: If we imagine three elementary
propositions p, q and r, then there are *eight possibilities* in terms of
the existence and non-existence of the *combinations*. If we arbitrarily
imagine the combinations p, q and p, r existing and the combinations
p, q, r and q, r not existing, then we have the following:

p, q exist   (not-exist)
p, r exist   (not-exist)
q, r not exist   (exist)
p, q, r not exist   (exist)

The next table then shows all the possible positive and negative facts, with the ones obtaining italicized:

p	q	r	
T	T	T	p, q, r exist
F	T	T	q, r exist
T	F	T	*p, r exist*
T	T	F	*p, q exist*
F	F	T	p, q not exist
F	T	F	p, r not exist
T	F	F	*q, r not exist*
F	F	F	*p, q, r not exist*

If we talk merely about truth functional conjunctions of existing states of affairs, then all such conjunctions stand on the same level and there is no way of distinguishing those *conjunctions* which exist from those which do not. It does not follow that because we have a certain number of existing states of affairs, therefore all possible combinations of these existing states of affairs must also exist. To distinguish between the *conjunctions* of existing states of affairs which exist and the *conjunctions* which do not exist it would be necessary for logical products of elementary propositions to be true or false within the possibilities provided by the truth or falsity of the elementary propositions, as indicated in the above table. (The only other alternative, it would seem, would be to restrict a single set of elementary propositions to representing a single *thing*, or states of affairs actually found to combine.)

In terms merely of truth functions, if the conjunction $p \cdot q \cdot r$ is true, then the conjunctions $p \cdot q$, $p \cdot r$, and $q \cdot r$ are all also true. But this by itself does not tell us that p, q and r represent states of affairs all found together in the same *thing*, or possibly two of them are in one thing and one in another. The analysis in terms of the truth of logical products will be necessary to make this distinction.

Wittgenstein does not pursue this matter, but there is one passage in particular which suggests that he intended to leave this door open. In speaking of the possibilities of existence and non-existence of n

states of affairs (and giving the formula for this) he says: "Of these states of affairs any combination can exist and the remainder not exist." (*Es können alle Kombinationen der Sachverhalte bestehen, die andern nicht bestehen*). (4.27B) It would appear from this that the combination corresponding to FFF, for example, might exist, and we would have the "existence" of three "non-existent" states of affairs. Along these lines it is possible to distinguish between the existence and non-existence of states of affairs and the existence and non-existence of *combinations* of states of affairs.

Just as facts can be understood as combinations of existing states of affairs which themselves exist, so positive and negative facts can be understood as the combinations of states of affairs which exist and the combinations of states of affairs which do not exist. The above table then shows that: (1) for three existing and non-existing states of affairs there are eight possible existing and non-existing combinations of them; (2) four of these are possibilities of existing combinations and four of them possibilities of non-existing ones; and (3) the total number of possible positive and negative facts together in such a world will be four, which is the same as the total number of possible positive facts. (If we took the total number of possible positive facts to be the *world*, and the total number of possible positive *and* negative facts to be *reality*, then the sum-total of reality would be the world. (2.063) We do not, of course, find the expression "possible facts" in the *Tractatus*, and there is no provision for finding combinations of elementary propositions true or false, independently of truth or falsity of the elementary propositions themselves, so that this entire procedure is only a *conjecture* about what Wittgenstein *might* have done.)

The source of the difficulty here goes back to an ambiguity in the nature of pictures, which, it will be recalled, picture both possible relations of *entities* and of *things*. (2.15, 2.151) If the entities are properties, qualities or sense-data, they are still distinguishable from the things, which are *combinations* of these. The difficulty of relating the two at the level of pictures returns to plague us at the level of elementary propositions and facts.

vii

In the *Blue Book* Wittgenstein says at one point: "If we look into the grammar of the word (*time*) we shall feel that it is no less astounding that man should have conceived of a deity of time than that he should have conceived of a deity of negation or disjunction." (p. 6)

In the *Tractatus* Wittgenstein does not conceive of a "deity of negation" or a substance for the substantive "negation" (much less a personification of such a substance). But the *Tractatus*, nevertheless, gives to negation a kind of "supreme status," for it connects the possibility of any kind of proposition with the possibility of negation. The logical framework of the world presupposed by propositions is the very framework unfolded by the operation of Negation. The non-existence which we must picture jointly with existence unfolds into the contradictory sense given by negation (*Verneinung*) and into the different truth functional senses given by Negation (*Negation*).

Negation, in other words, as the *Tractatus* conceives it, lies concealed in all picturing, thinking and saying, inasmuch as all picturing, thinking and saying represents reality with its polar character of existence and non-existence. And it is this same polar character of reality which furnishes the basis for generating all propositions from elementary propositions. To see the world as reality is already to see it as "containing" negation. But it may be wondered which has come first. Do we see it this way because there is no other way of seeing it? Or do we see it this way in order to justify the conception of propositions as necessarily true or false?

Elementary Propositions

Everything is partly true and partly false. Not so essential truth; that is pure and true throughout.

Pascal

εἷς δέ ἐστι λόγος διχῶς, ἢ γὰρ ὁ ἓν σημαίνων, ἢ ὁ ἐκ πλειόνων συνδέσμῳ.

(A proposition or a phrase may form a unity in two ways—either as signifying one thing or as consisting of several parts linked together.)

Aristotle

To make it perfectly clear that a sentence is an indivisible whole and not made up of any parts, a clear line of demarcation was necessarily drawn between the sentence and its so-called constituents, or, in other words, between what is real and what is unreal.

Prabhatchandra Chakravarti

Veritatis simplex oratio est.
(The language of truth is simple.)

Seneca

Factual existence is wholly indifferent to any and all variations in essence and everything that exists participates without petty jealousy in being and participates in the same degree.

Soren Kierkegaard

CHAPTER 7

Elementary Propositions

i

The *Tractatus*, it may be said, formulates its ontology in terms of the *minimum principles of symbolism*, or what is minimally necessary in order that signs may function as signs. These principles relate to what are conceived as the two fundamental aspects of language—*meaning* and *sense*, (or, roughly, what *a name stands for* and what *a sentence represents*.) Wittgenstein is concerned with signs which have fixed meanings and sense, or what he calls simple signs and elementary propositions. The simple signs are also called *names* (3.202) and the simplest propositional signs composed of them *elementary propositions* (4.21) or, in the *Notebooks* and the first translation of the *Tractatus*, *atomic propositions*.

Elementary propositions are functions of names as mathematical functions are functions of their arguments. Such propositions show the formal and structural side of the configuration of objects which has as its "content" the material properties of the world. (2.0231, 2.0272) They are the end result of the analysis of ordinary sentences, (4.221) the minimum possible order common to world and language. In *Some Remarks on Logical Form* we read (p. 162):

> But our analysis, if carried far enough, must come to the point where it reaches propositional forms which are not themselves composed of simpler propositional forms. We must eventually reach the ultimate connection of the terms, the immediate connection which cannot be broken without destroying the propositional form as such.

Elementary propositions are the equivalent in language of the "internal" structural nature of the material properties of the world. When they are true, they show the *essential nature* of material properties. Their irreducibly simple structures are the counterparts in articulation of simple phenomenal qualities. The "immediate connectedness" of the names in such a proposition is called by Wittgenstein a *hanging to-*

135

gether (*Zusammenhang*—a nexus, connection, coherence). (4.22) As objects in a state of affairs are likened to links in a chain (*Kette*), (2.03) so names in an elementary proposition are said to be a "chaining" or "chainwork" (*Verkettung*). (4.22) This must be understood to mean that both states of affairs and elementary propositions have purely "combinatorial" order, any one combination of objects or names being one case of all possible combinations of the same objects or names.

It is the capacity of both names and objects to be able to *hang together* (*zusammenhangen*) or *unite* (*verbinden*) which constitutes *form* and any one case of this which constitutes *structure*. Such combinatorial possibilities define the ranges of possible specific structures, any one of which may be in common in a given case between language and the world.

Wittgenstein, however, does not say (what, too hastily, we might have expected him to say) that "Names occur only in elementary propositions." But rather he says:

> It is only in the hanging together of the elementary proposition that a name occurs in a proposition. (4.23)

This way of putting it, (together with other indications elsewhere), suggests that the principle of "naming" is utilized by even ordinary propositions in such a way that names occur even in these only in the determinate connectedness in which they occur in elementary propositions. The combinatorial principle of the elementary proposition lies at the heart of even the propositions of everyday language. (We might say that even in the most ordinary statement "word order counts.") And this is related to the way in which names may *mean objects*, (3.203) even when they *stand for things*, (4.0311) and the way in which the propositions of everyday language "are in perfect logical order just as they are." (5.5563)[1]

Elementary propositions are the structural core of all material propositions, and they enjoy this unique status because they operate with the simplest possible syntactical device—"immediate combination." (4.221) The phrase "immediate combination" (*unmittelbarer Verbindung*) points to the simplest connectedness, linear combinatoriality, into which, in the *Tractatus's* view, every kind of spatial, temporal,

---

[1] Wittgenstein, as he vividly puts it, is not interested in separating "the hard from the soft," but in seeing "the hardness of the soft," or in "justifying the vagueness of ordinary sentences, for it *can* be justified." (*Notebooks.* pp. 44, 70)

colored, etc., structure can be projected. Indeterminateness can only be conveyed by a proposition when we see that a propositional element signifies a complex because then "we know (*wissen*) that the proposition leaves something undetermined." (3.24C) It is as if determinate connectedness must convey even indeterminateness, since it is not the propositional element which is complex, but what it signifies, and that this is complex has to be seen. (3.24C)

What distinguishes an elementary proposition from an ordinary proposition is that in an elementary proposition a sense is not "characterized" by symbols which may designate in different ways in accordance with a complicated conventional grammar, but is entirely a function of fixed signs with only combinatorial or logical grammar. The world, looked at in this way, reveals its essence, or existing structure, but loses its "physiognomic" aspect. In ordinary life we cannot dispense with "characterized" sense, any more than we can see all there is to see in a work of art simply in terms of geometry.

Wittgenstein says that it is on "purely logical grounds" that we know that there must be elementary propositions, (5.5562) for it is "obvious (*offenbar*) that the analysis of propositions must bring us to elementary propositions." (4.221) But what elementary propositions there are cannot be anticipated in advance. To the question "What determines what elementary propositions there are?" the answer is:

> The application of logic decides what elementary propositions there are. (5.557)

The actual possibilities for the structural description of the world have to wait upon what possible situations are actually pictured and projected into propositional signs and their essential character then revealed by logical analysis. There is no general form of elementary propositions (5.55) and no way of setting up a pattern for them in advance since "An atomic form cannot be foreseen." (*Some Remarks on Logical Form*. p. 163) The most we have to go on is that we do have a concept of elementary propositions "apart from their particular logical forms." (5.555)

A difference between *objects* and *names* is apparent again here. In the *Tractatus* objects form (*bilden*) the substance of the world (2.021) and their configuration forms (*bilden*) material properties (2.0231) and states of affairs. (2.0272) But it is *we* who form (*bilden*) systems of signs (5.475) and symbols (5.555) and propositions (5.4733) on the basis of what it is possible to do with signs. And it is in the course of our dealings with signs that we get to know objects and *find out (erfinden)* the forms of elementary propositions. (5.555C)

ii

While all propositions are composite (*zusammengesetz*), only *elementary propositions* have signs "hanging together" (*zusammenhangen*) or in "immediate combination" (*unmittelbarer Verbindung*). And while ordinary propositions represent complex things in complex situations, only *elementary propositions* represent the simplest things (*objects*) in the simplest situations (*states of affairs*).

This unique status of elementary propositions involves three special features:

(1) elementary propositions are *necessarily affirmative;* they are what must be available for the fundamental operation of Negation and hence cannot themselves be negative;

(2) elementary propositions must be *logically independent* of each other; they cannot contradict each other and cannot logically "follow" or be deduced from each other; (5:134)

(3) elementary propositions *cannot "exclude"* each other; two of them cannot make assertions about the same logical place, since there is room for only one state of affairs in one logical place.

Looking at these three points more carefully:

(1) *No negative elementary propositions.* Elementary propositions may be false, but not negative. It is conventional whether we assert positive facts or negative facts, for both may be asserted as "the way things are." If we assert the way things are not, that is an assertion of the way they are too, and they can also fail to be *that* way and hence such propositions may also turn out to be false. Elementary propositions, in other words, cannot assert *not* since in any case they assert *what* or *how.* This shows that true or false is, as it were, the real disjunction, and not positive or negative, for while we require both of the latter, it does not make any difference with them which is which, while the distinction of *true or false* holds fast in all cases.

Another way of putting the reason why there cannot be negative elementary propositions is because negation as an operation depends upon affirmation; it reverses the sense of a proposition, (5.2341) and we must have a proposition first in order to do this. Wittgenstein asks:

> Why should it not be possible to express a negative proposition by means of a negative fact? (E.g. suppose that '*a*' does not stand in a certain relation to '*b*'; then this might be used to say that *aRb* was not the case.) (5.5151A)

And his answer is:

> But really even in this case the negative proposition is constructed by an indirect use of the positive. (5.5151B)

(We conceive of '*a*' not standing in a certain relation to '*b*' by first conceiving of it standing in that relation.)

(2) *Elementary propositions logically independent of each other.* This is a consequence of states of affairs being independent of each other. (2.061) We cannot infer from the existence or non-existence of one state of affairs to the existence or non-existence of another. (2.062) Propositions, like situations, may be internally related, and in these cases the truth of one may follow from the truth of another. (5.131) All such deductions are made *a priori*. (5.133) But in the case of elementary propositions Wittgenstein says "One elementary proposition cannot be deduced from another" (5.134) and

> There is no possible way of making an inference from the existence of one situation to the existence of another entirely different (*ganzlich verschiedenen*) situation. (5.135)

The phrase "entirely different" here may be taken as meaning that the situations involve states of affairs of different forms.

This logical independence of elementary propositions is a corollary of the *Tractatus's* atomistic view of properties—the view that the occurrence of properties is entirely contingent. There is no necessary relation between the occurrence of any property and the occurrence of any other property. If elementary propositions were not logically independent, it would mean that, for example, from the color of a thing we could infer *a priori* something about its shape or about its duration.

(3) *Elementary propositions cannot exclude each other.* This formulation does not occur in the *Tractatus*, but in *Some Remarks on Logical Form* where the difference between elementary propositions (there called "atomic propositions") contradicting each other and "excluding"

each other is brought out. (p. 168) Wittgenstein there says that when he wrote the *Tractatus*, he believed that elementary propositions could not contradict each other and *also* could not "exclude" each other. What this means is that propositions making different assertions of the same form about the same situation had to be regarded as in every case contradictory. What he had come to propose was that contradiction was no longer to have to prevent exclusion also. Elementary propositions were to be allowed to be mutually exclusive.

This drastic attempt to revise the *Tractatus* was made to handle irreducible differences of degree of the same property through introducing numbers into elementary propositions. It was doomed to failure because it undercut the whole ontology of the *Tractatus* and could not serve as simply one additional qualification. "Impossible combinations," which were ruled out in advance in the *Tractatus* by not permitting their components to be elementary propositions at all were to be ruled out in the *Aristotelian Society* article by not permitting certain truth functional possibilities and leaving these spaces empty on the truth table. This was indeed too artificial a solution of the problem of representing continuity in a system which essentially forbids it.

iii

Elementary propositions may be said to have an implicit generality because they consist wholly of names which mean "formal objects." The substance of the world, as Wittgenstein conceived it, is not unique unrepeatable particulars (or individuals on the lowest level), but rather "formal simples," or the units of ultimate structure. We reach unique individuals only in terms of conjunctions of structures which are, in a certain sense, intrinsically general.[2]

It is Wittgenstein's view that there must be some kind of "logical

---

[2]The *Tractatus* is more "Platonic" than "Aristotelian" in its view that knowledge is not an abstracting from sense experience of particulars, but a *direct knowing of objects* as what "make possible" even sense experience. Forms are given with the world as the rational presuppositions of being acquainted even with particulars, rather than as immanently derived *from* acquaintance with particulars. The rationalistic tendencies of Frege are finally much more in evidence in the *Tractatus* than the empirical tendencies of Russell. As Wittgenstein wrote Russell: "the individual primitive signs (in the Theory of Descriptions) are quite different from what you believe." (*Notebooks*. p. 128) He might have added: "They have a formal rather than an empirical character."

articulation" in all propositions, and the absolute minimum possible articulation is simply arrangement of signs *per se*, (remembering that we only have an identifiable or determinate arrangement when we also have for those signs "all possible arrangements"). Elementary propositions are the most "singular" propositions possible which meet a minimum "bonding" requirement. Their generality is implicit because there are in the world innumerable identical possible instances of every structure (as, for example, there are innumerable possible instances of any shade of color or any shape). What amounts to saying the same thing is to say that the same elementary proposition may appear in innumerable conjunctions with other different elementary propositions and hence as part of the representation of innumerable different facts. What we ordinarily call particularity will show up only at the level of facts or as conjunctions of properties.

The notion of elementary propositions as formally simple makes it necessary to distinguish between them and *general propositions* or the kind of propositions which involve the concept *all* and which Wittgenstein labels as "fully generalized" (*vollkommen verallgemeinerte*) (5.526, 5.5261) or "wholly general" (*ganz allgemeinen*). (5.5262)

That elementary propositions and wholly general propositions have a great deal in common is indicated by the circumstance that the world can be described completely by either of them.

> If all true elementary propositions are listed, the world is completely described. (4.26)
> We can describe the world completely by means of fully generalized propositions, i.e. without *ever* (*irgend*) correlating any name with a particular object. (5.526)[3]

And he adds:

> The truth or falsity of *every* proposition does make some alteration in the general construction of the world. And the range that the totality of elementary propositions leaves open for its construction is exactly the same as that which is delimited by entirely general propositions. (5.5262)

There are thus two ways of describing the world, each of which

---

[3] The Pears–McGuinness translation gives *first* for *irgend*, which weakens the impact of Wittgenstein's statement. What he says is that we don't have *ever* to correlate a name with a determinate (*bestimmten*) object. (Has the term *quark* in modern physics ever been correlated with a particular quark?)

can do the job: a *formal* way and a *general* way. In each case we approach particulars, as it were, at a second remove, for in the *Tractatus* all representable or describable features are formal or general.[4] All that corresponds to particularity is *things*, which, because they are dependent upon states of affairs, (2.0122) can only be described as *facts* or conjunctions of essentially structural properties. Attempting to specify the particularity of a thing, we can only do it by way of "general" properties, represented in the last analysis by structures of formal names. (It might be said that the reason we *can* describe the world completely without correlating any name with a determinate object is because we *cannot* describe particular things except by further general descriptions.)

The condition that in describing the world we have two choices— to use formal names or to use the generality-sign to indicate all the values of given variables—shows that forms contain implicit generality (though it is real forms which make generality possible and not more or less arbitrary generalizing which we use to construct forms). The *allness* in the case of objects becomes explicit in the case of the generality sign. The relation between the two is brought out in the following passage from the *Notebooks*, (p. 76):

> If there are objects, then that gives us "all objects" too.
> That is why it must be possible to produce (*herstellen*) the unity of the elementary propositions and the general propositions.
> For if the elementary propositions are given, that gives us *all* elementary propositions, too, and that gives us the general proposition.—And with that has not the unity been produced? (Cf. 5.524)

(The most plausible interpretation of this is that if, for example, the elementary proposition which says "Red" is given, all the elementary propositions for all the other colors are also given—i.e. the whole color

---

[4] What is not representable or describable is, of course, the mere presence or existence of the world itself, *that* it is. This *thatness* (which is the fullness of particularity) is the ultimate presupposition even of logic, for if the world were not given, how could it turn out that logic is applicable to it? (5.5521) The general situation is that although we must presuppose the world in its particularity, we can only describe the particular by, as it were, detouring through what is not particular. We have no access to particularity or the ultimately individuated except through the formal and the general.

system—and with this we have the general propositions about color.)

Elementary propositions and wholly general propositions are so closely interrelated that Wittgenstein says that

> Indeed the understanding of general propositions *palpably* (*fuhlbar*) depends on the understanding of elementary propositions. (4.411)
> Generality is essentially connected with the elementary form. (*Notebooks*. p. 39)

What this says is that we could not "generalize" unless we could recognize forms. We could not, for example, make general statements about spatial properties unless we could distinguish space from time or space from color. And it is just these differences which the different forms of elementary propositions show. While in the wholly general proposition we talk about *all things* of a certain kind, in the elementary proposition we *show* just what that "kind" is. Wittgenstein says:

> The peculiarity of the generality-sign is first, that it indicates (*hinweisen*) a logical prototype (*Urbild*) and, secondly, that is gives prominence (*hervorheben*) to constants. (5.552)

The "logical prototype" is the possibility of a certain variable, while the "constants' are all the names which can appear in it.

Wholly general propositions, like elementary propositions, are "material" and can be true or false (unlike logical propositions which are tautologies and always true). That a statement is made about *all* of something does not, as Wittgenstein sees it, make the statement any less contingent.

> Whether I assert something of a particular thing or of all the things that there are the assertion is equally material. (*Notebooks*. p. 17)

All, in other words, belongs on the side of what is given, and assertions involving *all* are about the world and have the same forms as assertions about individual cases.

> That arbitrary correlation of sign and thing signified which is a condition of the possibility of the propositions, and which I found lacking in the completely general propositions, occurs there by means of the generality notation, just as in the elementary proposition it occurs by means of names.
> (For the generality notation does not belong to the *picture*.)

Hence the constant feeling that generality makes its appearance quite like an argument. (Cf. 5.523)

The *all* may be regarded as something like an *appendix* to a picture, saying, in effect, "Apply the same picture in all such cases." The picture already contains in its logical form just such a possibility of further applications, (though in any particular case it may turn out to be inapplicable, making the general proposition false).

It might be said that, strictly speaking, it isn't a proposition as such which is generalized, but rather the cases in which the same proposition may be applied. For a proposition to make sense it has to be possibly true, and this possibility of truth covers both the individual case and all such cases. Hence we do not have in a wholly general proposition a "general sense," although we do have a logical prototype *indicated by* or *contained in* (5.522, 3.24C) the generality-sign.

To illustrate this we may take the sentences: *This man is mortal* and *All men are mortal*. We can then say that what makes it possible for the word *man* to make sense with the word *mortal* in the first sentence is the same as what makes it possible for the word *men* to make sense with the word *mortal* in the second sentence. The word *all* indicates the very logical prototype which is present in the singular sentence (irrespective of whether either sentence is true or false). (The indeterminateness in the sentences arises from not knowing exactly what the words *man* and *mortal* mean.) We might say that the general proposition makes a truth claim for the whole range of cases permitted by the logical form of the singular proposition.

Wittgenstein distinguishes between the "essential general validity" of logical propositions and the "accidental general validity" of wholly general propositions.

> To be general means no more than to be accidentally valid for all things. An ungeneralized proposition can be tautological just as well as a generalized one. (6.1231)
> The general validity of logic might be called essential in contrast with the accidental general validity of such propositions as 'All men are mortal'. . . . (6.1232)
> The generality of the completely general proposition is accidental generality. It deals with all the things that there chance to be. And that is why it is a material proposition. (*Notebooks.* p. 17)

The difference here is that between describing general features of the world (5.526) and describing (or rather representing) the *scaffolding* of the world. (6.124) While the propositions with accidental general validity are still about the world, those with essential general validity are "about" nothing, but simply allow "the nature of the natural and inevitable signs" (*die Natur der naturnotwendigen Zeichen*) to speak for itself, (6.124) revealing nothing of what happens to be so, but only the *world-syntax for all happening*.

All valid logical propositions can be given in advance because they depend only upon the logical properties of the symbol, (6.126) involving only rules which deal with signs. (6.126B) Hence the striking peculiarities of logic:

> In logic process and result are equivalent. (Hence the absence of surprise.) (6.1261)
> In logic every proposition is the form of a proof. (6.1264)
> It is always possible to construe (*auffassen*) logic in such a way that every proposition is its own proof. (6.1265)

Logical propositions are clearly not "pictures," but only signs arranged in such a way that their representational features cancel each other out, leaving only the reflection of logical space within which representation is possible. (4.462B, 3.42C)

iv

An important key to the role of elementary propositions is supplied by the following passage:

> Even if the world is infinitely complex, so that every fact consists of infinitely many states of affairs and every state of affairs is composed of infinitely many objects, there would still have to be objects and states of affairs. (4.2211)

The point of this remark is that what is required is determinateness of sense and what makes that possible would have to be available even if the world were "infinitely complex." We have to have complete definiteness for what we *do* represent *even if* there is infinitely much we do *not* represent.[5]

---

[5] One feature of language being called attention to here may be this one: "English allows only a finite (though quite large) number of sentences only two words long. But it allows an unlimited number of sentences because there is no fixed limit on how long a sentence may be." C. F. Hockett and R. Ascher quoted in *Linguistics Today*, (N.Y. 1968), p. 55.

There are several ways in which the requirement of determinateness is expressed in the *Notebooks*. Wittgenstein says that the sense must be *complete;* it must be *completely definite* or *completely clear*. And he also says that "as much as we *certainly mean* must surely be clear" and what we do not mean is not part of *that* sense. (pp. 63, 67) What we do not know we cannot, of course, mean. Hence if we do not know infinitely many objects or infinitely many states of affairs, they cannot be part of what we mean when we talk about the world. What we say and mean is completely definite *however much else we may be ignorant of*. Definiteness of sense is not impaired by what we do not know which has no bearing on what we mean to say.

> The analysis must not make the proposition more complicated than its reference was from the first. (*Notebooks*. p. 70)

In this light we can contemplate that it is "possible" (which would seem to be "merely possible" in the sense of 2.0121C) that there are infinitely many objects in every state of affairs and infinitely many states of affairs in every fact. For nothing is lost by this since determinate sense does not depend upon this infinity of objects but upon what objects are *known* or *given*. (2.0123, 2.01231, 2.0124) Wittgenstein is not concerned with an infinity which we do not know and could not express, but with what is known or given, which is always finite.

It might be said that just this "mere" possibility of infinitely many objects and infinitely many states of affairs would be enough to upset a determinateness which depends upon always having *all* objects and *all* states of affairs. (5.524, 2.0124) To this the only reply would seem to be that the "possibility" counts for nothing at all since we cannot formulate sentences which are infinitely long, and even if such sentences were required they would not prevent the formation of sentences of finite length.

It is important in connection with this discussion to notice that, according to Wittgenstein, we are not in a position to say that there are or are not an infinity of objects. Such statements are pseudo-propositions. (5.534) We do not know ahead of time how many names there are with different meanings. (5.55B) Russell's Axiom of Infinity makes no sense because what it tries to say (i.e. that there *are* an infinite number of objects) in a correct notation would be shown by, (what does not happen), there being infinitely many names.

What the axiom of infinity is intended to say would express itself in language through the existence of infinitely many names with different meanings. (5.535C)

Having real names we have objects, and there is nothing that can be said about them except what the names of them can say. To imagine, for example, that we could say that they exist would be like imagining that a ruler could be used to measure itself. It is to confuse what makes a proposition possible with what it is possible to do with a proposition. If names are real names, *that* takes care of the being of what they refer to, and we deceive ourselves if we suppose that *being* or *existence* is still somehow more available as a concept than simple names. (In the case of *things*, as distinct from *objects*, a proposition which talks about a complex which does not exist is false and not nonsensical. (5.24))

What the Tractatus does identify as infinite is *logical space*. It speaks of the "infinite whole" of logical space, (4.463C) and it speaks of the "infinitely fine network, the great mirror of logic." (5.511) The always available possibility of repeating logical operations endlessly would of itself acount for this infinity of logical space. (5.2523, 5.43) Thus even with a limited number of elementary propositions there is no limit to the number of truth functional propositions which may be made out of them, including any number of possible negations even of one proposition. (5.43)

Wittgenstein also says that "A spatial object must be situated in infinite space." (2.0131A) This infinity would appear to be necessary as the guarantee that space is *not limited except by objects*, an absolutely necessary condition for the ontology of the *Tractatus*. Were space to be finite, it would have some intrinsic character limiting it other than structures of objects, and there is no possibility of either saying this or representing it in the *Tractatus*, since *objects* are the whole substance of the world.

v

The question *What is the nature of a proposition?* was for the early Wittgenstein not only the central question of philosophy, but also the key to the nature of the world. Anything found out about language was also found out about the world. (It is quite likely that the "picture theory" grew out of *this* conviction, rather than this conviction resulting from the "picture theory.") The conviction is most strikingly expressed

in an extraordinary sequences of sentences in the *Notebooks,* which
could serve as an epitome of the entire *Tractatus:*

> My whole task consists in explaining the nature of the pro-
> position.
> That is to say, in giving the nature of all facts, whose picture
> the proposition *is.*
> In giving the nature of all being.
> (And here being does not stand for existence—in that case it
> would be nonsensical.) (p. 39)[6]

This distinction between *existence* and *being* mentioned here in the
Notebooks has a much more subtle version in the *Tractatus.* There it
becomes the distinction between *what is the case (was der Fall ist)* and
what obtains (Bestehen), on the one hand, and *substance (Substanz)* and
reality (Wirklichkeit), on the other, (substance giving all possibilities of
different forms and reality giving them in the bi-polarity of *Bestehen*
and *Nichtbestehen).* But it also appears in an equally subtle way in connection with propositions. And it is there that we find Wittgenstein's
only use of the term *Existenz* itself. What has *Existenz* in the *Tractatus*
requires a closer look.

What we find is that it is only with regard to *propositions* and *loci
in logical space* that Wittgenstein uses the term *Existenz,* and here it
is used in two ways, doing duty for both *being* and *existence.* He says,
first, that it is the *Existenz* of a proposition and of its constituents which
guarantees (*verbürgen*) the *Existenz* of a logical place. (3.4) And then
he says that a logical place (like a geometrical place) is itself "the possibility of an *Existenz.*" (3.411) The full formulation which results
from this is that *the existence of a proposition guarantees the existence
of the possibility of an existence* (i.e. in the language of the *Notebooks,*
the existence of propositions guarantees *being as the possibilities of existence*). The intentional ambiguity of the term *Existenz* underlines the
point that we cannot drive a conceptual wedge between *a possibility
of existence* and *existence.*

But this is far from the end of the matter because Wittgenstein also
says that "in order to understand logic" we need an "experience"
(which he says is "not an experience") *that something is.* (5.552) That

---

[6] The distinction between *existence* and *being,* it is worth noting, is unknown
to classical Greek philosophy, but is brought out in scholastic philosophy, where
it underwrites the doctrine of creation. Cf. Etienne Gilson—*Being and Some Philosophers,* (Toronto, 1949), especially Chpts. 3-5.

is, in order to be able to speak of the "possibility of an existence" we need some relation to what the term *existence* ineffably indicates, (i.e. we have to have some meaning for this term), and this has to be presupposed by logic. The paradox which results is that it is only possible to speak of existence in terms of the "possibility of existence," while at the same time we cannot understand the "possibility of existence" unless we already have some (impossible to describe or even refer to) acquaintance with existence itself.

The "experience" *that something is* is "not an experience" because it is not namable or describable. It would have to be the experience of a *possibility* if it were to be describable. But it cannot be the experience of a possibility because it is the "experience" of just what is no longer possible, but *is*. We cannot, in short, speak about the "possibility of existence" without presupposing existence; and, on the other hand, we cannot speak about "existence" with presupposing the "possibility of existence."[7]

All this shows that it is incorrect to say that for Wittgenstein either "being comes before existence" or "existence comes before being." What perhaps we can say is that, if we wish to speak at all, "being comes before existence," but "in the silence" "existence comes before being." Wittgenstein is the "silent existentialist." He points to the priority of existence over logic, over sense and over being; but this *that something is* is altogether ineffable. What we have to "know" more certainly than anything else, there is no possibility of "knowing."

---

[7] Wittgenstein interprets the view that even God could not create what is contrary to the laws of logic as an expression of the realization that "we could not say what an 'illogical' world would look like." (3.031) The question whether God is bound by *what can be said* would, however, it would seem, remain open, "intellectualists" like Thomas Aquinas continuing to disagree with "voluntarists" like Duns Scotus on this new question as they did on the previous one.

The Self

What has history to do with me? Mine is the first and only world.

WITTGENSTEIN

. . . the subject does not lie in space and time, for it is whole and undivided in every representing being.

SCHOPENHAUER

. . . nothing is more occult than the absolute present.

CHARLES PEIRCE

Thou couldst not see the seer of the sight.

Dryg-Drya Viveka

Become pure seeing!

JALALUDDIN RUMI

CHAPTER 8

The Self

i

There are two discussions having to do with the self in the *Tractatus*. The first is in the passages dealing with what Wittgenstein calls the *metaphysical subject,* involving the question of "how much truth there is in solipsism," (5.6-5.641) and the second is in those dealing with the *ethical will,* involving the transcendental character of ethics and aesthetics. (6.4-6.43) These two separate discussions point to the two-fold transcendence of the self in terms of *knowing* and *willing* in the tradition of Kant and Schopenhauer.[1] Both the metaphysical subject and the ethical will are outside the world and cannot be described, the former because it is a single point without content at the limit of the world (5.641C) and the latter because it has only "ethical attributes" about which nothing can be said. (6.423A)

The two aspects of the self are radically different in the *Tractatus*. On the one hand, the *metaphysical subject* expresses the condition that the entire world is *my* world, (5.641B) while, on the other, the *ethical will* has no connection with the world at all and cannot even (*qua ethical*) have any effect on it. (6.375) On the one hand, there is a *self which is all world* and, on the other, a *self which is not world at all.* (For Schopenhauer these two are ultimately the same, but there is no basis for finding this in Wittgenstein.)

The metaphysical subject, to begin with, only "limits" the world, like the visual field oriented from the eye, when the eye is an ideal point at the limit of the field, in no way determining the form of the field. (5.6331) This "perspectival point" (as it were, at infinity) is the

---

[1] For example, Schopenhauer wrote: "On the one hand, every individual is the subject of knowing, in other words, the supplementary condition of the possibility of the whole objective world, and, on the other, a particular phenomenon of the will, of that will which objectifies itself in each thing." *The World as Will and Representation.* trans. E. J. Payne, (Indian Hills, Colorado, 1958), vol. 1, p. 278, note 5.

"philosophical *I*" which only expresses the world being my world and in no way affects or determines the world. The ethical will, contrariwise, is not a limit, but *changes* the limits of the world, as it were, changing the "perspectival point" and thereby changing what will count as facts and bringing us into an "altogether different world." (6.43B) While knowing is "necessarily connected" with what is known (so that it is in a certain way identical with what is known), ethical willing enters the world as a stranger, alien and powerless, having no connection with the world at all, and confronting, not its equivalent, but what appears as an "alien will."

It is this two-foldness of the self, as in one way identical with the world and in another having no relation to it at all, which defines the ethical problem. But before examining this we have to look more closely at the two aspects, beginning with Wittgenstein's special kind of solipsism.

ii

Wittgenstein's *solipsism* (or his conception of "how much truth there is in solipsism" (5.62A)) is especially striking in three ways:

(1) It denies the usual conception of the self as a thinking, representing being. (5.631A) Solipsism, in the sense of "I alone exist," is not correct.

(2) It recognizes not only *my world* but *the world,* and its correct expression is not that *there is only my world,* but that *the world is my world.* (5.62C)

(3) It holds that there is a genuine *I,* but this *I determines nothing* about my world or the world, but is identical with the former and is the "metaphysical limit" of the latter. (5.63, 5.641)

In order to understand this and to see how what the solipsist *means is* correct (5.62B) we have to see how Wittgenstein draws the line between the *objective* and the *subject.* This provides not only a key to what he has to say about solipsism, but also a basic insight into his whole philosophy. This line for him does not coincide with that between the *physical* and the *psychological* (since both of these in so far as they are complex and describable belong to the objective). Nor does it coincide with that between *the world* and *the thinker* (since there is no thinker and no need for any if thoughts simply mirror the world). Nor, finally, does it coincide with the line between *the world* and the *user of language*, since Wittgenstein recognizes no "user of language" (and, indeed, a distinction between *language* and *my language* parallels that between *the world* and *my world*).

What the line between the *objective* and the *subject does* coincide with is that between the *form* and the *content* of the world, or that between what can be directly expressed in language and what, in a certain sense, cannot be expressed in language at all. It is this distinction between the *public structural* character of the world and the *private experiential* character which is expressed in the distinction between *the world* and *my world*. *The world* is the world whose *form* and *structure* is mirrored in pictures and propositions; *my world* is the direct qualitatively experienced *content*, (the latter being that which, as it were—although Wittgenstein rejects this way of putting it—"only I experience").

The *Notebooks* abandon the notion that any kind of experience requires an experiencer. Wittgenstein there says that "all experience is world and does not need the subject" and, even further, that we do not need the subject even for individuation, for "Is not my world adequate for individuation?" (p. 89) If we can talk about *experience* at all, it falls under the heading of the structural and the sayable and hence under the heading of *the world;* and if we cannot talk about it, it falls under the heading of private content and hence of *my world,* and this latter, my direct qualitative experience, is *what I am*, no more and no less. (5.63) What solipsism correctly realizes (and what comes out in the way the limits of language mean) is that, nevertheless, there are not two worlds, but only one world and the *world is my world*, (i.e. the world of form and structure *is* the world which is directly experienced). The ontological expression of this, of course, is the formulation that substance is both *form and content*, (2.025) (content being that which is not contained in propositions (3.13) and is only "marked" by expressions (3.31)).

The denial of a thinking, representing subject has also been called the "no agent" view of thinking. G. E. Moore, reporting on *Wittgenstein's Lectures in 1930-33*, wrote:

> For he (Wittgenstein) said that "Just as no (physical) eye is involved in seeing, so no Ego is involved in thinking or having toothache;" and he quoted, with apparent approval, Lich-

tenberg's saying: "Instead of 'I think' we ought to say 'It thinks.' "[2]

Lichtenberg was saying that representing and thinking "happen," and we do not need to introduce a subject which *does* them. Wittenstein from an early date accepted this:

> The thinking subject is surely mere illusion. But the willing subject exists. (*Notebooks.* p. 80)

Why does Wittgenstein deny that there is any thinking representing subject? The reason is that, on his view, there is nothing for it to do because

> The connection between knowledge and what is known is that of logical necessity. (5.1362)

A subject is not needed to make this connection or to add anything to it. (There is a willing self, on the other hand, just because there is no connection between the will and the world.) The *I*, unlike the Cartesian *cogito*, does not appear as thinker, doubter or dreamer, but only as the "perspectival point" which establishes *the world as my world*, and otherwise does nothing at all.

iii

There are three main formulations of solipsism in the *Tractatus*. These are:

(1) *the world is my world;* (5.62C, 5.641B)
(2) *I am my world;* (5.63) and
(3) *solipsism coincides with pure realism.* (5.64)

All of these are connected with "the limits of my language," and indeed they all appear as comments on the statement:

> *The limits of my language* mean the limits of my world. (5.6)

The connection between what we cannot think and what we cannot say is what provides the key to "how much truth there is in solipsism." (5.61D, 5.62)

---

[2] In *Mind*, vol. lxiv, No. 253 (January 1955), p. 13. The entire series of three *Mind* articles is reprinted in G. E. Moore—*Philosophical Papers*, (London, 1959). For Lichtenberg see J. P. Stern—*Lichtenberg: A Doctrine of Scattered Occasions*, (Bloomington, Ind., 1959).

We begin with the first formulation—*the world is my world*. This statement can only be understood if we understand the basic distinction in the *Tractatus* between *form* and *content*, a distinction which cannot, of course, be specified (and is, strictly speaking, not even a "difference"). *The* world is entirely *form* and *structure* (since it is the totality of existing structures of objects (2.04)); *my* world, on the other hand, is entirely *content* (or sheer inexpressible qualitative experience). And what Wittgenstein says is that these two coincide, and that it is language at its limits which shows that they coincide.

What is "coordinated with" the *I* of solipsism is, not reality as logical form and structure (which Wittgenstein calls *Wirklichkeit*), but reality as *content* (which he calls *Realität* (5.64)). The point of solipsism is that *I* experience the world as *content* (or as sheer inexpressible qualitative experience). The distinction between form and content within substance (or within "what subsists independently of what is the case" (2.024)) is carried over into a similar distinction within reality between *reality as form and structure* and *as content*, and to underline this Wittgenstein uses a different word (*Realität*) for the latter. Since nothing can be said about content, and it cannot even be named, we cannot *talk about my* world except as *the* world.

The way in which "the world is my world" is understood when we see that the limits of language in actual use *mean* the limits of *my* world. Wittgenstein formulates the following sequence:

> *The limits of my language* mean the limits of my world. (5.6)
> The limits of the world are also the limits of logic. (5.61A)
> The limits of *the* language (the only language which I understand) mean the limits of *my* world. (5.62C)

We go here from "my language" to "logic" to "language" (or "*the* language," and it is worth noticing that it is the word *the* that is italicized and not, as the translation has it, the word *language*). The transition is from what *my language* means (having, as it were, *content* in mind) to what *language* can say in terms of logic, and finally to the *limits of the latter meaning what the limits of the former mean*. Wittgenstein is pointing out that it is through its logical "public limits" that language means the "private limits" of my world, and *this* is what shows that *the world is my world*.

It is what I cannot say which indicates what I cannot experience. If, for example, I am born blind and cannot therefore "recognize" blue and so cannot say—identifying something for the first time—"This book is blue," it is my inability to say this under these circumstances which *means* that I cannot experience blue. (Even if born blind, of course, I may learn to use color words and may, in another way, understand the sentence "This book is blue.") In a similar fashion my inability to say with sense "This book has a toothache" means that I do not experience *that*.

On the one hand then, all the content of the world is mine or content for the *I*, but, on the other hand, this cannot be said (since we cannot speak about content), but rather is *meant* by the border between what can be said and what cannot be said marking just the border between what I experience and do not experience. It is *not* that I cannot experience what cannot be thought or said (because this is exactly what I do, in some inexpressible way, in experiencing the *content* of the world), but rather that where I can no longer think or say *means* where I can no longer experience.

In the *Notebooks* there is a slightly different way of putting this which shows what Wittgenstein had in mind at the earlier date: (p. 49)

> The limits of my language mean the limits of my world.
> There really is only one world soul which I for preference call *my* soul and as which alone I conceive what I call the soul of others.
> The above remark gives the key for deciding the way in which solipsism is a truth.

Here the difficulties of talking about solipsism entirely in terms of language were avoided by thinking of one universal *I* which would do for all "experience of content." In the *Tractatus*, instead of this, we find the "metaphysical subject" and no reference to whether it is singular or plural (because, of course, nothing can be said about the subject and so nothing can justify this distinction). The *I* involved in solipsism has to be taken without any qualification, and *that* it comes in at all, as well *how* it comes in, has to be shown entirely by language.

iv

Wittgenstein's second formulation of solipsism identifies the *I* with *my world:*

I am my world. (The microcosm.) (5.63)

This same statement also appears in the *Notebooks* where it follows shortly after

> A stone, the body of a beast, the body of a man, my body all stand on the same level. (p. 84)

All these things are parts of *the world* (as structures of objects) and parts of *my world* (as content). What leads him to say that I *am* all of them?

In an entry only a few days later there is a clue to his thinking of that time: (p. 85)

> Now is it true (following the psycho-physical conception) that my character is expressed only in the build of *my* body or brain and not equally in the build of the whole rest of the world?
> This contains a salient point.
> This parallelism, then, really exists between my spirit, i.e. spirit, and the world.

The "salient point" here appears to be that what I experience is as much an expression of me as my body is. I have a certain world and that there is included in it just what there is in it reveals what I am in the same way that my having a certain body does.

Again this way of speaking is dropped in the *Tractatus*, and there this sentence *I am my world* leads directly to the metaphysical subject and to the point that

> The subject does not belong to the world; rather it is a limit of the world. (5.632)

Nothing is now said about the world as the *expression* of the subject or as the *experience* of the subject. Rather we have a simpler way of putting it, for the subject cannot even enter to that extent. The point now is that the subject appears as *none other than my world*. There is no other subject, for the metaphysical limit has no nature or content and *does* nothing. My world as what I experience *is my I*. The full range of my qualitative experience is just what I am, with nothing left over and nothing to be added. We could say "All I experience is all that I am," but we must immediately be on guard not to inject any "experiencer," for

> All experience is world and does not need the subject. (*Notebooks.* p. 89)

The psycho-physical parallelism mentioned in the *Notebooks* continues in the *Tractatus*, but in a more subtle version. It continues as the *content-form* parallelism or as the parallelism of *my world* and *the world*. Inexpressible first person experience still belongs to the *I*, but not as "psychological," rather as the *content of the world which is experienced as my world, but is only sayable as the world*. It is then *my world* which individuates *me* and not *I* who individuate my world.

The final formulation of solipsism—that "solipsism coincides with pure realism" (5.64) underlines the point that the metaphysical subject does not alter or influence or color the world in any way. The subject has no more place within *my world* (which in a sense is *all subject*) than it has within *the world* (which is *all object*). However we look at it

> The self of solipsism shrinks to a point without extension and there remains the reality (*Realität*) coordinated with it. (5.64)

The subject cannot be separated from *my* world, *or the world as directly experienced content*, and this is why Wittgenstein says *I am my world*. But it cannot be found anywhere within *the* world, or the world as form and structure, except at its limit when we find that the two worlds are the same. It is as if nothing could be said about a place from which a view is seen except, in the one case, the view itself, and, in the other case, that there is such a place. The world as altogether inexpressible *content* and altogether expressible *form* and *structure* requires such a limit point, which is in the one case identical with the whole and in the other required in order that the two sides may coincide.

v

The upshot of Wittgenstein's notion of the self is that the "psychological self" which thinks, represents, believes or says is dissolved into psychological states which are as factual as anything else and to describe which we do not need to bring in any subject at all. This comes out in one of the most discussed passages in the *Tractatus:* (5.542)

> It is clear, however, that '*A* believes that *p*', '*A* has the thought *p*', and '*A* says *p*' are of the form ' "*p*" says *p*': and this does not involve a correlation of a fact with an object, but rather the correlation of facts by means of the correlation of their objects.

The point here is that *A* and *p* are both facts, and in the cases mentioned are both of the same complexity. The facts are psychological states of affairs on the one side and propositional signs as states of affairs on the other. No subject has to be brought in. *A* is not to be thought of as either a subject or an object, but as a different *fact* in each of the cases mentioned—the *fact of believing*, the *fact of thinking*, the *fact of saying*, etc. Such psychological states are altogether parts of the world, in so far as they are describable.

The metaphysical subject is, of course, *not* a fact and has no composition. It bears a certain resemblance to Kant's "transcendental unity of apperception" (the "I think" which "must be able to accompany all our representations"). But Kant says:

> This pure original unchangeable consciousness I shall name transcendental apperception.[3]

Wittgenstein does not introduce the word consciousness (*Bewusstsein*), and it does not appear in the *Tractatus*. Nor is the metaphysical subject the "agent" of thought, or the source of the "unity" of thought. It expresses only something like the relation of *the world to me*—i.e. that *the* world is *my* world.

Besides thinking, representing, believing, saying, etc., which are ruled out as activities of the metaphysical subject (because they are distinguishable and describable), there are, however, other activities in the *Tractatus*, which might seem to require a "transcendental" grounding. These are (1) *naming* and *meaning* objects (3.203) which involves *knowing* objects; (2.0123) (2) *distinguishing between existence and non-existence* (which depends upon the "experience which is not an experience" (5.552)) and (3) *viewing and feeling the world as a limited whole* (6.45) and *becoming clear about the sense of life.* (6.521B) These "activities" would seem to be not "complex" and not describable.

As distinct from "*A* believes *p*" or "*A* says *p*," the case of "*A* names B" requires that B should be either a thing (if it can also be described) or an object (if it can only be named). If B is a simple object, we are tempted to ask what A is. Wittgenstein's answer would undoubtedly be that "naming" does not involve merely attaching a label; it means knowing the "ontological grammar" of the object, or what other objects it can combine with. But "*A* knows a logical form" would not involve a correlation of facts either.

---

[3] *Critique of Pure Reason.* Kemp Smith trans., (London, 1950), A 107, p. 136.

The solution to this difficulty must be that *naming with sense* is what, in effect, all language does, and the metaphysical subject is at the limit of this as it is at the limit of the world. We do not have to suppose a "user" of language here any more than for thinking and representing. A metaphysical subject does not have to *do* the naming, for it is language which does the naming. (The philosopher's *discussion of naming* is, of course, nonsense. (6.54))

The case seems to be different, however, with the distinction between existence and non-existence, or holding and not holding of states of affairs. The difference between a true elementary proposition and the same elementary proposition when it is false is the difference between the existence and non-existence (or "obtaining" or "not-obtaining") of the very same state of affairs. And this difference is, as it were, *no difference at all* since there is no experience or thought which can represent it. Nevertheless the distinction, resting on nothing experienceable, thinkable or sayable, *must be made* if we are to describe the world as it is.

The great purity and economy of the *Tractatus* hinges, perhaps more than on anything else, on the way in which it deals with this question. We require a fundamental distinction, which quite literally "makes no sense," between "sheer presence" and "sheer absence of the same." This difference is not logical or factual, not picturable or thinkable, not showable or sayable. *That* the world *is* Wittgenstein calls "the mystical." (6.44) And it would seem that it is *to a subject*. But here again the metaphysical subject does not have to *do* anything; it is simply "in the presence of" the world. The world is given to it with a kind of total immediacy which is altogether unthinkable.

Finally, closely allied to this, is the view of the world *sub specie aeterni* and the feeling of it as a limited whole. (6.45) Only the metaphysical subject, located outside the world, it would seem, could "see" or "feel" the world this way. At this point, it would also seem, the metaphysical subject would also have to become aware of itself and of its unique place. But certainly no provision can be made for this.

vi

We turn now to Wittgenstein's treatment of the *will*, and the key to this is that the important line for him is *not between voluntary and involuntary actions*, which, since they can be distinguished, must both be on the side of facts, but *between happenings and events of any kind and the ethical*. It is only as a bearer of the ethical that a *transcendent* will is involved. In any other way of speaking the will simply belongs to psychology as part of its apparatus of phenomenal description. But just as "the superficial psychology of our day" confuses the composite "soul," which is no soul, with the genuine non-composite subject, (5.5421) so "the will as a phenomenon is of interest only to psychology" (6.423B) and should not be confused with the will as "the bearer of ethical attributes" which is genuinely outside the world. (6.423)

Wittgenstein is quite clear in the *Notebooks* that the difference between what is ordinarily called "willed behavior" and "unwilled behavior" is *not* fundamental, since this difference itself is of a factual nature and *can* be described. The crucial passage in the *Tractatus* is the following: (5.631B)

> If I wrote a book called *The World as I found it*, I should have to include a report on my body, and should have to say which parts were subordinate to my will, and which were not, etc., this being a method of isolating the subject, or rather of showing that in an important sense there is no subject; for it alone could *not* be mentioned in that book.

What is important about this passage is that it tells us that the distinction between the parts of the body subordinate to my will and the parts not subordinate to my will has to be made *without reference to the subject* (since it alone could not be mentioned in the book). It must be possible to distinguish the two kinds of bodily happenings—those subordinated to my will and those not subordinated to it—without bringing in the subject. The motions of my body can be described as factual happenings, and if I can distinguish between those motions which are "produced" by me and those which are not, then there must be some factual basis for being able to make this distinction, and it must lie within the factual realm. If, for example, I consciously and voluntarily raise my arm, what makes the gesture "voluntary" as distinct from "involuntary" must be something describable, perhaps its being accompanied by certain muscular feelings or by certain ideas. Wittgenstein asks:

> Have the feelings by which I ascertain that an act of will takes place any particular characteristic which distinguishes them from any other ideas?

And his answer is: "It seems not!" (p. 87) (i.e. they are like all other ideas).

As the *Tractatus* sees it, to assert "I move my arm" is *either* the description of a factual process (in which case the *I* as subject does not come in) *or* it is evaluated as an ethical action in which case the *I* is held "responsible." And between these two there is no middle ground. The common conception of the will, which mixes the two together by treating the will as if it were simultaneously both object and subject, simply leads to confusion. "Being responsible for one's actions" is given a factual meaning, *as if it were possible to introduce the subject factually* in order to distinguish between voluntary and involuntary actions. But there is no need to do this, and if we are talking about the genuine subject, it cannot be done.[4]

In Wittgenstein's view the will-as-ethical is not any closer to my body than it is to anything else in the world, and, in addition, it is not any closer to the parts of my body that I can move than it is to the parts of my body that I cannot move. He tells us that "my body" is simply a part of the world like any other part of the world. (*Notebooks.* p. 82)

> The human body, however, my body in particular, is a part
> of the world among others, among animals, plants, stones,
> etc., etc.

The consideration that I am able to move my own body, whereas I am not, for example, able to move the sun, simply means for Wittgenstein that the factual situations are different in the two cases, and this can be brought out in the descriptions of the two cases as something we can represent. There is no need to introduce a transcendent subject to account for this difference.

Wittgenstein's position on this (divergent as it is from popular conceptions of the will) is summed up in these sentences from the *Notebooks* (p. 88):

> For the consideration of willing makes it look as if one part
> of the world were closer to me than another (which would
> be intolerable).

---

[4] Schopenhauer, maintaining the identity of will and body, also rejected any ultimate distinction between voluntary and involuntary movements of the body, merely linking the former with the brain and the latter with the autonomic nervous system. *World as Will and Representation. op. cit.*, vol. 2, pp. 245 ff.

But, of course, it is undeniable that in the popular sense there
are things I do, and other things not done by me.
In this way then the will would not confront the world as its
equivalent, which must be impossible.

The words *intolerable (unerträglich)* and *impossible (unmöglich)* indicate that the "popular" view of the will (like the superficial view of
the soul (5.5421)) is altogether inadequate because it does not isolate
the genuine subject. For the will-as-subject cannot intervene in a factual
way at some points and not at others. This would be "intolerable" and
"impossible." The will would then appear as fact or phenomenon,
which might be a way of talking in psychology, but has nothing to do
with the will as genuinely subject.

The "popular conception" of the will, Wittgenstein says, rests on
the error of regarding the will-as-subject as the "cause" of our "willed
actions." He follows Schopenhauer in rejecting this. (*Notebooks*.
p. 87)

The act of the will is not the cause of the action, but is the
action itself.

The will does not cause, but accompanies the action:

Does not the willed movement of the body happen just like
any unwilled movement in the world, but that it is accompanied by the will?

We cannot will without acting, but this does not mean that what we
try to do we can always do; it merely means that it makes no sense
to talk about "trying to will." To will is to act, even though *in thought*
the action may appear as the intention of the will. (p. 88)

vii

That everything can be looked at as object belonging to the world,
including my body and including the difference between the parts of
my body which "I move" and the parts of it which "I do not move,"
isolates the subject, or rather leads to the conclusion that there is no
subject. We are left with the *metaphysical subject*, which expresses
the world being my world and is identical with the sheer inexpressible
experience of the world, and the *ethical will* which cannot affect facts
as facts at all. The question remains: What is the relation between
them?

The *Tractatus* does not provide an answer, but there are various hints in the *Notebooks*. (p. 79)

> Good and evil only enter through the *subject*. And the subject
> is not part of the world, but a boundary of the world.
> As the subject is not part of the world, but a presupposition of
> its existence, so good and evil are predicates of the subject, not
> properties of the world.

In the *Tractatus* we do not read of "predicates" of the subject, and a single point could not have predicates, but the metaphysical subject and the ethical will still appear to be linked.

What appears to dominate Wittgenstein's notion of the self is a very strong visual analogy in which the metaphysical subject is a kind of ultimate "perspectival point" for the ontological, limiting the world, while the ethical will changes the "perspectival point" and hence changes the limits of the world, making it "altogether different." That thereby the world "waxes and wanes as a whole" (6.43A) suggests that "different perspectival points" are not of equal scope, but perhaps some include "more" than others. What this "more" might be is not clear, but a further clue is provided by an additional sentence in the *Notebooks*, not included in the *Tractatus*. (p. 73)

> The world must, so to speak, wax and wane as a whole. As if
> by accession or loss of meaning.

The Ethical and the Religious

. . . anyone nowadays who pays the slightest attention to his own experience finds it the experience of a non-knower, a non-canner.

SAMUEL BECKETT

The higher a system is the more powerless it is.

Zohar

In order that Good may pass into existence, Good must be able to be the cause of what is already entirely caused by necessity.

SIMONE WEIL

Whosoever names Paradise must look and point towards it.

stage direction for a
medieval morality play

I thought that what separated me from God was doubt. But perhaps it was beliefs . . .

E. ALEXIS PREYRE

CHAPTER 9

The Ethical and the Religious

i

The line between fact and value in the *Tractatus* is absolute and impassable. On the one side are the *facts* of the world, which are just what is the case and in themselves have no value, so that

> . . . what happens, whether it comes from a stone or from my body, is neither good or bad. (*Notebooks.* p. 84)

And on the other side is the *ethical will,* which alone is good or bad and which is unable to have any effect on the facts as facts, but can only alter the limits of the world. (6.43) The "solution to the riddle of life" (6.4321) must somehow encompass this absolute discontinuity.

The incommensurability of world and ethics for Wittgenstein rests on his view that

> All propositions are of equal value. (6.4)

because they are all equally descriptive of what is or is not the case. A description of the world, complete in every respect (so that *all possible* scientific questions have been answered), will still not have said anything about *what the sense of it all is or what value it has.* (6.52, 6.41) Good and evil do not belong to the world and cannot, as it were, get *into* the facts. The facts always remain just facts, just neutral.

> The world itself is neither good nor bad.
> Good and evil enter only through the *subject.*
> What is good and evil is essentially the I, not the world.
> (*Notebooks.* pp. 76, 79, 80)

The problem raised by the lack of relation between the ethical will and the world is that, while my will "penetrates" (*durchdringen*) the world,

> I cannot bend (*lenken*) the happenings of the world to my will. I am completely powerless. (*Notebooks.* p. 73)

167

The world is independent of my will, (6.373) and at the same time I am dependent on the world (or on what can be called God or fate). This *completely alien* position of my will in the world makes me "powerless."

But what does Wittgenstein mean by the statement "I am completely powerless"? This does not refer in the first instance to any factual lack of power (as if the world were, so to speak, overwhelmingly stronger than I am). It is not a confession of relative weakness. It refers rather to just the discontinuity between the ethical will and the world. To see this we might consider the case of my control over my body, and here at least it might seem that I am *not* "completely powerless." But this is not the point at issue. My "powerlessness" is not a question of what I can "control" or not, but of the impossibility of *ever translating the ethical qua ethical into facts*. Whatever is willed (however good or bad the willing) enters the realm of neutral fact on a precise par with every other fact. The ethical as ethical cannot be "factualized." There is no equivalent for "good" or "bad" anywhere in facts.

However much we may change the world, there are not, and never will be, any facts that can be said to be good or bad in themselves. We cannot, for example, say that biological life *per se* is a good in itself:

> For it must be all one, as far as concerns the existence of
> ethics, whether there is living matter in the world or not.
> And it is clear that a world in which there is only dead matter
> is in itself neither good or evil, so even the world of living
> things can in itself be neither good nor evil. (*Notebooks.*
> p. 79)

Nor can we say that "life" in the widest sense is good in itself, since life in this sense is the world (5.621) and the world is neither good nor bad. (Wittgenstein does consider the possibility that suicide might be evil in itself, but even here a doubt may be raised, and he asks "Or is even suicide in itself neither good nor evil?") *No* objective situation *per se* can be *intrinsically* any better than any other one. If we say that it is better to live than to die, this is not because life itself is intrinsically superior to death (there might be times when it would not be), but because this is the attitude which the ethical will takes toward facts which in themselves have no value. That we generally desire to live is a fact (if it is a fact) about us. The ethical only enters when we say, for example, that life is good, or it is good that we desire to live.

The statement which best sums up Wittengstein's sharp separation of fact and value is this:

> If the good or bad exercise of the will does alter the world,
> it can only alter the limits of the world, not the facts—not
> what can be expressed by means of language. (6.43)

The point here is not that we cannot alter the world; the point is that if willing *being good or bad* alters the world, it cannot be the facts that *this* alters. The difference between good and bad willing is not itself something which registers factually. Consequently the fundamental reason why "I cannot bend the happenings of the world to my will" and why "I am completely powerless" is that there is no way of writing into facts the values which I wish to ascribe to them.

The air of paradox which clings to this is because all day long we are changing facts to make them coincide with our values, and so it looks as if we bring the world into line with our values. But there are two points to notice about this: (1) that there is nothing about the facts *per se* which corresponds to the judgment of good or bad and (2) such a judgment may at any time be reversed in the light of entirely extraneous additional facts. Because there is *no connection* between the ethical will and the world it is always conceivable that any situation can be good or bad depending on circumstances over which we have no control.

We might suppose that there are psychological factors which could in some way bridge the gap. But in his *Lecture on Ethics*[1] Wittgenstein makes it clear that psychological facts are on exactly the same footing as any other facts

> . . . A state of mind, so far as we mean by that a fact which
> we can describe, is in no ethical sense good or bad.

There is no reason why any state of mind should be regarded as in itself good or bad (even states of extreme suffering, for example, have been regarded as "good for the soul").

Both in the *Notebooks* and in the *Tractatus* Wittgenstein avoids what might have been a serious source of confusion by rejecting the notion that happiness is "psychological" or is a "state of mind." In his view no criteria at all (either physical or psychological) can be

---

[1] In *The Philosophical Review*, vol. LXXIV, No. 1, (January, 1965) pp. 3-12.

found to distinguish between happiness and unhappiness. The difference between the two is a difference *in the whole world.*

> The world of the happy man is a different one from that of the unhappy man. (6.43C)

Happiness is connected with the "significance" of the whole world, and to "live happily" amounts to the same thing as to "live ethically." The desire for happiness is not a solution to any ethical problem, but merely another way of restating every such problem.

Finding ourselves in a world which is totally independent of the ethical will and in which we have "the feeling of being dependent upon an alien will" how is it possible to "live happily" and what is to be done?" We turn now to Wittgenstein's answers to these questions.

ii

His first answer is that *I must make myself independent of the world* by "renouncing any influence on happenings," and in this way *come into agreement* (in *Übereinstimmung*) *with the world;* "and this is what 'being happy' *means."*

> I am then, so to speak, in agreement with that alien will on which I appear dependent. That is to say: 'I am doing the will of God.' (*Notebooks.* p. 75)

As this formulation stands, it is sufficiently broad to fit any religion teaching "submission to the will of God," (provided that we do not inquire too closely what is meant by the "will of God"). But in the *Notebooks* it is not certain whether the "will of God" is to be identified with *the world of facts* (the "alien will" on which we appear dependent) or whether it is connected with the *meaning* of the world of facts. Hence we find (p. 75):

> In order to live happily I must be in agreement with the world.

But this is followed by the question:

> When my conscience upsets my equilibrium, then I am not in agreement with Something. But what is this? Is it *the world?* Certainly it is correct to say 'Conscience is the voice of God.'

Further on is this (p. 79):

> How things stand, is God.
> God is, how things stand.

But this way of speaking appears to be repudiated in the *Tractatus:*

> *How* things are is a matter of complete indifference for what
> is higher. God does not reveal himself *in* the world. (6.432)

And this picks up the other line of thought in the *Notebooks* about
God (pp. 73-4):

> The meaning of life, i.e. the meaning of the world, we can
> call God.
> To believe in a God means to understand the question about
> the meaning of life.
> To believe in a God means to see that the facts are not the end
> of the matter.
> To believe in God means to see that life has a meaning.

It is evident that we are confronted here by two different ways
of talking about God: (1) God as fate, or as the world of facts seen
as the product of an alien will independent of my will, and (2) God
as outside the world, as the meaning of the world—perhaps as the
ethical will, (the "voice of conscience"). Wittgenstein in the *Notebooks* seems to accept both these views and at one point actually says:
(p. 74):

> There are two godheads: the world and my independent I.

This is further supported by a comment made to Waismann:[2]

> *I ask Wittgenstein*: Is the existence of the world connected
> with the ethical?
> *Wittgenstein*: Men have felt a connection here and have ex-
> pressed it this way: God the Father created the world, while
> God the Son (the Word proceeding from God) is the ethical.
> That men have first divided the Godhead and then united it
> points to there being a connection here.

These remarks should warn us against a too hasty interpretation of
Wittgenstein in terms of Spinoza.[3] Ethics as "outside" the world, belonging to a transcendental subject and altering the boundaries of the
world—all this bears little or no resemblance to Spinoza. Wittgenstein

---

[2] *Philosophical Review, ibid.,* p. 16.

[3] Cf. B. F. McGuinness—*The Mysticism of the "Tractatus"* in *The Philosophical Review*, vol. LXXV n. 3, pp. 305-328, who makes the comparison between
Wittgenstein and Spinoza. But, as will be seen, Wittgenstein at this point is much
closer to Kant than to Spinoza.

in his *Lecture on Ethics* describes ethics as "supernatural," a view, to say the least, scarcely congenial to Spinoza. Even the phrase *sub specie aeterni* has a quite different meaning for Wittgenstein, since he is above all interested in the *limits* of the world, and *what is outside the limits*.

The two injunctions of the *Notebooks* to "renounce any influence on happenings" and to "follow conscience" should not be considered as incompatible, but actually as supplementing each other. In a quite traditional way the implication is that, *only if* we renounce any influence on happenings, *can* we follow conscience. What is good, if it is to be genuinely good, must be done *only* because it is good and not because of any concern for results. Being "in agreement with the world" is not mere resignation to whatever happens, but acting with a good will and at the same time being willing to leave the factual outcome in the hands of the "alien will." In such a view we are not required to believe that whatever happens is good just because it does happen, but rather that whatever happens is neither good nor bad, but only the ethical will is good or bad, and this will is obligated to act in accordance with conscience, even though, ethically speaking, this has no effect on the facts at all. Renunciation of influence on happenings is not submission to fate, (or to a Spinozistic necessitarianism), *but rather the recognition that ethics belongs to a completely different dimension from the facts.*

It is the very binding character of the ethical that it should *not* be concerned with results. Just this emphasis on doing what is right without caring what follows is the common element in such otherwise different ethical teachings as, for example, Stoicism, the Bhagavad Gita and the Sermon on the Mount. The ethical will, in recognizing its powerlessness *qua* ethical, actually affirms in the strongest possible way its *superiority to the world* and the uncompromising character of its imperatives. What appears as its powerlessness also appears as its *superiority to power—its power-freeness*. When Wittgenstein says "I am powerless," (recognizing the *I* primarily as the bearer of the ethical), this is not a lament of impotence, but a recognition of the incommensurability between the factual and the ethical (an incommensurability which is just what constitutes the significance of the ethical.)[4]

---

[4] If God as creator is "all-powerful," God as the ethical is "all-powerfree." This distinction comes out in the Old Testament in the contrast between the two most commonly used names of God—*Elohim* and *Yahweh*. One commentator says: "It is agreed by almost all scholars that the name *Elohim* signifies the putter-

Opting for the ethical and giving up the attempt to influence what happens may be seen as one path which leads to *living in the present,* which is called in the *Tractatus* the only genuine eternal life. (6.4311, 6.4312) The connection is that, when he no longer tries to influence events, a man "no longer needs to have any purpose except to live," and when this alone is his purpose, he is finally "fulfilling the purpose of existence." (*Notebooks.* p. 73) Not concerned with what happens, he is no longer then at the mercy of time and knows the happiness of living without fear or hope, for

> Only a man who lives not in time but in the present is hap-
> py . . . (*Notebooks.* p. 75)

iii

We can get an insight into Wittgenstein's ethical and religious thought through examining what he means by *absolute* or *ethical values,* as this is discussed in the *Lecture on Ethics* (delivered in late 1929 or 1930).[5] In this lecture, to explain what is meant by "absolute value," he cites as examples three particular "experiences" which for him have "absolute value." The first, which he calls "my experience *par excellence,*" is that "when I have it *I wonder at the existence of the world.*" The second is "the state of mind in which one is inclined to say 'I am safe, nothing can injure me whatever happens.'" And the third, which is mentioned, but not discussed, is "that of feeling guilty." (pp. 8, 10)

Speaking of the first two examples, Wittgenstein says that "the verbal expression which we give to these experiences is nonsense" since it involves misusing the words "existence," "wondering" and "safe." He says:

> But it is nonsense to say that I wonder at the existence of the

---

forth of power. He is the being to whom all power belongs. . . . God's personal existence, the continuity of his dealings with man, the unchangeableness of His promises, and the whole revelation of His redeeming mercy, gather round the name *Yahweh (Jehovah)*." R. B. Girdlestone—*Synonyms of the Old Testament,* (Grand Rapids, Mich., 1953), pp. 26, 38. The contrast is even more pronounced in the New Testament—between the two "masters," the "world" and God, the "world" not being the "original world," but the "fallen world," since in the "original world" (and in the world-to-be) the creation and the ethical are reconciled.

[5] *The Philosophical Review,* vol. LXXIV, No. 1, (January, 1965) pp. 3-12. All page citations in the text are to this article unless otherwise indicated.

> world, because I cannot imagine it not existing. . . . To
> be safe essentially means that it is physically impossible that
> certain things should happen to me and therefore it's nonsense
> to say that I am safe *whatever* happens. (p. 9)

And he points out that, although these experiences are facts, (in the
sense that, as experiences, they have a limited span, can be described,
etc.), they are not facts like any other facts because when it is urged
that they are just ordinary facts

> . . . I at once see clearly, as it were in a flash of light, not only
> that no description that I can think of would do to describe
> what I mean by absolute value, but that I would reject every
> significant description that anybody could possibly suggest,
> *ab initio*, on the ground of its significance. That is to say: I see
> now that these nonsensical expressions were not nonsensical
> because I had not yet found the correct expressions, but that
> their nonsensicality was their very essence. For all I wanted
> to do with them was just *to go beyond* the world and that is
> to say beyond significant language. (p. 11)

Wittgenstein presents his experiences as "examples" "to fix my mind
on what I mean by absolute or ethical value" because recalling a typical
situation in which one would use such a term as "absolute value" makes
what we say "concrete and, as it were, controllable." (p. 8) The examples point to what lies "beyond language" in three different directions: *sheer existence*, the *subject* and the *ethical*. These three kinds
of "transcendence" are, of course, central to the entire philosophy of
the *Tractatus*. What appears in terms of the ontological limits in the
Tractatus are presented as "experiences of absolute value" in the *Lecture
on Ethics*.

In the first direction lies the *existence of the world*, or the existence
of *anything* (whatever it is), here linked with "wonder" (while in the
Tractatus it is called an "experience which is not an experience" *that
something is*. (5.552A)) Like Leibniz, Wittgenstein wonders that anything exists at all, that there is something rather than nothing. That
something is the case or *is so* may be contrasted with that same state of
affairs or situation not being the case or not being so. But prior to this
is something even more fundamental: recognizing *that something is*
(not *is* relatively to the corresponding negative fact, but *is* absolutely).
While every particular something is experienced as "something being

the case" (and possibly not being the case), *that any something at all is* has no negative. Wondering about the existence *per se* of the world is not wondering about the existence of anything particular, but of *anything at all.*[6]

The sheer presence of the world, its *thatness*, cannot be said or experienced or thought. What is most evident is, as it were, most hidden. The primal miracle (as Wittgenstein calls it) that *the world is there*, (and what men mean by this, he says, "lies close to my heart"), is *not a fact or a truth or an experience*, but must be presupposed by all of that. It is not too much to say that the decisive insight of Wittgenstein's philosophy is that what is most important, most evident, most undeniable (that is, *that something is*) *cannot be said*. The *Tractatus* is a kind of stammering in the face of this overwhelming immediacy, both of form and content.

The second example of an "experience of absolute value"—the "experience of feeling absolutely safe"—points to another fundamental idea of the *Tractatus*, the idea that *the subject does not belong to the world*. The subject is a limit of the world (5.632) or, as the ethical will, lies completely outside the world. (6.43) It is, therefore, beyond the reach of facts. The *I* which cannot be confronted and which never appears as an object cannot be in any way impinged upon by anything in the world. It is outside of space and time, and, to the extent that we see that *that is what we are*, we are absolutely safe.

Wittgenstein rejects popular ideas which treat the subject as simply one more fact of a somewhat peculiar kind. (5.5421) What psychologists talk about when they talk about "personality" or "character" *cannot be the genuine subject*, for the genuine subject cannot be described, since it is not composite. It is not part of the web of fate. What is in the world is "my body," which is a neutral fact like any other fact.

> The human body, however, my body in particular, is a part of the world among others, among animals, plants, stones, etc., etc.
>
> Whoever realizes this will not want to procure a pre-eminent place for his own body or for the human body.
>
> He will regard humans and animals quite naively as objects

---

[6] It is at this point that Wittgenstein's philosophy has something in common with Heidegger's. What Wittgenstein merely points to, however, Heidegger talks about at ample length.

which are similar and which belong together. (*Notebooks*. p. 82)

What lies outside the world and hence outside of space and time cannot be subject to death. But this does not mean that it "survives" after death with an infinite temporal duration. It means rather that it *belongs to timelessness*, to the eternal present. (6.4311) (Wittgenstein might well have answered what the mystic Jacob Boehme did when asked where the soul goes after death: "There is no need for it to go anywhere.")

iv

The third experience of "absolute value"—that of "feeling guilty" —is not discussed in the *Lecture on Ethics*, but considerable light is shed on it by Paul Engelmann's *Memoir* of Wittgenstein and by Wittgenstein's own *Lectures on Religious Belief* (given about 1938).[7] In these lectures Wittgenstein takes as his prime example of religious belief the belief in the Last Judgment. How he came to choose this example is better understood in the light of a passage from the Engelmann *Memoir*.

> The idea of a God in the sense of the Bible, the image of God as creator of the world, hardly ever engaged Wittgenstein's attention (as G. H. von Wright rightly points out in his *Biographical Sketch*), but the notion of a last judgment was of profound concern to him. "When we meet again at the last judgment" was a recurrent phrase with him, which he used in many a conversation at a particularly momentous point. He would pronounce the words with an indescribable inward-gazing look in his eyes, his head bowed, the picture of a man stirred to his depths. (p. 77)

The *Lectures on Religious Belief* almost at the outset suggest:

> Suppose that someone believe in the Last Judgment, and I don't . . . (p. 53)

In the light of Engelmann's recollection it is not unlikely that the "someone" who believed in it was Wittgenstein himself. Later in the same lectures he defends the belief in these terms:

> Why shouldn't one form of life culminate in an utterance

---

[7] Paul Engelmann—*Letters from Wittgenstein with a Memoir*, (N.Y., 1967) and Wittgenstein—*Lectures and Conversations on Aesthetics, Psychology and Religious Belief*, edited by Cyril Barrett, (Berkeley, Calif., 1967).

of belief in a Last Judgment? But I couldn't either say "Yes"
or "No" to the statement that there will be such a thing. Nor
"Perhaps," nor "I'm not sure."
It is a statement which may not allow of any such answer.
If Mr. Lewy is religious and says he believes in the Last Judgment, I won't even know whether to say I understand him or
not. I've read the same things he's read. In a most important
sense I know what he means. (p. 58)

As in the *Notebooks, Tractatus* and *Lecture on Ethics* Wittgenstein
is here saying that such religious and ethical matters as the Last Judgment are in no way factual, and it does not make sense to say that there
will be or *will not be* (or *might be* or *might not be*) a Last Judgment.
What is being expressed by such a belief is the "culmination of a form
of life," and if somebody expresses such a belief, Wittgenstein may not
know how to take it, but knows "what he means."

It is clear from others' reminiscences of Wittgenstein, as well as
from his own published letters, that the theological expression "living
under judgment" would aptly describe his life. The intensity of his
thought and of his search for clarity could only have grown out of a
driving sense of moral urgency. We have a memorable picture in Norman Malcolm's *Memoir* of the fierce demands which he made on himself, his "absolute relentless honesty" and his "ruthless integrity."[8] All
this was undoubtedly closely connected with the "experience of feeling guilty" as an experience of "absolute value," and this guilt may well
have been one of the mainsprings of the stern demands which motivated
his existence.

We may suppose that, if Wittgenstein *had* discussed the "experience of feeling guilty," as he did the other two such "absolute experiences," the discussion would have followed roughly the same lines. He
would have rejected *ab initio* any significant description of the experience. And it would not have been a feeling guilty about anything
in particular, but a sense of falling short of some total requirement,
where we could not specify what the requirement is, how it arises, or
how and why we fail to meet it, (although, of course, various theological statements purport to do this). Any psychological account of

---

[8] Norman Malcolm—*Ludwig Wittgenstein—A Memoir*, (Oxford, 1958), p. 27.
G. H. von Wright in an essay included in the same volume describes Wittgenstein
as saying that "The thought of God . . . was above all for him the thought of
the fearful judge." (p. 20)

such a feeling would have to be rejected as missing the point of the absolute value of the experience.

The "experience of feeling guilty" might presumably be contrasted with the happiness which a good conscience brings about. There is in Wittgenstein's view some kind of "internal" punishment and reward in connection with ethics, as is evident from this passage:

> When an ethical law of the form, 'Thou shalt . . .' is laid down, one's first thought is, 'And what if I do not do it?' It is clear, however, that ethics has nothing to do with punishment and reward in the usual sense of the terms. So our question about the *consequences* of an action must be unimportant.—At least those consequences should not be events. For there must be something right about the question we posed. There must indeed be some kind of ethical reward and ethical punishment, but they must reside in the action itself.
> (And it is also clear that the reward must be something pleasant and the punishment something unpleasant.) (6.422)

"Feeling guilty" would not, however, have the absolute significance which Wittgenstein ascribes to it if it came only as a punishment for specific bad acts of will. It presumably would have to make us question even the "goodness" of our supposed good actions and just in this would lie its inexpugnable claim.

While "feeling guilty" might involve a range of feelings all the way from a "vague sense of discontent" to "suffering the torments of the damned," the *sui generis* aspect would remain inexplicable. For the simple hedonist there would be an appearance of paradox in the circumstance that it is an *unpleasant* experience (which even comes at times as a punishment) which is regarded by Wittgenstein (and others) as an experience having "absolute value." Such a person might be driven to saying that "unhappiness" can make us "happy," a way of speaking fostered by some psychologists. For Wittgenstein, however, "feeling guilty" would have to be the prototype of "unhappiness," the signal that we do not "live happily" and do not "follow conscience" and, above all, that *the blame for this rests with us*. In this sense, the experience might almost be a synonym for "feeling responsible" or "being responsible" and hence for the "ethical" itself.

The three experiences which Wittgenstein gives as examples of experiences having "absolute value" may all, he points out, be easily translated into the religious mode, in which terms they will seem to become part of a "great and elaborate allegory."

> For the first of them is, I believe, exactly what people were referring to when they said that God had created the world; and the experience of absolute safety has been described by saying that we feel safe in the hands of God. A third experience of the same kind is that of feeling guilty and again this was described by the phrase that God disapproves of our conduct. (p. 10)

We seem, he says, to be dealing with similes, but when we try to find out what the similes are similes *for*, there is nothing there,

> And so what at first appeared to be a simile now seems to be mere nonsense. (p. 10)

The gap between the *Lecture on Ethics* (1929 or 1930) and the *Lectures on Religious Beliefs* (1938) is shown by the difference between regarding a religious belief as a seeming simile which is really nonsense and regarding it as "the culmination of a form of life."

v

We can sum up Wittgenstein's early ethical and religious views in roughly this way:

Happiness lies in the realization that the meaning of life lies "outside" of space and time and that "the facts of the world are not the end of the matter." (*Notebooks*. p. 74) The world as a whole *has* an "outside" and seeing it in this way is seeing it *sub specie aeternitatis*, which is the basis for the good life.

> The usual way of looking at things sees objects as it were from the midst of them, the view *sub specie aeternitatis* from outside.
> In such a way that they have the whole world as a background. Is this it perhaps—in this view the object is seen *together with* space and time instead of *in* space and time? (*Notebooks*. p. 83)

At the end of the *Tractatus* Wittgenstein uses the expression "the sense of the world" which, he says, "must lie outside the world." (6.41A) Throughout the book it has been propositions which have sense, and their sense is what they assert, what they stand for. To ask *what is the sense of the world?* is to ask what does the world say? what does it stand for? or perhaps what is it all about? how does it hang together?

Wittgenstein tells us that the facts do not, and cannot, provide an answer to this question or these questions, because the facts are accidental and in their own terms do not "make sense." The facts only contribute to setting the problem; they do not contribute to its solution. (6.4321) And even if *all* possible scientific questions were answered, we feel that the problems of life would remain "completely untouched." (6.52) The reason for this irrelevance of the facts to the solution of the problem of life, Wittgenstein says, is that the problem does not lie in *how* the world is (i.e. in its factuality), but in *that* it is. But *this is not a problem* because there is no question that can be asked about it.

There are two apparently contradictory movements here: (1) to realize that the solution of the riddle of life lies outside space and time (6.4321) and (2) to see from *that* perspective (because it is only from that perspective that it can be seen) that there *is* no riddle. (6.5) All our questions will only ask *how* and hence will only provide more facts. But this is not what we want, for we are wondering *that* the world is, and for this there is no question. And seeing that there is no question constitutes the "answer." It is what Wittgenstein calls the "mystical" which unveils the "question which is no question" and which is "answered" in this way.

Wittgenstein says three things about the *mystical:* (1) it is *that* the world is; (6.44) (2) it is the "feeling of the world as a limited whole;" (6.45B) and (3) it is "the inexpressible" which "shows itself." (6.522) These are all something like the *sense of the presence of the world*— its simply being there—its content anteceding all questions. The "sense of the world" must lie in its directly perceived content, about which nothing can ever be said, but which simply shows itself. The riddle vanishes when we realize that *we are in the presence of this overwhelming immediacy,* and nothing that we can do or say is more important than that.

The System of the Tractatus—Ontology

Perhaps the philosophically most relevant feature of modern science is the emergence of abstract symbolic structures as the hard core of objectivity . . .

HERMANN WEYL

So it can be said that *sensible qualities* are in fact *occult qualities* and that there must be others *more manifest* which could render them understandable. Far from understanding sensible things only, it is just these which we understand the least.

GOTTFRIED LEIBNIZ

περὶ δὲ τὸ παρὸν ἑκάστῳ πάθος, ἐξ ὧν αἱ αἰσθήσεις καὶ αἱ κατὰ ταύτας δόξαι γίγνονται, χαλεπώτερον ἑλεῖν ὡς οὐκ ἀληθεῖς. ἴσως δὲ οὐδὲν λέγω· ἀνάλωτοι γάρ, εἰ ἔτυχον, εἰσί,

(There is more difficulty in proving that states of feeling which are present to a man and out of which arise sensations and opinions in accordance with them, are also untrue. And very likely I have been talking nonsense about them, for they may be unassailable.)

PLATO

Necessity is a slightly degraded image of impossibility; and existence, of necessity.

SIMONE WEIL

CHAPTER 10

The System of the Tractatus—Ontology

i

There are four clearly distinguished "ontological levels" in the *Tractatus:*

substance (Substanz) —
    form and content (2.025)
    all possible states of affairs (2.0123, 2.033)
    all imagined worlds have in common (2.022)

reality (Wirklichkeit) —
    existence and non-existence of states of affairs (2.06)
    world as pictured and spoken about (2.12, 4.01)
    form is logical form (2.18)

essence (Wesen) —
    disclosed by possibility of each individual case (3.3421)
    same for proposition, description and world (5.4711)
    essential is what is in common (3.341)

world (Welt) —
    all that is the case (1.)
    totality of facts not of things (1.1)
    totality of existing states of affairs (2.04)
    sum-total of reality (2.063)

While this may seem like an unnecessarily complex metaphysical framework, it will be found that all four "levels" are indispensable.

What is in many ways the most fundamental distinction of all appears within the category of *substance*—that between *form* and *content.* The other three "levels" all have to do with *form* and *structure.* It is a fundamental point throughout the book that we cannot say anything about *content* at all and that *reality, essence* and *world* all involve only form and structure. When content is put aside, we have to do mainly with possibility, or possible structure, which is *form* and existing structure which is *essence.*

We can look at all four "levels" in terms of possibility in this way:

substance — all possibility (and content)
reality — logical possibility (possibility "bi-polarized")
essence — existing possibility (logical place indicated)
world — totality of existing possibility

The important transition from *all* (applied to possibility) to *totality* (applied to facts) is discussed in the chapter on *The Limits of the World*.

And finally we can look at the four "levels" in terms of language and propositions:

substance — what is *named* (required for *determinateness*)
reality — what is *shown* (required for *logical form*)
essence — what is *shown* and *said* (required for *sense*)
world — what is *truly said* (required for *truth*)

The best way to understand these categories is in terms of three fundamental contrasts running throughout the book—those between (1) *form* and *content;* (2) *form* and *essence* and (3) *reality* and *world*. We turn now to a discussion of each of these three.

ii

In the *Tractatus* it is only *form* and *structure* that can get into words; *content* as such is altogether private and inexpressible. We could not tell a person blind from birth *what green is as an experience* or what the difference between red and green as experiences is. We could say that red and green are different, but we would not be talking about *content*, but about red and green as parts of an objective color system (or about red and green as they enter into language or into a "system of sameness and differences"). Nothing can be predicated of content as such. To say "This is the same color as I saw yesterday" is not to make a statement about the *contents* of two private experiences, but rather a statement about objective phenomena which are viewed *structurally*.

Wittgenstein's view in the *Tractatus* is that content is "private," and language cannot be "private."[1] If I have never "experienced" green,

---

[1] The whole point about the impossibility of a private language in the *Philosophical Investigations* is implicit in the *Tractatus's* distinction between *form* and *content* and the impossibility of saying anything about the latter, although Wittgenstein approaches the question from a very different point of view in his later philosophy.

no amount of talk about it will tell me *what it is,* but the grammar of the word, its use in relation to other words, may still be entirely comprehensible. The blind person will be as able to talk about green as anyone else; what he lacks (the "experience" of the ineffable content of green) is just that about which nobody can say anything.

Metaphysics has traditionally attempted to *say what content is in general,* calling it "matter," "ideas," the *"ding-an-sich,"* "reason" (dialectical or otherwise), "will," etc. In this century we have had Peirce's *firstness,* Whitehead's *feelings,* Bergson's *elan vital,* the phenomenalists' *sense-data,* and still others. From Wittgenstein's point of view all these are attempts to express the inexpressible and so doomed to failure. It makes no sense to say "We know what content is" or "We do not know what content is." All we can say is that content shows itself and it cannot be expressed. Content does not get into language; what gets into language are simply *samenesses and differences,* and we leave it to the persons who understand the language to fill in the content.

For Wittgenstein the "experience which is not an experience" *that something is* is the "experience" of content, the "experience" which comes before logic and language. (5.552A) Content is *there;* it is the *presence* of the world, and it must be there before we can say anything. But content as such cannot be named or described, for it cannot be "recognized" or "identified." What we put into words is not content; *it is the structure which goes with content.* We leave it to each speaker and hearer to fill in the content from his own experience, if he has such experience, but it is not *this* that he is talking about. For nothing can be said about content; it remains wholly inexpressible.[2]

The possibility of a blind person understanding all there is to know about color, or all that we can put into words about color, shows that when we talk about color, we are not talking about content. The "logic of color" (that, for example, it is spatial objects which are colored, and not temporal durations or psychological states) can be understood by those who have never had any "color experience." And if two colors are called by the same name, it can be understood that they are being treated as the *same* even if we never "experienced" them. It is true that the blind person will not be able to pick out colors or

---

[2] Plato's *Theaetetus* is the *locus classicus* for the impossibility of "recognizing" or "identifying" content. In Moritz Schlick's lectures on *Form and Content,* (1932) clearly written under the influence of Wittgenstein although they do not mention Wittgenstein, we have a classic modern statement.

apply color words directly to colors, but the possibility of substituting
a tactile coding for the colors shows that it is the *structures* which are
needed for the language and not the specific "color content." All we
can communicate in any case are the structures, and the experienced
contents simply accompany these.

Content is so ubiquitous, for it is our entire experience of the world,
that it may seem paradoxical when we are told that we cannot talk
about it, since it may seem that we talk about nothing else. But it is,
after all, not our qualitative experiences that we talk about, but *objects
with properties, a pattern which we must continue to apply even when
we are talking about material properties themselves.*

It might be asked: Why should not content be dropped altogether
if it cannot even be mentioned and if all we ever talk about is structure?
The answer is because content *is* given; it belongs to the substance of
the world, (2.025) and our inability to speak about it does not mean
that it is not present and presupposed by our language. Content must
be counted as belonging to the world because it *does* belong to the
world. Accompanying what we say, which moves in the realm of
structural possibilities, is what does not involve possibility and is not
possible to say. The effort to *say content* is futile, not because there is
no content, but because language is not adapted to saying it (whatever
that would mean) and, in addition, because there is no need to say it.
(Have we ever attempted to describe the aroma of coffee and failed?
Wittgenstein asks in the *Philosophical Investigations.* (610))

To say (as behaviorists are sometimes inclined to do) that all "subjective" or "private" experiences are "illusions" or "have no reality"
rests upon a misunderstanding. It supposes that it is possible to refer
to such experiences in order to deny them. And, in addition, the private
experience is being described (as an illusion) and if such a description
is to make sense, there must be some way of finding out whether the
private experience *is* an illusion or *is not* an illusion (although the person giving the description in this case has in mind no such possibility,
and there is no such possibility). The word *illusion* is being misused,
as the *Philosophical Investigations*, approaching the same problem from
a different point of view, would point out.

But, beyond this, the denial of *content* (or, what amounts to the
same thing, of "first-person experience" or of what Wittgenstein calls
"my world") leaves no room for the limitations on the use of language
which affect a person without first-hand experience of *content*. What,

for example, prevents a blind person from driving an automobile is also what prevents him from reading sign-posts, although not from talking knowledgeably about driving automobiles, or from understanding the sign-post when it is read to him. Such an instruction, (however given), as "Turn right at the green" cannot be followed by a blind person, not because the same instructions could not be coded in some other way, but because we could still distinguish between any other coding and *this* one, and the distinction could only be made on the basis of content. In the terminology of the *Tractatus* the expression *green* marks a form *and* a content (3.31) and even objects, which we name, retain external properties, (2.01231, 2.0233) which are not "structural."

The entire "realm of content" or *my world* (5.6) — just what is not present and not needed in the robot—is present side-by-side with the "realm of form" or *the world* in the *Tractatus*. This "immediately enjoyed actuality," as Whitehead described it, cannot, however, be expressed as such, for its only possible expression lies in public, logical structures. In the words of Heracleitus, quoted at the beginning of the first chapter, "it is necessary to follow the common" even though "the many live as though they had a private understanding." In Wittgenstein's language there is no private understanding, no private description, or, as he phrased it in the *Philosophical Investigations*, finally no private language. Whatever *can* be expressed is expressed in a common coin, and whatever *is* expressed *can* be expressed and thus reveals the common coin.

Wittgenstein's refusal to speak about content prevents calling it illusory or real, phenomenon or epiphenomenon, public or private, *or anything else*. He tells us specifically that it cannot get into language.

> A proposition contains the form, but not the content of its sense. (3.13E)

In the *Notebooks* he is still able to say:

> Names signalize what is common to a single form and a single content. (p. 53)

But in the *Tractatus* even this road is closed, for names there have no relation to content. All that is permitted is that *expressions* may "mark" (*kennzeichnen*) a form and a content. (3.31)

An expression is the mark of a form and a content. (3.31D) An *expression* (in distinction from a *name*) is a word or phrase appearing in an unanalyzed proposition. The word "green," for example, points to the "experienced" content green, as well as to the form of color, and that particular structural possibility of that form.

The world as "immediately experienced," or *material properties as content,* is what we cannot talk about. What they are structurally, as states of affairs, is what we can talk about. But somewhere in between material properties as content and objects as structures lie what are in some respects content and in some respects form and structure—that is, *things.* Things have a kind of "reduced form," or a "form of independence," because although they occur in situations (rather than in states of affairs), they occur in *all possible* situations and this connects them with states of affairs, so that their form of independence is, after all, a "form of dependence." (2.0122) While *objects* are fully determinate, not having more than one form each, *things* share in forms only because there is a limitation on the possibilities of their occurrences in situations.

The following table shows this duality of *content* and *form* in the *Tractatus,* the parentheses indicating the ambiguous status of *things* (as distinct from *objects*):

Content		*Form*
(things)	names	objects
material properties as experienced	elementary propositions	states of affairs
(things in situations)	ordinary propositions	objects of thought in states of affairs
(things)	truth functional propositions	facts

As this table brings out, things have a dual status because, on the one hand, they are *named like objects,* and, on the other, they are *described like facts.* They have the "recognizability" and "identifiability" of objects and at the same time the "complexity" and "describability" of facts. They are simple, in so far as they are named, and complex, in so far as they are conjunctions of material properties or states of affairs.

Wittgenstein tells us that substance is both form and content (2.025) and that it is the configuration of substance or objects which *forms* (*bilden*) both material properties and states of affairs. The material properties may be regarded as the "external properties" of the objects (2.0233) and the states of affairs as showing their "internal properties." (2.01231) (The use of the same word *forms* (*bilden*) for both may well suggest that even the term "material properties" has no meaning apart from *form* even though substance "can only determine a form and not any material properties." (2.0231))

Material properties (although that term is only used once in the *Tractatus*) cannot be dispensed with because they are the link between things-as-objects and things-as-facts. It is because things, as well as being quasi-objects, also are conglomerates of material properties or states of affairs that they can be further described in propositions with new senses. (Final analysis requires only that the intended sense be determinate, so it will be possible for things still to be named as objects in a proposition which is fully analyzed, although no things can be named in elementary propositions.)

There is a necessary ambiguity in the term *thing*, arising from whether the thing is to be taken as a simple or a complex, for it can always be taken either way although not in the same proposition. That things have this ambiguous status (and hence can be distinguished from both *objects* and *facts*) is what justifies putting them on the side of content. On the other hand, it is only material properties that are "experienced" as the inexpressible content of the world. We can name objects and things-as-objects even though we "cannot put them into words." And we can describe facts and things-as-facts. But material properties *as content we can neither name nor describe*. Hence it is this latter (the *what* of the world) which is altogether private and incommunicable.

iii

The distinction between *objects* and *things* also introduces another central distinction—that between *form* and *essence*. Wittgenstein says that

> The possibility of its occurring in states of affairs is the form of an object. (2.0141)

and he also says

> It is essential to things that they should be possible constituents of states of affairs. (2.011)

Objects are entirely formal, what correspond to pure names; and the words *essence* or *essential* do not occur in connection with *them*. There are no "accidental" possibilities for objects; they can only occur in connection with each other. Things, on the other hand, have a certain independence, (2.0122) (as if they could be recognized in isolation by themselves), but it is necessary for them that they should be able to form the same kinds of immediate combinations as objects do.

This helps to indicate the difference between *form* and *essence*. Broadly speaking, *form* usually means *all possibilities*, while *essence* means *possibilities found to exist*. Form is what is known and given as what logic has to deal with, (2.0121C) while essence is what is discovered or disclosed. (3.3421) We cannot picture or talk about the world at all without making use of form and logical form, while it is in the course of doing this that we discover something about what is the essence of the world and what is essential to pictures and propositions. In regard to the world especially it can be said that form is the *possibilities of existence* (what possibilities could exist), while essence is the *existence of possibilities* (what possibilities do exist).

It should be noted that it is almost entirely with regard to pictures, propositions and symbols that Wittgenstein speaks of what is *essential*. For what contrasts with what is essential is what is accidental, which is primarily the non-structural, adventitious aspect of language. (And, indeed, there is a certain analogy between the form-content distinction and the essence-accident one.) To illustrate his use of the terms *essence* and *essential* three quotations will serve:

> . . . what is essential in a proposition is what all propositions that can express the same sense have in common. (3.341A)

> It belongs to the essence of a proposition that it can communicate a new sense to us. (4.027)

> A proposition communicates a situation to us, and so it must be *essentially* connected with the situation. (4.03B)

Here we have (1) what is in common between all expressions with the same sense; (2) what is in common between all propositions and (3) what is in common between propositions and the world. What we have to do with in all three cases is a "commonness," which is not a form, but involves in all three cases *sense*. Essence in the *Tractatus*, it often will be found, is connected with *sense*, which is the way in which we represent a single possibility of the world. (4.031) Propositions have logical form, or what corresponds to *logical form*, (3.315) but they also have *sense* which may be shared. There are, in other words, necessary common features which are *not* formal ones, and these are essential.

The place where *essence and form coincide* is in the case of the *general form of a proposition* which is also the *essence of a proposition*. (5.471) The general form of a proposition, (which is the general nature of a proposition presupposed by all propositions), is the same as the essence of a proposition, (which is what all propositions have in common). This general form or essence is that a proposition says: *Matters stand so and so* (or *Such and such is the case*).[3]

Although there is a basic identity between the logical forms of the world and the logical forms of propositions, there is no identity between the form of the world and the general form of propositions (and this is just what is conveyed by the word *general*). The general form of a proposition does not correspond to the form of the world, but to the essence of the world. There is no form of all propositions, giving something like *all possible senses* or the totality of all possible arrangements of names. The general form of a proposition, in other words, is not the "sense of its senses" (any more than the form of the world is the "forms of its forms"), but rather that propositions all assert how things are. Wittgenstein says that what is essential to all propositions is not what is essential to all possible senses, but what is essential to the *expression* of all possible senses. (4.5)

There is in the *Tractatus* no "all possible logical forms" and no "all possible senses." We do not know the composition of elementary propositions in advance because we do not know "the number of names with different meanings" (5.55) or the logical forms that we will invent. (5.555) It is not possible to lay down definitions or rules for guaranteeing that propositions have sense. All we know is that they must have logical form (i.e. show all the possibilities of existence and non-existence of states of affairs of the given objects) and also must have the general form of a proposition (i.e. assert the existence of one of these states of affairs).

---

[3] *Es verhält sich so und so.* The German verb here carries the notion of a relation or a certain element of constraint. It is worth noting that *sich verhalten* can be used as a psychological term referring to human or animal behavior and can also be applied to chemical reactions.

The general form of a proposition is not able to distinguish between elementary propositions (which are true or false by virtue of their senses as compared with the world) and truth functional propositions (which are true or false by virtue of the truth or falsity of the elementary propositions). As regards truth or falsity, all propositions stand on the same level, even though as regards sense, all sense comes from elementary propositions. (5.2341) Since all elementary propositions are truth functions of themselves, (5.B) we can take an elementary proposition as a true or false assertion about the world and also use it as an assertion about its own truth or falsity. ("*p* is true' has no sense different from "*p*" and has the same truth values.)

In every proposition something of the form of the world is *shown* and something of the essence of the world is *shown* and *said*. (In order to be able to *say anything* language must be able to *show what* it is saying (4.022, 4.461) and also to show *more* than it is saying. (4.121)) A tautology, in effect, tries to show and say the complete essence of the world, while a contradiction tries to say the complete form of the world. The former is, as it were, so "loose" that it describes everything, the latter so "restricted" that it describes nothing. We require a "proto-conjunction" for a logical form and a "proto-disjunction" for an essence, but neither can be framed for an entire world.

The *Tractatus* envisages the world as suspended between *form* and *essence*, or between the requirement of determinate sense supplied by all possible structures of given forms and the "in common" possibilities which are actually said to exist or found to exist. It is logical form which links the two by polarizing the possible structures into their possibilities of existence and non-existence. Each meaning and sense are provided by making the *all* immanent at every point, so that, however many objects and elementary propositions we have, we always have *all* objects and *all* elementary propositions. (5.524) Thus the world is always "closed" as a field of possibilities, while, on the other hand, it remains "open" as to what possibilities happen to exist.

It is basic to Wittgenstein's point of view that *we* do not determine possibility. We only deal with what turns out to be possible as this is disclosed by essence and given by the forms of the world and the form of reality. If any sign may be used at all, it then has all the further uses which it is possible for it to have, and this is in no way determined by us. The dual nature of pictures and propositions, as being identical in form with what they represent while at the same time agreeing or disagreeing in structure, displays the gap between form and essence. It is this gap which is opened by the disparity between *objects* and *names* to be discussed in the next chapter.

iv

The distinction between *reality* and *world* is as fundamental as those between *form* and *content* and *form* and *essence*. Reality *(Wirklichkeit)* is the term used by Wittgenstein for the ordinary world around us when it is seen as including both existence and non-existence, and for every existence its corresponding non-existence. In his *Notes on Logic* (1913) Wittgenstein tells us why he needs this category when he says:

> The chief characteristic of my theory is: *p has the same meaning as not-p* . . . (*Notebooks.* p. 94)

In the *Tractatus* (where *propositions* do not have meaning) this becomes:

> The propositions '*p*' and '*not-p*' have opposite sense, but there corresponds to them one and the same reality." (4.0621)

Reality is the world as having the character that it permits opposite senses for one and the same "reference." Or, as Wittgenstein puts it:

> The existence and non-existence of states of affairs is reality. (2.06)

But there is more involved than this, as the following sequence of statements brings out:

> The totality of existing states of affairs is the world. (2.04)
> The existence and non-existence of states of affairs is reality. (2.06)
> The sum-total of reality is the world. (2.063)

How, we may ask again, if reality is the existence and non-existence of states of affairs, can the "sum-total of reality" be just existing states of affairs? Or, phrasing the question slightly differently, how can existing and non-existing states of affairs add up to just existing states of affairs?

The answer is that existence and non-existence *of the same do not count as two, but as one*, because there is no way of distinguishing between them in a picture or in a logical picture, and consequently when we have pictured an existence, we have at the same time pictured that same non-existence. This will still not give us the same total for both existing and non-existing states of affairs as for existing ones, however, unless every non-existence also counts as "some other existence" (of course, with *its* nonexistence).

We can say, therefore, that, while there is nothing in reality which corresponds to *not*, there is always *something* there which settles simultaneously both the existence and non-existence of any possibility which is pictured as being there. It is only if in the case of non-existence "something else is there instead" that existence and non-existence can always add up to existence. To take a specific example: to both *red* and *not-red* there corresponds in reality *just one color*, which may turn out to be red or the non-existence-of-red-in-the-form-of-any-other-color. The point is that *whatever color is there* (red or any other one) it is one and the same color which makes *red* true or false and *not-red* true or false. The logical form of reality is always "one state of affairs present and all other states of affairs of the same form absent, whatever the one state of affairs may be."

We can see from this that there are two points which have to be borne in mind about what Wittgenstein calls *reality:* (1) there is nothing in reality corresponding to absence or nothingness, for we logically picture reality, and, from the standpoint of what we *can* picture, '*p*' and '*not-p*' are the same; and (2) reality, nevertheless, always has the form that only one possibility is present, and this one excludes all other possibilities of the same form, and this is what is meant by the *logical form* of both pictures and propositions.

Wittgenstein mentions, as an alternative way of speaking, that he also calls the existence of states of affairs a positive fact and their non-existence a negative fact. (2.06B) (Again it should be noted that he does *not* say, as many commentators have imagined, that the existence of a *single* state of affairs is a positive fact and the non-existence of a single state of affairs is a negative fact, since a fact is a *combination* of states of affairs, or what corresponds to a truth function and not what corresponds to a single elementary proposition.) That this is an *alternative* to calling reality the existence and non-existence of states of affairs is evident from the consideration that there are no negative facts in reality and no negative states of affairs. Negative facts only appear *after* we have the general operation of Negation and resulting truth functions and hence after we have established a *different logical place* for the negation of an elementary proposition.

The two ways of speaking about the world—as *facts* (which includes both positive and negative facts) and as *reality* (which includes both existing and non-existing states of affairs) run parallel in the case of pictures, (for we picture facts and we also picture reality (2.1, 2.12)), but they part company when it comes to propositions. Propositions picture reality, (4.021, 4.06) but they have a sense that is independent of facts. (4.061) This is necessary because, while propositions must be able to picture and assert as true any possibility, it must be entirely the world which settles the question of truth or falsity.

This gives us the fundamental difference between *reality* and *world*. *Reality* is the world as pictured before we have truth functions: it gives us all possibilities of different forms, in the logical form of one-possibility-excluding-all-other-possibilities-from-any-one-logical-place, while *world* is positive and negative facts with the possibility of true and false propositions about both of them. If we have all positive facts, we automatically have at the same time all negative facts (there being for every positive fact one and only one corresponding negative fact (1.12, 5.513)). Hence while the world is "all that is the case" (*alles, was der Fall ist*) (1.) or merely positive facts, it is also "the totality of facts," an expression, however, which will not be able to distinguish between the *totality of positive facts* and the *totality of positive and negative facts*.

For some time in the *Notebooks* Wittgenstein was bothered by the duality of positive and negative since he saw that this duality could not "exist," but did not see how to get away from it. But then it dawned on him that

> If all the positive statements about a thing are made, aren't all the negative ones already made too? And that is the whole point. (p. 33)

Positive and negative facts were here seen to be in complete symmetry. But this is only possible when we have the kind of negation which affirms precisely what is not there, and that is all. The more basic requirement of a world which permits being represented thus truly or falsely (which is the basis for such negation) has to be met in another way. And it is for this that the distinction between *reality* and *world* had to be introduced.

Reality is, as it were, the "representable" world, the world which "makes logic possible," by establishing "logical places," having the character that they permit one structure of objects of a given form to exist while excluding all other structures of the same form. Propositions picture the world in this way, the existence of the proposition guaranteeing the existence of the logical place. (3.4)

Reality is, therefore, the bridge between *substance* and *world*, an indispensable bridge because it links *possibility* and *existence*, the completeness of one with the arbitrary exclusiveness of the other. Reality has, as it were, one foot in the realm of "all possibility" and the other in the realm of "arbitrary existence," and just this is what is meant by "logical form." Possibility, we might say, is tied to existence in this way through what has the form of "one-possible-structure-existing-and-all-others-of-the-same-form-not-existing." And this form embraces simultaneously all possibility and all existence, since all possibilities may be cast in this form, and when they are, they give us the complete plenum of possible existence as it is represented by pictures and propositions.

While reality may be described as the "way we represent the world," it is more fundamental that the world *can* be represented this way (and that it *can* be represented this way we know *a priori* because we cannot think illogically (5.4731, 6.33)). Reality, in other words, is not to be understood as a "projection" onto the world, but as the objective status of the world as pictured and spoken about. Logic is not a human invention, but it is the logic of the world, and it can be applied to the world because the world already has that character. Wittgenstein says:

> Logic is prior to every experience—that something *is so*. It is prior to the question 'How?' not prior to the question 'What?' (5.552B, C)

> And if this were not so, how could we apply logic? We might put it this way: if there would be a logic even if there were no world, how then could there be a logic given that there is a world? (5.5521)

This can be read as meaning that logic is not prior to substance (whether as form or content), though it is prior to "sayable" existence. And the same may be said about reality—that it is not prior to substance, but is prior to "sayable" existence. For if logic did not have this status, it would not be possible to apply it to the world; it would remain irrelevant. That it *can* be applied shows that there being a world does make a difference, and hence the world itself as reality must have those characteristics which logic requires.

The System of the Tractatus—Epistemology and Language

. . . without language man could never have come even to his senses.

MAX MÜLLER

We are striving for the essence that hides behind the fortuitous.

PAUL KLEE

Since we can think only thought, and all the words we use to speak of things can express only thoughts, to say there is something other than thought is therefore an affirmation which can have no meaning.

HENRI POINCARE

. . . ideas are so alike when you get to know them.

SAMUEL BECKETT

And how try to *ask* whether THAT can be expressed which cannot be EXPRESSED?

WITTGENSTEIN

CHAPTER 11

The System of the Tractatus—Epistemology and Language

i

The *Tractatus* understands thought and language as essentially ways of representing the world and then investigates how they represent in accordance with two basic premises:

1—that representation is only possible by means of underlying structural identities; and

2—that these structures must be in the logical form of possibilities of existence and non-existence.

Metaphysically, this requires that the world have *substance* (or fixed form) and *reality* (bi-polarity of existence and non-existence). With these two conditions met, thought and language may represent possibilities of existence and non-existence and still fail to represent those possibilities which actually do obtain.

In so far as sense experience can itself be represented pictorially, it also must take place according to these same principles. And in so far as it cannot be represented pictorially, it is the direct private experience of content about which nothing can be said and which cannot be represented. The "representable" side of sense experience belongs to the *form* of the world, while the non-representable side is the unsayable *content*, which has no place in language.

In the course of the book seven different kinds of representation or picturing are discussed, five of them in the sphere of language. It is helpful to see all seven listed together.[1]

---

[1] This table helps to bring out the importance of Wittgenstein's distinctions between *situations* (*Sachlagen*) and *states of affairs* (*Sachverhalte*) and also between *presenting* (*vorstellen*) and *representing* (*darstellen*). It is only by very careful attention to these distinctions that Wittgenstein's conception of the intricate relation beween possibility and existence can be understood.

(1) *pictures* — present (*vorstellen*) that entities are related (2.151)
present (*vorstellen*) possibilities that things are related (2.151)
present (*vorstellen*) situations in logical space—existence/non-existence of states of affairs (2.11)
represent (*darstellen*) possible situations in logical space (2.202)
represent (*darstellen*) possibilities of existence and non-existence of states of affairs (2.201)

(2) *thoughts* — logical pictures of facts (3.)
contain possibilities of situations (3.02)
propositions with sense (4.)

(3) *propositions* — express thoughts in perceivable way (3.1)
projections of possible situations as forms of sense (3.11)
present (*vorstellen*) states of affairs (4.0311)
represent (*darstellen*) situations (4.031)

(4) *completely analyzed propositions* — elements are simple signs or names (3.202)
elements correspond to objects of thought (3.2)
configurations of elements correspond to configuration of objects (3.203)

(5) *elementary propositions* — concatenations of names (4.22)
assert existence of states of affairs (4.21)
contain all logical operations (5.47)
cannot give composition in advance (5.55)

(6) *truth functional propositions* — all propositions truth functions (5., 5.3)

(7) *logical propositions* — represent (*darstellen*) scaffolding of world (6.124)
show formal properties of language and world (6.12)
recognized as true from symbols alone (6.113)

What all representations share is that they all involve objects and determinate structures, though in different ways. This can be seen from the following:

representations	constituents	standing for
(1) *pictures*	elements corresponding to objects (2.13)	correlated to entities (2.1514)
(2) *thoughts*	(unknown)[2]	objects of thought
(3) *propositions*	words (3.14)	things properties relations
(4) *completely analyzed propositions*	names (3.2, 3.201)	objects of thought
(5) *elementary propositions*	names (4.22)	objects
(6) *truth functional propositions*	elementary propositions (5.)	facts or combinations of existing structures of objects
(7) *logical propositions*	sense-cancelling truth functional propositions	framework of world

This table shows that every kind of representation involves substance or objects, *except* ordinary propositions, which only involve them when they are completely analyzed. This is another way of saying that every kind of representation involves determinate structure, although in the case of ordinary propositions this structure is *hidden*. Objects, however, come in in different ways, and we can distinguish the *objects in a picture* (2.13) from the *objects of thought* (3.2) and both from *objects* named by the names in elementary propositions. (4.22)

---

[2] " 'Does a *Gedanke* consist of words?' No. But of psychical constituents that have the same sort of relation to reality as words. What those constituents are I don't know." (Letter to Russell. *Notebooks*. p. 130)

At the center of this conception of structure is Wittgenstein's notion of objects and representations as "containing possibilities" (2.014, 2.203, 3.02, 3.13C) and also his notion of the elements of pictures and of propositions as "corresponding to" objects and to the objects of thought. (2.13, 3.2) In the *Tractatus* before "correspondence" (or rather, identity of structure) can give truth, we need it to establish determinate meaning and sense. Pictures and propositions have to invoke determinate structure even in order to represent what is indeterminate (and this is the "hardness" contained in the "soft," the vagueness of ordinary propositions which *can* be justified). The *Tractatus's* epistemology tells us that there is no representation at all which is not based on the principle of determinate structure and there is no such structure without simple objects or something which "corresponds to" simple objects.

ii

The basic idea of Wittgenstein's epistemology is that both pictures and ordinary propositions represent *things-in-situations* by representing them as *objects-in-states-of-affairs*. The picture does it by having objects "corresponding to" its elements, (2.13) while the proposition does it by having the elements of the propositional sign (words) "correspond to the objects of the thought." (3.2, 3.14) We can suppose that the elements of a picture might be, for example, lines, colors or tones, and it is these which are "correlated to" entities in the world. (2.1514) The "objects of the thought," on the other hand, will be things, properties and relations, as these are named in "completely analyzed" propositions. (3.2, 3.201, 3.202) The elements of pictures enter into determinate structures when they have pictorial form, just as the elements of propositions acquire determinate structure when they enter the propositional bond.

Propositions appear in the *Notebooks* as *standards* or *measures* of the world. Thus we have

The proposition is a measure of the world. (p. 41)

A proposition is a standard with reference to which facts behave. (p. 97)

This way of putting it, however, suggests that perhaps a proposition *imposes* something on the world, while what the *Tractatus* stresses is that the world itself is intrinsically so "measurable." We do not, therefore, find this formulation in the *Tractatus*, except with reference to a picture which Wittgenstein says is "laid against reality like a ruler." (2.1512) The objects and structures of the *Tractatus* are known and given as the substance of the world, and what we picture and say has to correspond to them.

The way in which a proposition in the first instance represents is this:

> In a proposition there must be exactly as many distinguishable parts as in the situation that it represents.
>
> The two must possess the same logical (mathematical) multiplicity. (4.04)

What is notable about this is that Wittgenstein does not say here about ordinary propositions (what applies only to elementary propositions) that they must have the same multiplicity as *states of affairs*. Ordinary propositions represent *situations,* and it is *things,* and not objects, which are in situations, (2.0122) even though when we talk about the *possibility* of situations, then it is *objects,* and not things, which are involved. (2.014) Propositions, nevertheless, represent situations by presenting them as states of affairs, (4.0311A) and the critical question in understanding Wittgenstein's conception of propositions is how is this done? It can only be done if everything which a proposition "refers to" in a situation is *named* as an "object of thought." That this is what Wittgenstein has in mind is shown by his statement that

> The configuration of objects in a situation corresponds to the configuration of simple signs in the propositional sign. (3.21)

The unexpected intrusion of the word "configuration" here (a word which is only used in three other places in the book, all of them having to do with objects as substance) shows that "objects in a situation" (like words in a propositional sign) are not a structure like "objects in a state of affairs." They do not "hang together" that way *until* they are named as "objects of thought" when the proposition is "completely analyzed," and *then* their determinate structure is revealed. It is *only at this point that the situation is presented as a state of affairs.*

An illustration may suggest how this is done. But first it has to be clearly understood that a "completely analyzed proposition" is not an elementary proposition. A "completely analyzed proposition" still represents a situation (and does not, as an elementary proposition does, assert the existence of a state of affairs (4.21)). A "completely analyzed proposition" *apes* an elementary proposition because it too consists only of names, but what it names are not objects, but "objects of thought." In the "completely analyzed proposition" all the "semanticity" is stripped from type differences, so that words of all types function semantically merely as names, the differences of types, (or the *kinds* of words which they are), being expressed now only syntactically. In an elementary proposition, on the other hand, there *are* no more type differences, (i.e. we are dealing only with signs and not symbols), and all signs which can combine at all stand on the same level both semantically and syntactically.

If we consider now the proposition "The house is red," when this is "completely analyzed," it names two "objects of a thought," corresponding to the two objects in the situation—house and red. That one of these is a *thing* and the other a *property* is shown now, not by the names, but by the *order* of the names, by the word *red* coming after the word *house*. (If *red* came before *house* in English we would be describing an object "by giving its external properties," rather than describing reality "by its internal properties." (4.023D)) We may say that when a *thing* like a house and a *property* like red are named in a "completely analyzed proposition," they are named as "objects of a thought," and the difference in kind between them is conveyed only by the arrangement of the names (or some other suitable syntactic device). It is in this fashion that a *situation* is *represented* by being *presented* as a *state of affairs*.

In order to communicate a situation, Wittgenstein says, a proposition has to be *essentially connected* with it by being its logical picture. (4.03) Since situations *per se* do not have form or structure, this can only be done if propositions make use of the principle upon which the possibility of propositions is based—namely, that "objects have signs as their representatives." (4.032) As a logical picture of a situation, a proposition treats things, properties and relation as "namable simples," conveying their type differences by syntax. Thus in between the unanalyzed proposition (in which we do not know what the meanings of words are) and elementary propositions (in which meanings are the coordinates of property spaces) lie the "completely analyzed propositions" (in which we have names, but they are still of different kinds). (We see, for example, that a name "stands for" a relation, not from the name or from the meaning of the name, but from the name being between other words. The meaning is the *specificity* of what is named, not the *role* which it plays.)

There is no way of getting from a completely analyzed proposition to an elementary proposition. Wittgenstein says that

> It is obvious that the analysis of propositions must bring us to elementary propositions which consist of names in immediate combination. (4.221)

This is, of course, up to a point, just what a completely analyzed proposition is—names in immediate combination. And it is indeed the way in which all propositions resemble elementary propositions since names occur in all propositions only in the "hanging together" of the elementary proposition. (4.23) An elementary proposition, however, has *only* combinatorial syntax, and *all* arrangements of its names are of equal significance and equal possibility.

This shows what the difference between a completely analyzed and an elementary proposition is—that, whereas in a completely analyzed proposition a different arrangement of the terms may not provide a sense, in the case of an elementary proposition any arrangement of the terms will continue to give a sense. This is the difference between a logical syntax, which still requires certain combinations to be singled out, and a purely "combinatorial syntax" in which all possible combinations are of equal significance. It is only with elementary propositions that we have the latter.

The same difference comes out with regard to *logical form*. When an ordinary proposition has been reduced to its form by the use of variables, what we get is a *class* of propositions which *corresponds to* a logical form. (3.315) These will be, for example, propositions of the subject-predicate form or of the relational form. Wittgenstein does not say that these *are* logical forms, but rather that they *correspond to* logical forms. It is only elementary propositions which actually *have* logical forms *per se*, and these logical forms always have the character of "one-possible-combination-holding-out-of-all-possible-combinations-of-the-same-given-objects." In the logical form of an *elementary proposition* even the distinction between subject and predicate does not have to be preserved since *the entire proposition is, in effect, the predicate*. (The proposition no longer says, for example, "This is blue," but simply "Blue.") And no distinction between "thing-terms" and "relational terms" needs to be preserved, since all terms are "object-terms" which amounts to saying that *all relations are combinatorial*. (The difference in relations between "ab" and "ba" is actually pictured, and neither relation has to be itself named.)

iii

The basic way in which a picture is distinguished from a thought or a proposition is that a picture has three different forms (or involves three different kinds of possibilities), while a thought or a proposition has only one form plus a sense. (3., 4., 3.3) In the case of a picture we have to consider its *pictorial form*, (whether it is spatial, temporal, colored, etc.); its *representational form*, (the "standpoint" from which it represents) and its *logical form*, (the possibilities of existence and non-existence of the structures which it shows). But in the case of a thought or a proposition all these are telescoped into one form—logical form—and a sense. A thought or a proposition has only one *way* of repsenting—the logical form of picturing.

A more careful examination of these differences brings out the following:

> a picture is said to *present a situation* and to *represent a possible situation* (both in logical space) (2.202, 2.11)

> while a proposition is said to *present a state of affairs* and to *represent a situation* (4.031, 4.0311)

The difference indicated here is that a proposition absorbs all possibility into itself and just by presenting a sense establishes a possibility as one out of a range of all possibilities of the objects involved. Whereas in a picture a definite pictured situation is used to represent a possible situation in the world, in a proposition a possible state of affairs is used to represent a definite situation in the world.

This becomes clearer in the following passages:

> A picture contains the possibility of the situation that it represents. (2.203)

> A proposition . . . contains the possibility of expressing its sense. (3.13)

To this may be added:

> Instead of, 'This proposition has such and such a sense,' we

can simply say, 'This proposition represents such and such a situation.' (4.031)

We now have that, whereas a picture (or a thought) "contains the possibility of a situation," a proposition "contains the possibility" of representing a situation.

This brings out that, as might be expected, a proposition is at a further remove from what it represents than a picture is. This is underlined in the following statement from the *Notebooks:*

> It is clear that the closest examination of the propositional sign cannot yield what it asserts—what it can yield is what it is capable of asserting. (p. 40)

How the proposition gets to be at this further remove is explained by Wittgenstein in his discussion of how a possible situation is projected into a propositional sign by "thinking the sense of the proposition." (3.11) He tells us that "what is projected is not itself included, but its possibility is" (3.13B) and this means that only the *form and not the content* of its sense is projected into a propositional sign. (3.13E) (It should be noted that we *cannot* say that only the form and not the content of the *possible situation* is projected, because situations do not have forms, and it is only in terms of states of affairs that we can speak of *all possible situations.* (2.0122)) Wittgenstein tells us that it is "thinking the sense" of a proposition which separates the form of a sense from the content of a sense and puts only the former into the propositional sign.

The impossibility of speaking about *content* (either in ordinary language or in the philosophical description of language) comes out strongly here. Wittgenstein tells us that

> A proposition contains the form, but not the content, of its sense. (3.13E)

And since

> A thought is a proposition with a sense. (4.)

this must also be true of a thought. But the operative word is *contains* (*enthalten*), and there *is* a content of the sense even if it is not "contained in" the proposition or the thought as a proposition. The word *red,* for example, does not express the *content* of red as a sheer qualitative experience because this cannot be expressed, but it does *contain the possibility of representing red* and the possibility of expressing that sense. (3.13B, C)

This shows in a still more concrete way the difference between a picture and a proposition. A picture may actually contain the color red and in this way represent the possibility of that color in the world. The word *red,* on the other hand, is not itself red, and the sentence "This is red" does not represent a possibility in the world, but rather (since it is a sentence with a sense) itself has a possibility of representing something in the world. In a certain sense the *content* of red is in the picture (although it is not this which makes it a picture), while in the thought and the proposition are only the *possibility* of the content. (3.13B)

We must recall again here that a thought is both "a logical picture of facts" (3.) and a "proposition with a sense." (4.) Light is shed on why Wittgenstein puts it this way by a sentence from the *Notebooks:*

> Now it becomes clear why I thought that thinking and language were the same. For thinking is a kind of language. For a thought too is, of course, a logical picture of the proposition, and therefore it just is a kind of proposition. (p. 82)

In the *Tractatus* a proposition is called a logical picture of a *situation,* (4.03C) while a thought is called a logical picture of *facts,* (3.) and we may wonder about this difference. But the difference is that a thought "contains the possibility of the situation of which it is the thought," (3.02) while the proposition only contains "the possibility of expressing its sense," (3.13C) (which means the possibility of representing a possible situation). We might say that the proposition has to be applied or has to be thought, while the thought already has this status.

iv

The phrase "it is obvious" (*es ist offenbar* or in one case *offenbar ist*) occurs five times in the *Tractatus* in the following connections: [3]

---

[3] The word *obvious* (*offenbar*) also occurs on two other occasions: Wittgenstein speaks of the inner connection between propositions in an inference "becoming obvious" when expressed in simplest possible truth functional notation, (5.1311) and he speaks of the attempt to state elementary propositions *a priori* leading to "obvious nonsense." (5.5571) Compare also the use of the expressions "it is clear" (*es ist klar*), *einleuchten* and *von selbst verstehen.*

It is obvious that even in an imagined world there must be some kind of objects. (2.022, 2.023)

It is obvious that we perceive (*empfinden*) a relational proposition ('aRb') as a picture, the sign being obviously a likeness of what is signified. (4.012)

It is obvious that the analysis of propositions must bring us to elementary propositions consisting of names in immediate combination. (4.221)

It is obvious that Frege's and Russell's "primitive signs" of logic are interdefinable and therefore not primitive. (5.42)

It is obvious that the so-called law of induction is a proposition with a sense and not a law of logic. (6.32)

What is meant by the statement that it is *obvious* that in analyzing propositions we must come to elementary propositions? What makes this obvious? In another place Wittgenstein says:

If we know on purely logical grounds that there must be elementary propositions, then everyone who understands propositions in their unanalyzed form must know it. (5.5562)

We may wonder why there *must* be elementary propositions and what are these "purely logical grounds"? The answer is that elementary propositions appear as the "simplest kind of proposition," (4.21) being nothing but *the simplest combinations of the simplest signs*. The questions transform themselves into the question: What justifies simple signs?

To this question the *Tractatus's* answer is:

The requirement (*Forderung*) of the possibility of simple signs is the requirement of the determinateness of sense. (3.23)

(Here *Forderung*, translated by Ogden *postulate*, might also be rendered *demand*.) It is determinate sense we are after. But why does this depend upon simple signs? Apparently for the same reason that if there were no objects, then

In that case we could not sketch out (*entwerfen*) any picture of the world (true or false). (2.0212)

Objects are what make simple signs possible; determinate sense goes with simple signs; and all three are necessary to picture the world. The conclusion seems to be that the world has a determinate character because otherwise we could *not* picture it, but also there is nothing that guarantees that we *can* picture it other than its having a determinate character.

A little more light is shed in the *Notebooks*, particularly in this passage:

> It does not go against our feeling that we cannot analyze PROPOSITIONS so far as to mention the elements by name; no, we feel that the WORLD must consist of elements. And it appears as if that were identical with the proposition that the world must be what it is, it must be definite. Or in other words, what vacillates is our determinations, not the world. It looks as if to deny things were as much as to say that the world can, as it were, be indefinite in some such sense as that in which our knowledge is uncertain and indefinite. (p. 62)

This paragraph is immediately followed by the assertion that

> The world has a fixed structure.

If we are inclined to wonder *why* the world cannot be indefinite, the most we can get out of this is that we *feel* that it cannot be. But we may then wonder why we feel this way. And this seems to be involved with the nature of meaning. Wittgenstein asks and replies:

> Is it or is it not possible to talk of a proposition's having a more or less sharp sense?

> It seems clear that what we MEAN must always be *"sharp."* (p. 68)

Here the word *mean* applies to propositions, as in the *Tractatus* it does not, but Wittgenstein is expressing the same idea in the *Tractatus* when he says:

> What a proposition expresses it expresses in a determinate manner, which can be set out clearly . . . (3.251)

> Everything that can be thought at all can be thought clearly. Everything that can be put into words can be put clearly. (4.116)

The notion that *any* sense can be made fully determinate seems to lead to the paradoxical result that if we mean something indefinite, then the indefiniteness must be *sharp* too (just *that* is then what is intended). The indefiniteness becomes definite in so far as *that* is exactly what we mean. This suggests that it would be necessary to distinguish between ambiguity or indefiniteness which is *meant* and ambiguity or indefiniteness which is *not meant* and which can always be removed by philosophical clarification. (4.112E, cf. 3.24C) With this caveat Wittgenstein's view is that, although we may not express ourselves clearly and may not mean anything even when we think we do, (6.53) *any sense can be seen to be clear when it is logically clarified.*

To say that "what we MEAN must always be *sharp*" seems to say that what we mean, whatever it is, is singled out and delimited by the act of meaning. It acquires a status as a *one*, however complex it may be or however many parts it may have. What is *meant* cannot *per se* be "blurred" because *there is no act other than meaning to determine what* anything *is.* What is referred to is *ipso facto* sharp for the particular sense involved. It is as if there may be maps of any scale at all, all equally *sharp,* and though the maps may be "blurred" (e.g. the colors blotched or smeared) what they refer to cannot be finally "blurred" since the nature of mapping and what is "mappable" does not permit and could not depict *that.* For how would an *indefinite* boundary be shown except as a departure from, or in terms of, the possibility of a definite one? *Indefiniteness* and *definiteness* cannot be equally fundamental or they would be indistinguishable. (Analogously, the unintentional blurring of a photograph is recognized *as a blurring* presumably because we have some notion of what these things would look like if they were not blurred.)

What are the "purely logical grounds" on which we know that there *must* be elementary propositions? They seem to be the joint requirements of simple signs and determinate sense as presuppositions of logic, (6.124) which taken together will give us elementary propositions. Wittgenstein calls the representation (*Vertretung*) of objects by signs the principle (*Prinzip*) upon which the possibility of all propositions is based, (4.0312) and when these signs *mean* objects, (ie. have that simple terminal reference), their possible combinations *are* elementary propositions.

v

It is time now to summarize what the *Tractatus* says about *meaning* and *sense*, Wittgenstein's fundamental distinction taken over from Frege.

As regards *meaning* (*Bedeutung* and *bedeuten*):

1 — It is *signs, proto-signs, symbols, names, expressions, words, functions, fundamental concepts* and *negation* which are said to have *meanings*. (And *names, words, expressions, truth possibilities, philosophy*, the *limits of language* and the *exploration of logic* which are said to *mean*.)

2 — And we *give*, (6.53) *choose, arbitrarily determine*, (3.315) *recognize*, (5.02) *know*, (4.243, 6.2322) and *explain* (3.263, 4.026) *meanings*.

As regards *sense (Sinn):*

1 — It is *pictures, propositions, propositional signs, facts, symbols, truth functions, rules, languages*, the *world* and *life* which represent, express or have *sense*.

2 — And sense is *represented*, (2.221) *thought*, (3.11) *expressed* (3.13, 3.142, 3.34, 4.002, 4.5) *understood*, (4.021) *shown*, (4.022) *communicated*, (4.03) *characterized*, (5.25) *affirmed* (4.064) and *determined* or *undetermined*. (4.063, 4.431)

Some of the important points which Wittgenstein makes in connection with this contrast are: (1) *meanings* involve samenesses and differences which cannot be said but simply have to be seen, (5.53, 4.243) while everything that can result from relations between meanings is a matter of *sense;* (2) we do not need to *know* what the *meanings* of the words we use are in order to express *sense;* (4.002) (3) *meanings* of words have to be explained to be understood, but propositions can be understood without their *senses* being explained; (4.026, 4.021) (4) we can choose what *meanings* we want arbitrarily, but this will be limited by the possibilities of *sense* which arise from what can be done with these meanings. (3.3, 3.342, cf. 2.0122)

The fundamental contrast which Wittgenstein has in mind can be shown by means of a short table:

Meaning	*Sense*
names have meanings (3.203) but *what* they mean—objects—cannot be stated (3.221)	propositions have sense (3.3) but sense is not *contained* in them (3.13)

name *means* an object but *stands for* a thing (4.0311)	propositions *express* sense by *presenting* states of affairs to *represent* situations (4.031)
determinate logical combination of meanings corresponds to determinate logical combination of signs (6.2322)	sense of a proposition is agreement and disagreement with possibilities of existence and non-existence of states of affairs (4.2)
meanings are the same or different, but identity of meaning cannot be asserted, but only marked (6.2322)	there are two opposite senses for one and the same reality (4.0621)

This table helps to bring out that in the *Tractatus's* simplest possible language the term *object* is virtually a synonym for *unit of meaning* or *simplest meaning*, while the term *sense* covers the ways in which *sheer combinations* of such meanings may and may not exist. We might be tempted to conclude that objects are only "hypostatized meanings" and that we could, if we chose, simply substitute the word "meaning" for the word "object." What prevents this, however, is that a combination of names with meanings must be able to fail to agree with a combination of the very same objects which these names mean. A name cannot fail to mean an object, but it can fail to mean it in the correct relation to other objects. We can fail to give a *sign* a meaning, (6.53) but a *name* is only a name if it has a meaning, and so objects are always present with names, although not always in the combinations which the meanings are in. We might say that meaning is separated from objects only to the extent that sense is separated from states of affairs.

What Frege called "concepts" appear in the *Tractatus* as thoughts and propositions, assertions about *how things are*. And Frege's notion of "objects falling under concepts" becomes in the *Tractatus* "objects with intrinsic possibilities of combination." Conceptual words (or adjectival expressions) which appear to "name" properties are to be thought of as descriptions of objects which may be, if we wish, replaced by combinations of names of further objects. (It is in order to carry through the reduction of concepts to structures of objects that Wittgenstein has to introduce the distinction between *objects* and *things*, which is not found in Frege, although there are a number of places where it is implicit.)

The Limits of the World

I have managed in my book to put everything firmly into place by being silent about it.

WITTGENSTEIN

ἀρχὰν γὰρ οὐδὲ τὸ γνωσούμενον ἐσσεῖται
πάντων ἀπείρων ἐόντων

(For there could not even be an object set before knowledge to begin with if all things were unlimited.)

PHILOLAUS (frag. 3)

Paradox is the most true.

LAOTZU

As soon as thought stops one dies and is reborn elsewhere. Take heed of this, followers of the Way.

Platform Scripture 17

The only proper way to break an egg is from the inside.

PARVA GALLINA RUBRA

CHAPTER 12

The Limits of the World

i

Many philosophers in different parts of the world still regard the early Wittgenstein as a positivist. But this view is seriously in error, for, although Wittgenstein shares in the austerities of positivism, it is for reasons quite other than (and, in a sense, even opposite to) the positivist ones. Wittgenstein's purpose was to distinguish *what can be said* from *what cannot be said*, not in order to *deny* what cannot be said, but in order to *mean* it. He states this in so many words:

> (Philosophy) will mean what cannot be said by representing clearly what can be said. (4.115)

It was *what cannot be said* which was the most important to Wittgenstein. He was not concerned to destroy metaphysics, but rather, through a certain kind of metaphysical construction, to *point to the unsayable*. By clearly delimiting what a *fact* is he intended to bring out *what there is that is not facts*. In a way strikingly analogous to negative theology he was engaged in what might be called *negative metaphysics*.[1]

In order to understand the *Tractatus*, therefore, we have to become aware of what cannot be said at the same time that we become aware of what can be said. And (apart from logic which cannot be said, but can be *shown* (4.121)) *what cannot be said* falls under four main headings:

(1) *the content of the world* — immediate qualitative "private experience," which is the *what* which is not projected into propositions (3.13) and which comes before logic; (5.552)
(2) *the subject* — which is *a* limit of the world and (as the metaphysical subject) *the* limit of the world and which occurs in philosophy because "the world is my world;" (5.632, 5.641)

---

[1] Wittgenstein's relation to the positivists is somewhat analogous to Socrates's relation to the Sophists. The resemblances in each case conceal the much profounder and more important differences.

(3) *the ethical* — which is the same as the aesthetic and which is transcendental and cannot be put into words; (6.42, 6.421) and

(4) *the metaphysical* — Wittgenstein's own propositions, which are
   only understood when it is seen that they are nonsensical (*unsinnig*). (6.54)

All these four lie outside what can be represented or said and hence
outside the world. That they *do* lie outside can only be shown by
showing that the world *has limits and that they do not lie within these
limits.* In order to establish this Wittgenstein must speak of the "limits
of logic" and the "limits of language," and he must also show that the
world is an *all* and also a *totality.* We have first to look at the question
of *limits* in general in the *Tractatus* and then at the question of *all* and
totality and the difference between them, and why we must have both.

ii

So much in the *Tractatus* turns on the question of *limits* that it is
important to examine the major ways in which *limits* appear in the
book. (Italics in the following list are mine.)

(1) Empirical reality (*Realität*) *is limited by* the totality of objects.
   The limit also shows itself in the totality of elementary propositions. (5.5561)

(2) The limits of the world *are* the limits of logic. (5.61A, 2.0231,
   cf. 5.143C)

(3) The limits of my language *mean* the limits of *my* world. And the
   limits of language *mean* the limits of my world. (5.62, 5.6)

(4) The subject *is a* limit of the world; the metaphysical subject *is the*
   limit of the world. (5.632, 5.641C)

(5) The ethical will *alters* the limits of the world. (6.43)

(6) The mystical feeling is the *feeling* of the world as a limited whole.
   (6.45)

(7) Philosophy *sets limits* to what can be thought and to what cannot
   be thought. (4.114) (In the *Preface* this appears as: "Thus the aim
   of the book is to set a limit to thought, or rather—not to thought,
   but to the expression of thoughts . . ." (p. 3))

This list suffices to show the central importance of *limits*. But it is equally apparent in the words *all* and *totality* with which the book opens:

The world is all (*alles*) that is the case. (1.)

The world is the totality (*Gesamtheit*) of facts, not of things. (1.1)

The significance of these two key words *all* and *totality* will be discussed in the next section. They are mentioned here to show that *the* world is always a limited world. "Objectivity" requires finiteness.

We now examine the above seven cases of limits in the order in which they are listed here.

(1) It is an important point that Wittgenstein does not say, what we might expect, that "The world is limited by the totality of objects" or "Reality (*Wirklichkeit*) is limited by the totality of objects." Instead he says:

Empirical reality (*Realität*) is limited by the totality of objects. (5.5561)

Why is the word *Realität* used here, a word which only appears at one other place in the book, where it is said to be what is coordinated with the *I* of solipsism? (5.64) The answer is that *Realität* is objects as both form and content, while *Wirklichkeit* and *Welt* (*world*) are objects merely as form (and structure). And the word *empirical* (*empirische*) emphasizes that we are to think of this *Realität* apart from the subject. In a comprehensive sense substance is limited. This is not in conflict with the view that we cannot give the number of names with different meanings (objects) (5.55) and in addition that it makes no sense to talk about the number of all objects. (4.1272F)

(2) The limits of the world, secondly, are the *same* as the limits of logic. (5.61A) This is because logic deals with all possibilities, excluding none, (2.0121C, 5.61C) imposing on them logical form, which means preventing more than one such possibility of the same form from being present simultaneously. (6.3751) (A temporal object and a spatial object forming one structure is ruled out as a possibility, while two colors being at the same place in the visual field at the same time is logically impossible.) We cannot think these impossibilities and the world cannot contain them. This is how contradiction appears in physics, and contradiction is the "outer limit" of propositions. (5.143)

Logic, indeed, "pervades the world" because it is involved in every state of affairs and in the sense of every proposition. Two quotations from the *Notebooks* are helpful here:

> And it is clear that the object must be of a particular logical kind; it is just as complex or as simple as it is. (p. 70)

> Every *real* proposition shows something, besides what it says about the universe, for if it has no sense it can't be used; and if it has sense, it mirrors some logical property of the universe. (p. 107)

The language of the *Tractatus* is far more precise than this because it distinguishes between the *form of an object* and the *logical form of reality* (and of propositions) and also between the *sense* of a proposition and the *logical form* of a proposition. In other words, it distinguishes between *substance* (structures) and *reality* (existence and nonexistence of these structures). But the *Notebooks* help to show the genesis of Wittgenstein's views and how he saw logic as involved with every object and every proposition.

(3) When we go from logic to language, thirdly, the limits of language *mean* both the limits of *my* world and of *the* world. (5.6, 5.62) When language has specific meanings, it is *my* language, and, because it is also logical, it is language. The border between what my language can and cannot say *means* simultaneously, therefore, the border between what I "experience" and do not "experience" and between form and structure which can be thought and cannot be thought. *My world* (experienced content) and *the world* (logically pictured form and structure) coincide, and this is shown by the limits of language as form and structure, (the only language which I understand), *meaning* the limits of *my world* "as I alone experience it."

What the *Tractatus* tells us here is that the world which I publically speak about can be seen to be the same as the world which I privately experience through the limits of what I can say about the former pointing to the limits of what happens in the latter. The truth of what the solipsist means is shown by my not being able to say certain things *meaning* that I am not able to experience certain content.

(4) The subject appears as a consequence of the world being my world (5.641B) and because "no part of our experience is at the same time *a priori*." (5.634A) Something more than logic is needed to have a world, something which corresponds to the contingency of sheer existence, and this is the subject, which, as subject, is not conditioned

in any way by logic and could not be inferred from anything within the realm of objects. The subject, as subject, has no nature and nothing in common with the world, (in the same way that nothing about the eye could be inferred from the nature of the visual field). (5.633, 5.6331) The subject is in no way part of the world, but sets the limit which expresses the contingency of experience or the world as being my world.

(5) and (6) Finally, the altering of the limits of the world by the ethical will and the feeling of the world as a limited whole (6.43, 6.45C) tells us, as clearly as it is possible to that *the world as a whole has an outside*, even if nothing at all can be said about this "outside." Ethically and in some way connected with feeling, we ourselves, furthermore, *are* outside the world. That this conclusion is part of the main import of the book is evident not only with these thoughts near the end (which strictly are unthinkable) but from the very start where the world is spoken of as a "totality." Wittgenstein, in his own role as philosopher, is also always looking at the world "from outside." We have to consider now what justifies or requires this position, or why the world has to be an *all* and a *totality*.

iii

Viewing or feeling the world as "a limited whole" in the *Tractatus* (6.45) is the complement of speaking of it as "all that is the case" and as "the totality of facts." (1., 1.1) That the world has to *be* such an *all* and such a *totality* arises, it will be seen, from the very nature of Wittgenstein's analysis of propositions and the way they are related to each other. It is a direct consequence of understanding all propositions as truth functions of elementary propositions. (4.51, 5.3) For in order to generate truth functions we are always compelled to take some *all* of propositions or to take elementary propositions as a *totality*. The ontological aspect of this is that

> If objects are given, then at the same time we are given *all* objects. (5.524)

and

> If all objects are given, then at the same time all *possible* states of affairs are also given. (2.0124)

For logic must deal with *all possibilities*, (2.0121C) just as the world must always be a *totality* of those of these possibilities which exist.

We return to this in a moment, but first consider the difference between *all (alle)* and *totality (Gesamtheit)* as Wittgenstein uses these two terms.

A careful scrutiny of the text will show that where *possibilities* are involved Wittgenstein never speaks of a *totality*, but always of *all*, while in the case of what exists or of propositions he usually speaks of both *all* and *totality*. Thus we have *all possibilities*, (2.0121) *all possible situations*, (2.0122) *all possible occurrences of an object in states of affairs*, (2.0123) and *all possible states of affairs*. (2.0124) But, on the other hand, we have *all the facts* and the *totality of facts*, (1.11, 1.1) *all that is the case* and the *totality of existing states of affairs*, (1., 2.04) *all elementary propositions* and the *totality of elementary propositions*, (4.52) and, in addition, the *totality of true thoughts*, (3.01) the *totality of propositions* (4.001) and the *totality of true propositions*. (4.11)

Broadly speaking, *totality* means different items "taken together," while *all* means items which are not necessarily different and are not "taken together." More simply, *all* means "none left out even if not all are different," while *totality* means "taken as a whole and all must be different." (We can clearly have an *all* that is not a *totality* as we can have a *totality* that is less than *all*.)

The reason there is *no totality of possibility* is because each possibility does not count just once, but the same possibilities are available for each logical place of the same logical form. *Logic* deals with *all possibilities* in just this way, but the *world* shuts out all but one possibility from each logical place, and we may then speak of a "totalling" of what exists.

This same distinction between *all* and *totality* sheds light on the crucial difference between *world* and *reality* and also helps to explain the intricacies of wording, which shuttle back and forth between *all* and *totality*, in the first five sentences in the book.

In the very first sentence of the *Tractatus* the world is called "all that is the case," and then this is immediately followed by the sentence in which it is called "the totality of facts." We might wonder why we have these two different descriptions of the world at the very start and what is the difference between them. The answer is that the expression "totality of facts" cannot distinguish between a totality of positive facts and a totality of positive and negative facts. These are one and the same totality, as the totality of existing and non-existing states of affairs (*reality*) is the same as the totality of existing states of affairs (*world*). (2.063, 2.04, 2.06) The reason the latter two are the same is because there is nothing whatever in a state of affairs (nothing which can be represented or thought) which corresponds to the difference between the existence of a state of affairs and the non-existence of that very same state of affairs. They are "one and the same reality." (4.0621C) We might say that, whatever is there, is there with its existence and non-existence, having exactly the same nature in each case. And this applies also to facts. There is no way whatever in thought to distinguish between a positive fact and the corresponding negative fact. Hence to say that "The world is the totality of facts" (1.1) cannot tell us unequivocally that what is meant is the "totality of positive facts." To say the latter Wittgenstein must say: "The world is all that is the case." (1.)

It is evident from this that there is no totality of non-existing states of affairs or of negative facts which is different from the totality of existing states of affairs or the totality of positive facts. Whatever states of affairs or facts there are in the world, each logical place is occupied by two indistinguishable alternatives until such time as the truth functional operation of negation establishes the negative as a *different* logical place, about which separate statements may then be made. The sum-total of reality is the world (2.063) just because every proposition pictures one and the same reality with two conceptually indistinguishable senses. When we look at the two senses, we speak of *reality*, but when we look at only positive senses which exist, we speak of *world*, and the former do not "add up" as any more than the latter, since the non-existent states of affairs have no independently representable character.

Wittgenstein goes on to say:

> The world is determined by the facts, and by their being *all* the facts. (1.11)

> For the totality of facts determines what is the case and also all that is not the case. (1.12)

Here the "totality of facts" is the totality of positive facts, for in a moment a fact is described as "the existence of states of affairs," (2.) and it is, therefore, the totality of positive facts which determines both positive facts and all negative facts.

Just exactly what this means is well stated in the following entry from the *Notebooks:*

> If all the positive statements about a thing are made aren't all the negative ones made too? And that is the whole point. (p. 33)

But why does Wittgenstein stress that the world is determined, not only by the facts, but by the facts being *all* the facts? The following indicates the answer—that this is the way propositions are given to us:

> Propositions comprise all that follows from the totality of all elementary propositions (and, of course, from its being the *totality* of them *all*). (4.52)

What this tells us is that when elementary propositions figure as truth arguments of truth functional propositions, the elementary propositions are not taken in complete isolation from each other, but their truth possibilities have to be set up *all together*. Two elementary propositions "*p*" and "*q*," for example, are not written side by side as having just *two* truth values each (TF and TF). Rather they are taken *as a totality* and written as having *four* truth possibilities in this status of being *taken together* (TT, TF, FT and FF). In terms of truth possibilities we might say that every elementary proposition affects every other one. (With three elementary propositions, eight truth possibilities, with four sixteen, etc. (4.27))

This is the basis of Wittgenstein's notion of the world as a *totality*. Facts (both positive and negative) are what correspond to truth functional conjunctions (or logical products), and they constitute a totality because they are the result of taking elementary propositions as a totality, with each one referring to a different logical place and "all taken together." The only facts that are available are those which correspond to truth functional propositions which depend upon a totality of elementary propositions (4.52) and a totality of *all* of them when, if we have any of them, we always have all of them. (5.524)

We could, if we wished, describe the world completely by simply giving (*Angabe*) all elementary propositions and then giving all of these which are true. (4.26) We would then be, in effect, listing "all that is the case" (i.e. all the existing properties of the world), and no question of totality would arise. But no question of *facts* would arise either. If we want facts (combinations of existing states of affairs or structures of existing structures of states of affairs (2.032)), then the elementary propositions must be taken as a totality or "taken together" in terms of their truth possibilities. "All that is the case" and "the totality of facts" are, from this point of view, two different ways of describing the world, both of which may be complete.[2]

The *Tractatus* brings together the "all possibilities," which are the "facts" of logic (2.0121C) with the "totality of facts" which is the existing world. It is the background of "all possibilities" which permits the structural representation of what just happens to exist by enabling us always to understand it as a selection from those "all possibilities." The contingent and accidental character of the world attaches only to sheer existence as such, while everything about the nature of the world belongs to the realm of possibility, which is neutral to existence and non-existence. It is *substance*, or what is fixed and unchangeable about the world, which provides the "all possibilities" as "all possible structures," while it is *reality* which provides the bi-polarity of existence and non-existence as the basis for "logical places" which permit both. The totality of these logical places will be the same as the totality of existing states of affairs (since every place is occupied by something) although which states of affairs exist will not be found until we have true elementary propositions.

iv

An important distinction between *thought* and *language* in the *Tractatus* can be brought out by comparing what Wittgenstein says in the text about the nature of philosophy and what he says in the *Preface* about the aim of his own book.

In the text he says of philosophy that

> It must fix the limits of (*abgrenzen*) what can be thought (*Denkbare*) and through this of what cannot be thought (*Undenkbare*). (4.114A)

> It must circumscribe (*begrenzen*) what cannot be thought (*Undenkbare*) from within through what can be thought. (4.114B)

---

[2] It is essential to this point of view that elementary propositions be such that they do not "exclude" each other—i.e. that we do not, for example, have *red* at exactly the same time and place as we have *blue*. It was this restriction that Wittgenstein proposed to relax in his *Aristotelian Society* article on *Logical Form*. Supplementary Volume IX, (1929), pp. 162-171.

In the *Preface*, on the other hand, we find this:

> Thus the aim of the book is to set a limit to thought, or rather
> —not to thought, but to the expression of thoughts: for in
> order to be able to set a limit to thought, we should have to
> find both sides of the limit thinkable (i.e. we should have to be
> able to think what cannot be thought). (p. 3)

On the one hand, he tells us that philosophy fixes the *limits of what
can be thought*, and, on the other, that the aim of the *Tractatus* cannot
be to fix the *limits of thought* (for that cannot be done) but only to
set a limit to the *expression* of thoughts.

In order to make sense of this we must first distinguish between
what can be thought (which philosophy must limit) and *thought* (which
philosophy cannot limit). We can limit the thinkable, but not thinking,
for to limit the latter, Wittgenstein says, we would have to be able
to "think the unthinkable," or *get beyond thought in the realm of possible thought*, which cannot be done.(It is the possibility of thought
which circumscribes thought, and not thought which circumscribes the
possibility of thought.) Thought, it must be remembered, is limited by
the world's forms and possible structures and by logical form, (i.e. by
what is thinkable).

In the *Preface*, then, the further contrast is drawn between *thought*,
which we cannot limit, and the *expression of thoughts*, which we can
limit. The question arises as to what is the relation between what *can*
be thought (the thinkable) and the *expression* of thought. Here it is
important that Wittgenstein says that the expression of thought *is already* only the *possibility* of the expression of thought, and this is
clearly stated at 3.31C where a proposition is said not to contain its
sense, but to contain only the *possibility of expressing its sense. A proposition and the possibility of that proposition are one and the same. But
between a thought and the possibility of that thought a distinction can
be drawn.* This is because a proposition depends upon thinking (3.11)
while a thought depends upon facts. (3.) A proposition (and a thought
as a proposition), as it were, establish their own possibility in the process of being thought, but it takes the *world* to establish the possibilities
of thought as a logical picture. And new objects and new facts may
always show up.

From this it can be seen that the *thinkable* does not coincide with
thought in the same way in which the *expressible* coincides with *what*

is expressed. Thought still contains a "content" which language does not. A thought can never be of anything illogical (since illogical thought is impossible), (3.03, 5.4731) but there is more in a thought than logic. On the other hand, there is no more in language than just the possibility of expressing what is thought.

This helps to explain Wittgenstein's critical dual definition of thoughts:

A logical picture of facts is a thought. (3.)

A thought is a proposition with a sense. (4.)

To understand why we need both of these definitions we must recall that a logical picture is "a picture whose pictorial form is logical form." (2.181) Wittgenstein does not say that it is a picture which *has only* logical form, but rather that it is a picture which has *that kind* of pictorial form. Thoughts have in the first definition in that way the same content which is in pictures. In the second definition, however, thoughts are simply the *possibility* of expressing this. The dual nature of a thought itself supplies the transition from a certain kind of a picture (in which, as it were, the content of the sense is still recognizable) to a proposition which must have this content of the sense attached, for it is only a *possibility* of expressing its sense. (3.13C)

To illustrate this, we might say that, whereas the thought of a red house still, as it were, contains the "content" which would permit us to recognize a red house, the proposition "The house is red" contains only the possibility of expressing this thought (or only the form, and not the content, of this sense), and consequently from the proposition alone, without the content of the thought which it expresses, we would *not* be able to recognize the red house. At the same time the thought itself is also the proposition with the more "conceptual" character which could be understood even by a blind person who could not recognize a red house.

This brings out that it is not quite correct to say that for Wittgenstein thought and language are structurally identical, and that is all there is to it. Structurally they are identical, but thought still has in it something which is not in a proposition and cannot get into a proposition. This helps to explain why we can limit what *can* be thought, but cannot limit thought. It is the structure of thought, the possibility of the expression of thought (which is the same as the expression) which can be limited, while the content of the sense of a proposition cannot be limited.

The complete immanence of the rules of language within language, once meanings have been given to signs, is a cardinal tenet of the *Tractatus*. *All* we can do is to give meanings to signs, and then all the rest takes care of itself with all possible uses then provided and any possibility as good as any other. (5.473A, 6.124) *We* cannot determine what may be done with signs once meanings have been given, for anything that *can* be done *may* then be done. This is why Wittgenstein says "we cannot give a sign the wrong sense" (5.4732) and "Any possible proposition is legitimately constructed." (5.4733) Language *in* use provides its own possibilities *of* use, and there is no further court of appeal.

The *Tractatus* aims to set a limit to the expression of thoughts by "elucidating" the limits which are in language and in the world, not by *prescribing* what the limits of the world should be in accordance with some theory about the nature of language. It aims not to set up a perfect language, but to make clear how, even in ordinary everyday language "the nature of the natural and inevitable signs speaks for itself." (6.124) For there is no possibility of "improving" language as a whole, since language defines its own possibilities in terms of what we can think, and they are all equally possible. Philosophy and the *Tractatus* only serve to make this clear.

v

We come finally to the *metaphysical*, or Wittgenstein's own propositions, which, he says, if properly understood, are seen to be *nonsensical (unsinnig)*. (6.54) The announcement, reserved for the next to the last entry, that the book itself has no sense confronts us with the paradox that the very way in which the *Tractatus* distinguishes what can be said from what cannot be said is by statements which finally must be recognized as *themselves belonging to what cannot be said*. It is, in other words, only through statements which have no sense that we can elucidate (*erläutern*) (4.112C) what sense is.

This final revelation that Wittgenstein's system is itself nonsensical, heralds an ultimate defeat unless we accept the implicit distinction between *sense* and *apparent sense* (paralleling that between *propositions* and *pseudo-propositions* (4.1272, 5.534) and between *logical form* and *apparent logical form* (4.0031)) and then grant that *there is a kind of apparent sense in which the appearance of sense holds up long enough to reveal what sense is by revealing that there is no sense in attempting to say what it is.* Wittgenstein's own propositions, unlike traditional "metaphysical propositions," (6.53) are, in their own lack of sense, the final surety for the "truth" of what they can only appear to say, a truth which now no longer attaches to an image, but is the thing-itself. (5.5563)

The proper function of philosophy should be to make thoughts, which otherwise would be cloudy and indistinct, clear and sharp. (4.112E) We appear then to have "philosophical propositions," and traditional philosophy has supposed that there are indeed such propositions, and that they have sense. Of this mistake of traditional philosophy Wittgenstein has three things to say. First of all:

> Most of the propositions and questions to be found in philosophical works are not false but nonsensical . . . Most of the propositions and questions of philosophers arise from our failure to understand the logic of our language. (4.003)

And in another place he says that the failure to recognize the same sign as different symbols leads to "the most fundamental confusions" and "the whole of philosophy is full of them." (3.324) And, finally, at the end of the book he says that "the correct method in philosophy" would be

> whenever someone else wanted to say something metaphysical to demonstrate to him that he had failed to give a meaning to certain signs in his propositions. (6.53)

Looking at the propositions of the *Tractatus* in the light of these three ways in which traditional philosophy, in Wittgenstein's view, has generated nonsense, it would seem that the *Tractatus* propositions cannot be nonsensical because of a "failure to understand the logic of our language" or because of a failure to distinguish different symbols in the same signs (since it is just these matters which are being "elucidated"). It must be then that they suffer from failing "to give a meaning to certain signs." But, we may ask, what signs? What signs in Wittgenstein's own propositions has he failed to give a meaning to (and failed knowing that he has failed)? The answer seems obvious—it is the word *object* itself, the word for the fundamental case of meaning, the very prototype of meaning. To say that Wittgenstein has not given a meaning to *this* word of all words is to say that all of his own propositions do not make sense. (For logic presupposes that names have meaning, (6.124) and in the *Tractatus* their meaning must be objects. (3.203))

It would now seem that if the propositions of the *Tractatus* reveal that the word *object* has no meaning, then they demonstrate, not the validity of that way of looking at the world, but rather the complete failure of it and hence the failure of the attempt to distinguish what can be said from what cannot be said. How are we to conclude the "truth" of what is apparently said from our inability to say it? Could we not as plausibly conclude the "untruth" of what is apparently said from our inability to say it?

But this is a superficial way of looking at the matter. If *all* language in actual use involves statements about *objects*, then this itself is not something we can say, and *seeing* that we cannot say it is to understand what it attempts to say. Using the illicit word *object* (which Wittgenstein says expresses only a "pseudo-concept," (4.1272)) and thereby saying *nothing* because objects *are* simply named, is apparently referring to a class. But there is no classification in logic. (5.454) We cannot possibly get behind ultimate names to call what they refer to *anything* as a class, as the word *object* attempts to do. (Names can be classified, (3.142) but not what names refer to.) We talk about *objects*, only to understand finally that what is the ultimate basis of all "talking about" cannot itself be "talked about."[3]

If the term *objects* is meaningless in this way, then, strictly speaking, we cannot talk about objects, but, nevertheless, there are, in an ineffable way, objects. It is simply that we cannot refer to them "generally" as the word *object* tries to. The *Tractatus* propositions are nonsensical in a way which leaves intact what they are trying to say. Their failure to say what they try to say is itself the best evidence for what they try to say.

It should be borne in mind that understanding that the propositions of the *Tractatus* are themselves nonsense does not, in Wittgenstein's

---

[3] These difficulties with the word *object* are not unlike similar difficulties with the word *Being* in traditional philosophy. Is *Being* to be regarded at the largest class, in which case it expresses the most abstract and empty of concepts? Or on the other hand, does the term not refer to the most real and the most concrete? Cf. Joseph Owens—*The Doctrine of Being in the Aristotelian "Metaphysics,"* (Toronto. Pontifical Institute of Medieval Studies. 2nd edition. 1963).

view, result in understanding that the entire point of view of the book is to be discarded. He intends rather that *this understanding* is a *vindication* of the point of view of the book, setting, as it were, a final seal upon its truth. An earlier passage supports this, a passage quite startling in its claim:

> That utterly simple thing which we have to formulate here, is not an image of the truth, but the truth itself in its entirety. 5.5563)

The book, in other words, is *not constructing a metaphysical picture* of the world or of the relation of language and the world; it is *revealing* the nature of *all* pictures and hence of the world. If it were presenting a *theory* about language and the world, then discovering that what it says is nonsense would, of course, be fatal. But if what it formulates is "not an image of the truth but the truth itself," then, it is at least conceivable, that discovering that what it says cannot be said is just what removes the final veil. Discovering that we cannot *talk about* objects would mean that we finally understood *what objects are.* We understood their absolute presuppositional status. And the system of the *Tractatus,* discovered to be without sense, would then not crumble piece by piece, but rather would vanish all at once, as a shadow which we had imagined only to enable us to see what otherwise could not be seen. That the "picture of all pictures" was no picture would leave us, not less, but more enlightened, for we would then understand that all propositions *are* truth functions (5.) and that all are of equal value. (6.4)

In regard to *Wittgenstein's paradox,* however,—that he can only say what sense is by statements which have no sense and therefore which have to be overcome (*überwinden*), (6.54B)[4]—it is important to notice again the distinction between thoughts and language. The failure may be in the *expression of thoughts,* for in the *Preface* he says that

> the *truth* of the thoughts that are here set forth seems to me unassailable and definitive. (p. 5)

Hence while the *propositions* of the *Tractatus* are said to be non-

---

[4] The "Wittgenstein paradox" should be compared with the "Frege paradox" that "the concept *horse* is not a concept." (*Philosophical Writings of Gottlob Frege;* Oxford, 1952, p. 46) Wittgenstein avoids Frege's paradox by distinguishing between *objects* and *things,* but does not escape his own paradox that "the concept *object* is not a concept."

sensical (and so cannot be true or false), the *thoughts* which are communicated are said to be definitely true. (And we recall that "The totality of true thoughts is a picture of the world." (3.01)) It would appear from this that thoughts may be true even when they cannot be meaningfully expressed in propositions. (Wittgenstein at this point must then be talking about a thought as "a logical picture of facts" (3.) and not about a thought as "a proposition with a sense." (4.) What may fail must be the projection of a thought into a proposition.)

From this point of view it is only in language that the paradoxical character of the *Tractatus* appears, while we know what Wittgenstein's thought is, and this is not paradoxical but, he says, true. While the *word object*, therefore, has no meaning, it must be that in *thought* we know in concrete instances what objects are, and Wittgenstein's thoughts about them are straight-forward, even though when they get into language the result becomes nonsensical. (This might be due to the inevitable character of language or to Wittgenstein's failure to express himself better; the *Preface* suggests that it is the latter.) And, furthermore, we are *not* told that "everything that can be *thought* can be *expressed* clearly," but only that

> Everything that can be thought at all can be thought clearly.
> Everything that can be put into words can be put clearly.
> (4.116)

In order to understand Wittgenstein's thoughts (which are not nonsensical) we have to transcend his propositions (which are nonsensical), for what he means in thought has not gotten into language except in this nonsensical way.

The Change in Wittgenstein's Philosophy

. . . simplicity is the most deceitful mistress that ever betrayed man.

HENRY ADAMS

The danger is in the neatness of identifications.

SAMUEL BECKETT

I have come, alas, to compare words by which we so nimbly cross the space of a thought to light planks flung across an abyss, which hold for our passing over, but not for stopping.

PAUL VALERY

If things and thoughts were not only amalgamated, but integrated, then a higher dimension would be reached, and both would show new qualities.

ERIC GUTKIND

One final effort and painting too will have its picture which will carry us beyond all pictures.

GIORGIO DE CHIRICO

O sancta simplicitas!

JOHN HUSS (at the stake)

CHAPTER 13

The Change in Wittgenstein's Philosophy

i

There is a striking continuity and an equally striking change between Wittgenstein's early philosophy and his later one.[1] The writer of the *Tractatus* became in the second half of his philosophical life the severest critic of his own earlier ideas, but at the same time he succeeded in carrying out in a different way many of the same themes. The best introduction to the *Tractatus* is likely always to be Wittgenstein's own *Philosophical Investigations*, but it will equally remain true that the latter will be best understood in terms of the former.

In the opening sections of the *Philosophical Investigations* (up to section 143) Wittgenstein tells us both what is right with the *Tractatus* and also what is wrong with it. What he says about St. Augustine's notion of how language is learned can be applied to the *Tractatus*—that it embodies a philosophical concept of *meaning* which

> does describe a system of communication, only not everything
> that we call language is this system. (3)[2]

The *Tractatus* may now be seen as setting up something like a primitive model of a language which might illumine ordinary language. But this, of course, is not what Wittgenstein supposed he was doing when he wrote the *Tractatus*. For the *Tractatus* purports to present, not a model

---

[1] The course by which the change came about can be traced in Wittgenstein's *Philosophische Bemerkungen*, (Oxford, 1964), and in *The Blue and Brown Books*, (Oxford, 1958), and also in G. E. Moore's *Wittgenstein's Lectures in 1930-1933*, (*Mind*, vol. lxiii, nos. 249 and 251, and vol. lxiv, no. 253, reprinted in Moore's *Philosophical Papers*, (N.Y. 1962)). We are not concerned here with how the change occurred and the development of Wittgenstein's thought, but only with the similarities and differences between the two stages in so far as these may help to shed light on the *Tractatus*. A more detailed study of Wittgenstein's later philosophy is a subject for a sequel to the present book.

[2] The numbers in the citations in this chapter, unless otherwise indicated, refer to *sections* (and not pages) in the *Philosophical Investigations*.

of a simplified language, but rather the *essence* of all language (and indeed the "essence of the world" (5.4711)). In his later investigations one of the main questions Wittgenstein asks himself is how he could have been led to think that one particular model could be the essence of all language? Where did that idea come from? How could it have seemed so convincing?

His answer is that a certain picture of language (a picture of language as a picture) had *forced itself on him,* inexorably dictated by paying attention to just certain forms in language. This had led him to imagine that what we call "propositions" and "language" have a formal unity (108) which could be found in a "state of complete exactness" reached by a "final analysis" of ordinary language. (97) It had seemed that

> Thought is surrounded by a halo.—Its essence, logic, presents an order, in fact the a priori order of the world: that is the order of *possibilities,* which must be common to both world and thought. But this order, it seems, must be *utterly simple.* It is *prior* to all experience, must run through all experience; no empirical cloudiness or uncertainty can be allowed to affect it.—It must rather be of the purest crystal. But this crystal does not appear as an abstraction; but as something concrete, indeed, as the most concrete, as it were the *hardest* thing there is. (*Tractatus Logico-Philosophicus* No. 5.5563)

Under the spell of this picture Wittgenstein had accepted the "superstition" that there is something peculiar or unique about language and thought, (110) imagining the essence of language to be a "non-spatial, non-temporal phantasm" embodying such an a priori order of the world. (108) He had imagined that language contained an ideal order, "which *must* be found in reality" "for we think we already see it there." (101) Ordinary words like "sentence," "name," "word" and "picture" had come to have a peculiar metaphysical significance, quite removed from what they ordinarily mean. (97)

A particularly important mistake of the *Tractatus,* he says, was supposing that "naming" is an "occult process" and that names have a very special queer relation to the word, which could be stated by saying that "a name ought really to signify a simple." (39) Instead of imagining this we should see that

we call very different things "names"; the word "name" is

used to characterize many different kinds of uses related to one another in many different ways. (38)

To say, as the *Tractatus* in effect did about all except "logical words," that "every word in language signifies something," he now sees says nothing whatever "unless we have explained what distinction we wish to make" (as, for example, the distinction between words in particular language-games and words without meanings). (14)

Wittgenstein's fundamental desire, so pronounced in the *Tractatus*, to treat all language on the same level, reaches its natural culmination in the later philosophy, for here he renounces even the paradoxically "nonsensical" language of the *Tractatus* and the special vocabulary which it had required. The *Tractatus* had been concerned with the "essences" of names, sentences, pictures, thoughts, language, but Wittgenstein now says that what philosophers call the *essence* of a thing should not be thought of as a hidden metaphysical reality, but only as the use of a word "in the language-game which is its original home." (116) Giving up the notion of some "inner" essence of language (its "pictoriality"), he could at last treat all language equally. No ontological substance is required, no completely determinate sense or absolute simplicity. Wittgenstein's new motto is: *Sufficient unto the use of an analogy is the simplicity thereof.*

The *Tractatus* would have been on the right track if it had presented its conception of language as such a relatively simple model or analogy, that is

> as what it is, as an object of comparison—as, so to speak, a measuring-rod; not as a preconceived idea to which reality *must* correspond. (131)

Here Wittgenstein's life-long notion of language as a measuring-rod is applied to the way in which we describe language, rather than to the way in which language describes the world, or the way in which pictures are laid against reality. (2.1512) Language-games are (from one point of view) models, and thus to a certain extent "idealized" or "simplified" descriptions, but they are analogical, (not logical), models and do not reveal any single core of language, for there is no single core. As the *Philosophical Investigations* puts it:

> Our clear and simple language-games are not preparatory studies for a future reorganization of language—as it were first approximations, ignoring friction and air resistance. The lan-

guage-games are rather set up as objects of comparison which are meant to throw light on the facts of our language by way not only of similarities, but also of dissimilarities. (130)

A few of the main differences which go with this shift from the earlier to the later philosophy can be seen from the following comparisons:

Tractatus	*Philosophical Investigations*
all propositions are truth-functions. (5.)	there are countless irreducibly different *kinds* of propositions. (23)
only one final sense for each proposition. (3.25)	same proposition may have different senses in different language-games. (23)
a name means an object. (3.203)	one example of what may accompany a name is a paradigm used with it in a language-game. (55)
pictures are logical representations of the world. (2.182)	pictures are useful or misleading analogies. (131)
language always expresses thoughts about things. (3.1, 3.11)	language does not always express thoughts and is not always about things. (304)
philosophy clarifies by making thoughts sharp and by setting limits to what can be thought or to expression of thoughts. (4.112, 4.114, p. 3)	philosophy is purely descriptive, clarifies by reminding or rearranging. (126, 109)

The shift from *logical pictures* to *language-games* is a shift from the *requirement of final analysis* (logical simplicity) to an *instrument of description*. Ordinary language cannot be analyzed *into* language-games (as it can be analyzed into elementary propositions in the *Tractatus*); it can only be analyzed *by means of* language-games. While elementary propositions were, in a certain sense, *internal* to ordinary language, or presupposed by it, language-games remain *external* to language, merely to be used to see more clearly the way language works. No primitive tribe will ever be found playing one of Wittgenstein's language-games; this is only something we can imagine, a new way of understanding language, through a multiplicity of "minimum language activities," some seemingly a good deal more imaginary than others, but none to be found in just that *isolation* and *completeness* in actuality.

ii

Since so much emphasis is placed on the differences between the two stages of Wittgenstein's philosophy, it is important to recognize the equally striking continuity between them, even before we discuss the fundamental nature of the change.

In his later philosophy Wittgenstein is still concerned with (1) *complete clarity* (though no longer as a "state of complete exactness"); (2) the *essence of language* (though no longer as a hidden ideal structure); (3) *possibility* (though "actual possibilities" and not "all possibilities"); and (4) *complete and simple models* (though now a multiplicity of them, and not one ontologically "final" one). These are all ways in which the *Philosophical Investigations* is entirely the heir of the *Tractatus*.

But there is also another basic continuity. In his later philosophy Wittgenstein shifts from taking the *indicative* mood to taking the *imperative* mood as fundamental in language and, coincident with this, from emphasizing *forms* to emphasizing *rules*. But the way in which he later talks about *rules* is markedly similar to the way in which he earlier talked about *forms*. In place of implicit *logical forms*, which must look after themselves, we now have implicit *rules of usage*, which also must look after themselves. And, as in the *Tractatus*, there was nothing which determines the applications of language, but only the possibilities of application, so in the *Philosophical Investigations* there is nothing which *determines* the application of rules. Within language we still have an *irreducible presupposition* which is necessary for meaning (now provided by rules instead of by forms), and between language and its application there is still an *unbridgeable gap*, which is necessary for the possibility of error (though now it is between rules and the application of rules, rather than between signs and giving signs meanings).[3]

A still more basic continuity lies in Wittgenstein's continued rejec-

---

[3] "What I always do seems to be—to emphasize a distinction between the determination of a sense and the employment of a sense." (*Remarks on the Foundations of Mathematics*. II-37)

tion of explanations of language in psychological terms or in terms of immediate private experience. (In this way he remained faithful to the Frege tradition.) The *Tractatus* altogether by-passed private experience of "content" by treating pictures, thoughts and language as *intrinsically structural*. And so in a similar way the *Philosophical Investigations* sets aside private "mental processes" to show language as *intrinsically conventional*. "Following a rule" is no more to be understood psychologically in the *Investigations* than "combinatorial structure" was in the *Tractatus*. In each case psychological experiences may *at the most* sometimes be said to "accompany" language, but never to "determine" it.

> And hence also "obeying a rule" is a practice. And to think that one is obeying a rule is not to obey a rule. Hence it is not possible to obey a rule "privately"; otherwise thinking one was obeying a rule would be the same thing as obeying it. (202)

Language-games, unlike what elementary propositions refer to, have no ontological status. They are heuristic devices. But, they must also, Wittgenstein says, be "noted" as "final phenomena," without attempting to explain them further by means of our experiences. (654-5) The language-game, he says, should be looked upon as a "proto-phenomenon," which needs no further justification. Hence it has *all the irreducibility and finality of the elementary proposition, but without the latter's ontological claim to ideal simplicity*.

Obeying rules, whatever rules it is we obey, as this is understood in the later philosophy, is a *custom inherent in our behavior*, in very much the same way that *forms are inherent in the world and in language* in the *Tractatus*. We cannot get behind this to some further reason or cause why we obey rules, any more than we can explain why there are forms of the world and of language in the *Tractatus*. There is simply a certain regular "connection" between our language and our behavior, paralleling the "connection" between forms of language and forms of the world in the *Tractatus*. (If we found creatures who made sounds, but with whom there was no such regular "connection" between their sounds and actions, Wittgenstein says we would not be inclined to call the sounds they made "language." (207))

Obeying a particular rule has somewhat the same status in the *Philosophical Investigations* as *naming* has in the *Tractatus*, for just as there is no intermediary between names and the world in the latter case, so there is no intermediary between a rule and the action which obeys it in the former. If we ask in regard to the *Tractatus:* How do we know that we have applied a name rightly? the answer was that there is no possible appeal beyond the last naming (for it is not possible to give a sign the wrong sense (5.4732)). And similarly in regard to the *Investigations* if we ask: How do we know that we have applied a rule rightly, the answer is that there is no appeal beyond the last interpretation. Language finally "connects" with action directly as before it finally "connected" with the world directly.

Wittgenstein's later view involves a kind of "linguistic occasionalism"—not between mind and body, but between language and action. There is a relation here which is neither causal nor a matter of interpretation or choice, but is a matter of *agreement in what we do,* where what we do includes what we say. Words have to be able to influence people directly without intermediary and in a non-causal fashion, although natural capacities and certain kinds of training (which themselves take place with words and without intermediary) are also presupposed. The rules of a technique, Wittgenstein says, do not play the part of propositions of natural history, even though the technique is a fact of natural history. If we are able to form rules of a technique, they are rules because they *are acted upon* and can be acted upon in different ways, and not because they are *interpreted.* Learning to obey a rule is made possible by our natural reactions (as learning not to touch a hot stove is) and by training in technique (as learning to ride a bicycle is). But this does not explain how there happens to be such a custom as "obeying a rule," any more than describing how we learn to ride a bicycle explains how there happens to be such an activity as bicycle-riding. Applying a rule is something which in the end has to be done directly and blindly. It is always possible to have different interpretations of *any* rule, and, *in addition,* there are different ways of acting on *any* interpretation, so that in the end we are simply confronted by no transition, but only a jump from rule to action.

Such a notion of rules sets a certain limit on description and definition (as Wittgenstein's notion of *forms* set a limit on description and definition in the *Tractatus*). There is an "agreement in doing" which cannot itself be described because it is presupposed by any description and because any description of it will always be only an interpretation of it. Because we *describe by means of a rule* we cannot describe the rule (any more than we can "measure" the standard measure). "Describing a use" is more basically "using a description," for it presupposes that we are able to describe and have been trained to use that instrument when here too there is no natural necessity for it, but only an "agreement in practice."[4]

iii

Wittgenstein, it is apparent, in his later philosophy is still trying to understand language and to understand it in accordance with certain broad principles which remain the same. But a radical reorientation has taken place which he himself called a "turning round." He tells us that

> The *preconceived idea* of crystalline purity can only be removed by turning our whole examination round. (One might say the axis of reference of our examination must be rotated, but about the fixed point of our real need.) (108)

We have to ask: What is this rotation? And what is the "fixed point of our real need"?

The "fixed point," it is apparent, is the need to get clear about language and, indeed, to attain "complete clarity." (And he now says that "complete clarity" means that philosophical problems should *completely* disappear. (132-3) They *did not* completely disappear in the *Tractatus* because certain words were still being used in "unheard of" ways.) Now how is the "axis of reference of our examination" to rotate about this point? In this way: instead of trying to see how language can *possibly* be connected with the world, let us look at language as *already* interwoven with the world in innumerable different ways and then try to see *why it is that we fail to understand this*. Instead of looking for one supposed peculiar relation between language and the world we must look at the actual multiplicity of language activities. The prob-

---

4 Empirical linguists are sometimes impatient that there cannot be a definition of *rule* in the ordinary enough way in which Wittgenstein uses the term. They forget that "giving definitions" is itself a language activity and itself involves certain rules. Unless we could "follow a rule" we could not do that either. A definition of "rule" can, of course, be imposed, but it will always be a limitation for some particular purpose of the use of the word *rule*, and this will be a different matter from describing the way the word *rule* is normally used. In addition, the concept of a rule, like concepts in general in Wittgenstein's later philosophy, has "blurred edges" where it may or may not be used, and even when it is used quite properly, it only marks "family resemblances" between certain cases. For all these reasons no definition can be given that would in any way satisfy some linguists.

lem of how language *can* be related to the world will disappear when
we see clearly that it *is* related in many different ways, and ask why
we suppose otherwise.

With this "turning round" the supposed hidden structural identity
between language and the world of the *Tractatus* appears as a case of
reading into the world what *belongs only to one way of representing
the world*. What happened in the *Tractatus* was that

> We predicate of the thing what lies in the method of rep-
> resenting it. Impressed by the possibility of a comparison, we
> think we are perceiving a state of affairs of the highest gen-
> erality. (104)

In other words, we compare language to a model with exact meanings
and fixed rules and then we suppose that, because this can be done,
this is the way the *world* must be. But the compulsion lies only in the
model, which, as it were, makes us think that we see its "shadow" in
the world, and that this *must* be there, for otherwise, we ask ourselves,
how *could* the comparison be made?

The enormous importance of language, as the later philosophy sees
it, does not depend upon structure, but upon the interweaving of language with so many human activities and the deeply rooted nature of
the conventions involved. "Describing objects" Wittgenstein now sees
as one of the things which we naturally do, and this means that it is
"actually possible," and there is no need for it also to be "metaphysically
possible."[5] It is not logic, but grammar by which, he now says, essence
is expressed, (371) and grammar involves the actual possibilities for the
uses of words, as we have learned them or been trained to employ them,
rather than the "ideal possibilities" which were hypostatized in the
Tractatus.

A specific and fundamental way in which the *Tractatus's* notion of
language as a logical picture breaks down is presented at the very outset of the *Philosophical Investigations*, where Wittgenstein considers the
case of *commands* or *giving and obeying orders*. Here it comes out that
there is no reason why we have to have a picture or a proposition in

---

[5] Language-games are to a certain extent "ideal," but they are not "metaphysically ideal," because none of them claim a final ontological status. It is doubt-
ful, for example, whether a tribe having a language with only four words—*block,
pillar, slab* and *beam*—is an *actual possibility*. People who had reason to build with
these things would undoubtedly have other words too. But what Wittgenstein
describes is certainly "conceivable" as a simplified model.

order to give or obey orders, and, in addition, there is no reason to suppose that commands are not just as "primitive" a kind of language as any other or that there is any logical impossibility in having a language consisting entirely of commands, for such a language is entirely conceivable. (We might, for example, easily construct it in robots.)

The book begins with just such an example of a "command language," (the "builders' language"), which, in a remarkable *tour de force* makes four devastating points simultaneously against the *Tractatus's* conception of language: (1) that it is possible to communicate adequately with expressions of only one word (structure is not required for sense); (2) that a single name can be a command (which is more than meaning an object); (3) that a command need not have a propositional form (a single word command is not a logical picture, nor does it have to be regarded as a "condensation" of a logical picture); (4) that we can imagine a whole language without propositional forms and, to top it off, this imaginary language could consist wholly of names, none of which ever appeared in propositions (inconceivable in the *Tractatus*).[6]

This case of the "builders' language" shows us a conceivable complete language, to which what the *Tractatus* has to say about language simply does not apply. And at the same time it introduces something analogous to "following rules," which Wittgenstein finds involved in a great many language activities. In fact *rules* occupy an analogous place with regard to language-games to what forms occupy with regard to logical pictures.

As *forms* are "possibilities of structure" in the *Tractatus* (2.033) so we might imagine *rules* as something like "possibilities of use." But this can be misleading because possibilities are not "contained in" a rule (as objects, for example, "contain" the possibility of all situations in the *Tractatus* (2.014)). Wittgenstein, nevertheless, looks at *rules* in a presuppositional way, analogous to the way in which he earlier looked at *forms*. For rules to function it "must be possible" for us to follow them—whatever this may mean in regard to having certain natural capacities, having learned something and there being such a common practice.

These possibilities also set limits (again analogous to the limits in

---

[6] "We translate an order at one time into a proposition, at another into a demonstration and at another into action." (459)

the *Tractatus*). To say this, however, is not to make a metaphysical statement (the limits are not metaphysical), but merely to put forward a certain picture or one way of looking at it. Wittgenstein brings this out in the following passage:

> What do I mean when I say "the pupil's capacity to learn *may* come to an end here?" Do I say this from my own experience? Of course not. (Even if I had such an experience.) Then what am I doing with that proposition? Well, I should like to say: "Yes, it's true, you can imagine that too, that might happen too!"—But was I trying to draw someone's attention to the fact that he is capable of imagining that?—I wanted to put that picture before him, and his *acceptance* of the picture consists in his now being inclined to regard a given case differently: that is, to compare it with *this* rather than *that* set of pictures. I have changed his *way of looking at things*. (Indian mathematicians: "Look at this.") (144)

When we say that in order to carry on a certain language activity it "must be possible" to teach it and learn it, (386) Wittgenstein says, we are not talking about a metaphysical possibility or requirement; we are adopting a certain picture. (And the *Philosophical Investigations* also only puts before us certain "ways of looking" which have nothing to recommend them other than that they permit us to "see clearly.")

The question "*Can* we learn such-and-such?" (which is all that interests philosophy) remains a different question from the question "How *do* we learn such-and-such?" (which asks for factual information). The former question involves a clarification of the meaning of the word *learn*, to find out, for example, whether the word *learn* is appropriately used in that particular case. This is done by calling to mind the way the word *learn* is used in other cases and noting analogies and disanalogies. It may then turn out that the word suggests a certain picture which leads us to expect other features to be present which are not present, and this may then give rise to unnecessary problems.

What we have been doing is "getting clear" about the "grammar" of the word *learn*—that is, recalling under what circumstances it is used and what sorts of pictures go with it. The contrast made in the *Tractatus* between conventional *grammatical form*, (which is likely to be misleading), and *logical form*, (the underlying possibilities of sense), is here replaced by a contrast between the pictures suggested by "surface grammar" (which may be seriously misleading) and "depth grammar" (the actual possibilities for use of the word.) In the course of the latter kind of analysis we "assemble reminders" of a variety of uses of a word to prevent us from being led astray by a picture suggested by just one use. It is, in other words, no longer a matter of what is *logically possible*, but of a "way of looking" which establishes what is to be regarded as *actually possible*.

iv

Perhaps nothing is more startling in Wittgenstein's later philosophy than the metamorphosis which his notion of *pictures* has undergone. Pictures can now be false, (604) bad, (136) misleading, (171) and idle; (291) they can hold us captive, (115) obtrude upon us, (397) force themselves on us, (425) and take us in; (p. 184) and they conflict (402) and collide. (141) Pictures, in other words, have become highly questionable accouterments of language, producing at times disastrous misunderstandings, as they did for Wittgenstein himself in the *Tractatus*.

The *Philosophical Investigations* speaks of "using" pictures and of "calculating" with words and turning them "sometimes into one picture, sometimes into another." (449) And it also speaks of having a "clear picture" of the circumstances under which we would say something. (282) But, contrasted with this, are the pictures which arise in philosophy, especially when we introspect:

> When we look into ourselves as we do philosophy we often get to see such a picture. A full-blown pictorial representation of our grammar. Not facts, but as it were, illustrated turns of speech. (295)

In these cases (as, for example, when we "stare at" our own pain) such a picture "with its ramifications stands in the way of our seeing the use of the word as it is." (305) Instead we see looming before us a picture of what we are doing which is actually a "grammatical fiction."

There are three pictures in particular which Wittgenstein attacks in his later philosophy: (1) the *picture of the ideal*; (89-142) (2) the *picture of the inner experience*; (242-316) and (3) the *picture of logical necessity*. (143-242) (The last named is more thoroughly investigated in the *Remarks on the Foundations of Mathematics* and in the unpublished *Mathematical Notes*.) These give rise to three imaginary notions of language (1) the *ideal language*, (2) the *private language* and (3) the *logical language*—(involving the *ideal object*, the *inner object* and the *logical object*). Wittgenstein himself had fallen victim to two of these pictures in the *Tractatus* (though not to the picture of the private language).

To break the spells of these pictures it is necessary to look more closely at how words actually function in concrete cases.

(1) In the case of the *ideal language* closer examination will show that there are *many different kinds of names* and *sentences* (i.e. we use *these* words in many different ways), and none of these is, in some absolute sense, more "basic" than the others.

(2) In the case of the *inner experience* or the *inner process* we will see that the grammar of "name and object" which seems to force itself on us is not applicable, but instead generates insoluble difficulties.

(3) In the case of *logical necessity* we will find this to be a mythical idea generated by deeply conventional "agreements in usage."

Speaking of *pain* Wittgenstein introduces a distinction not found in the *Tractatus*. He says that we have an *idea (Vorstellung)* of pain, which "enters into the language-game in a sense; only not as a picture." (300) And then he adds:

> An idea (*Vorstellung*) is not a picture, but a picture may correspond to it. (301)

The word *Vorstellung* (which does not appear in the *Tractatus*, though *vorstellen* does) is not needed if language expresses only thoughts which are "logical pictures of facts," or if the elements of thoughts correspond to objects. Once the notion of "ultimate names" is abandoned, however, we can look at how the words *thought, pain* and *idea* are used, without worrying about what they "stand for."

In the later philosophy it is possible also for Wittgenstein to look at *concepts* in a new way. In the *Tractatus* proper concepts are ultimately functions of names. But in the *Philosophical Investigations* a concept becomes something like *a picture with which one compares objects,* or something like a technique for describing or portraying objects. There are now natural limits to concepts rather than "logical" ones. (71) And Wittgenstein can say that

> Concepts . . . are the expression of our interests and direct our interests. (570)

Understanding *concepts* as functions of *objects* has been replaced by
understanding objects in terms of the ways concepts permit us to look
at them.[7]

The *Philosophical Investigations* can be seen as something like a
sustained warning against the dangers of unacknowledged analogies
generated by favored uses of language. We permit "strong" grammar-
generated pictures to obscure the varieties of language-meanings. In the
Tractatus Wittgenstein had said that:

> Everyday language is a part of the human organism, and is
> no less complicated than that. (4.002B)

In the *Philosophical Investigations* he might have said that it is part of
human activities and no less complicated than they are. In the early
philosophy everyday language "disguises thought" so that

> It is not humanly possible to gather from (everyday) language
> what the logic of language is. (4.002C)

In the later philosophy *certain uses* of everyday language confuse
thought, and most of all precisely those uses which lead us to suppose
that everyday language as a whole "disguises thought." A certain "distrust of grammar" remains for Wittgenstein the "first requisite of philosophizing" (*Notebooks*. p. 93) although now not because it *disguises*
an ultimate picture, but because it *creates the illusion* of an ultimate
picture.

v

The *Tractatus* imagines an *Ur-world* of structural possibility as
the essential core of language, thought and the world. This Ur-world
of fixed forms and logical "bi-polarity" is conceived as hidden within
the ordinary world of things and situations in the same way that an
"essential language" of names, elementary propositions and truth functions is hidden within ordinary language. The Ur-world is, in effect,
the totality of everything that can be said with both final truth and
falsity about the world. It is the world as matrices of determinate structures in the further field of the two possibilities of existence and non-
existence. In the Ur-world we have both positive and negative facts,
(all combinations of existing and non-existing combinations of objects),

---

[7] "When language-games change, then there is a change in concepts, and with
the concepts the meanings of words change." Wittgenstein—*On Certainty*. sect. 65.

while *the* world is positive facts. The Ur-world is the *essential world*, the "immanent form of objectivity" common to every possible world.

Everything in the *Tractatus* is, as it were, "doubled" to provide a determinately simple prototype in this essential world, this Ur-world of all possibilities. Thus we have:

> proto-things (objects) and proto-signs (names)
> proto-pictures (logical forms or what corresponds to them)
> proto-situations (states of affairs)
> proto-propositions (elementary and truth functional propositions)
> proto-conjunction (logical form as existence and non-existence)
> proto-disjunction (sense as asserted existence)
> proto-negation (the "general" operation of Negation)

The *proto-world*, or *essential world*, which Wittgenstein later called a "phantasm" or *Unding*, (108) was, it seemed, what was needed to permit *complete exactness of reference* along with the *possibility of error*, the two absolute requirements which the *Tractatus* had somehow to reconcile. It is the former of these requirements which Wittgenstein later examined so intensively and repudiated.

The Ur-world is predicated finally on what the *Tractatus* calls the "requirement" or "postulate" (*Forderung*) of determinateness of sense. (3.23) But what, we may ask, is the source of this "requirement?" Is it indeed merely generated by one particular picture of a use of language? Can we be persuaded that Wittgenstein has gotten to the bottom of its hold over him (and so many others) in his criticism of it in the *Philosophical Investigations?*

The long tradition of Western philosophy would suggest otherwise. The *theoretical vision* (an etymologically redundant phrase) itself appears to be wrapped up with the demand for ontological reference. Even if we decide for the "priority of the practical reason," which in this case means for the priority of *rules* over *forms*, or of *forms of life* over *ontological forms*, we have not thereby established that the "ontological demand," suitably formulated to permit other kinds of language, is no more than a misleading picture. Even if the attempt to understand *all* language in this way was mistaken, was it mistaken to understand *some* language in this way?

In the later philosophy a picture-of-the-world is *itself* a picture, or, putting this another way, the *Tractatus* is seen as based on *a picture of the application of pictures*. And since there is nothing necessary about the application of any picture, *this* picture came to appear as also arbitrary or conventional. Pictures then appeared as analogical rather than logical. But, it may still be pointed out, that even analogical pictures, in so far as they purport to describe the world, may be ontologically revealing without landing us back in another picture of the application of pictures.

While theoretical vision and its ontological demand do not require that "speaking about the world" supply the model for *all* language, neither does it seem that this is just "one more picture." Being able, in some sense, to describe anything that we choose to describe, (even when the word "describe" is used in many different ways), suggests not only that this one particular use of language may mislead us, but also that "talking about objects" may be something like a "preferred model," perhaps for further good reasons. The gravitation of our understanding toward "objectification" may do more than confuse us, since it may represent also the insistence that *everything shall be "in front" of us in some way or another*. And Wittgenstein's own final conception of philosophy itself as purely descriptive stands as testimony to this. For even if his own "descriptions" have only the status of "recommended analogies" for "seeing clearly," they still involve "objetification," as indicated by the expression "seeing clearly."

Unacknowledged analogies suggested by our grammar may make us fail to understand the "workings of our language," but, when these analogies point so strongly in the same direction, we may suspect that more is at work than misleading pictures. It is as if we try to represent everything as different "kinds of objects" where all that is obscured is that *they really are different*. The preference for the name-object pattern, even if it gives a misleading impression of the unity of language, may testify to the value of the objectivizing tendency which allows us to "confront" everything (including, for example, even that which the religious tradition teaches cannot be "confronted").[8]

If, we may ask, the *Tractatus* was not successful in attempting to assimilate language to pictures, is the *Philosophical Investigations* any

---

[8] The statement "God is not an object" is already a self-contradiction since it appears to be *talking about something*. And even if the statement makes only a "grammatical" point, what it has to do with is more than grammar. A prohibition against talking about God *ought not to tell us anything*.

more successful in attempting to assimilate pictures to language? The discovery that language does not always function in the same way and that we need to "see clearly" the enormous variety of different kinds of language-activities does not remove the key place of pictures, if "seeing clearly" itself somehow involves approximating to "the way things are," where, as the language itself suggests, the paradigmatic case of this is clear perception. The visual analogies which we have in language (*point of view, representing, seeing clearly*, etc.) may indeed be so deeply ingrained in language for good and sufficient reasons, and if we *cannot* do without pictures or models, this may attest, not so much to weakness of thought, as to the striving for the synoptic clarity and unity which we have in perception.

Wittgenstein's philosophy, in both of its phases, exemplifies just such a marvelous interaction of "saying" and "seeing." Although language is always the center of his concern, it is also always his aim to "see clearly" how language functions. And the expression to "see clearly" (or to arrive at a "perspicuous representation") is, as it was for Plato and Descartes, more than just another dangerously concealed metaphor. If the metaphor misled him into supposing that complete clarity of representation was the secret essence of all language, what the metaphor suggested still remained for him the aim of philosophy. The "visual" import of Wittgenstein's conception of philosophy is, in a sense, as strong at the end as it was at the beginning.

When the conception of language itself as a "logical picturing," or a kind of "rational seeing," broke down with the realization that there are no logical pictures since there is no one final (only possible) way by which pictures may be related to what they picture, Wittgenstein did not abandon looking for "models" of the different ways in which language functions. The notion of a language-game is still that of a "clear and simple" description of one possible "whole language." And by means of *these* pictures he still tried to "see clearly" because in each of these was still represented just one, as it were final, thing which could be done with language. While the "formal unity" of language as a whole disappears, the "unity" or "completeness" of each separate language-game remains.

Like the philosophy of Kant, of which it so often reminds us, Wittgenstein's philosophy moves from uncovering the presuppositions of the theoretical or scientific vision in the *Tractatus* to describing the wider areas of human language-practice in the *Philosophical Investiga-*

tions. The "presuppositional method" is similar in both accounts. But what is the relation between them? The latter book suggests that it "supplants" the former. But Wittgenstein did not live to write his "third Critique," and perhaps there was more to say about how the theoretical vision is related to practice.

vi

A central impulse of Wittgenstein's philosophy from the start is the attempt to find the *limits of facts*. And this is done through uncovering the presuppositions of meaning and sense. Language which is already meaningful is a precondition for speaking about facts, as possibly existing and non-existing structures of objects is a precondition of their existence. Hence meaning is not itself a fact, but what makes possible talking about facts. (And hence also the expression "theory of meaning" is a total confusion because it treats meaning as itself a fact.)

The *Tractatus* sets limits to facts not only in the direction of *meaning and logic*, but in the directions of *immediate experience* (which cannot be expressed), the *subject* (which is the condition for immediate experience), and all *values*—ethical and aesthetic (about which nothing can be said). All these are clearly marked off as *outside the realm of facts*, because outside the realm of possible description.

In the later philosophy the same impulse is at work in a different way, for here countless entirely sensible uses of language, other than those of describing facts, are singled out, and, in addition "description" itself is shown to have manifold meanings. The possibilities of what can be done with language far exceed the boundaries of the particular uses of language involved in science, in such a way that there can be no kind of an "explanation" of any of them. Language-games are not themselves facts to be explained. (654)

It is always basic to Wittgenstein's point of view to defend the *integrity and ultimacy of language*. This meant denying the possibility of special privileged kinds of language—and specifically *metalanguages* in the *Tractatus* and *private languages* and *ideal languages* in the *Philosophical Investigations*. His view that *there is no intrinsically privileged way of speaking* was extended even to the structural and logical language of the *Tractatus* itself at the end of that book, and then in a thorough and consistent way in the *Philosophical Investigations*. We gain only an *illusory transcendence* in supposing that there can be a *language about language* or a *language of immediate experience* or a *purely logical language*. Just as a "picture of a picture" is only one more picture, so "language about language" is just more language. (If we supposed that there could be—except in an altogether superficial sense— a "music of music" or an "art of art" or a "seeing of seeing" we would be making a similar mistake.) The most we can do is to use language to put forward certain pictures of the uses of language which may help us to sort out these uses.

A consequence of this, maintained by Wittgenstein throughout, is that there can be no special rules for the application of language and, in addition, no way of guaranteeing the application. *All possibilities* for the application are either contained within language and must all be equally permissible (*Tractatus*) or go along with our acceptance of the rules which we learn when we learn language. (*Philosophical Investigations*). There is no further court of appeal for using language other than how it *can* be used, but then also no guarantee whatsoever in how it *can* be used that it *will* be used this way. *Between possibility of use and actual use nothing can be introduced which is not simply a further possibility*. (In the *Tractatus* all semantic and syntactic possibilities are available *before* application. And in the *Philosophical Investigations* all *being able to use* is, as it were, complete before actual use.)

What Wittgenstein said about logic and its application in the *Tractatus*—that they must not "overlap," but nothing must come between them (5.557)—can be extended to what he says about language-activities in the *Philosophical Investigations*—that what we are *able* to do with language must not "overlap" with what we do with it, (for otherwise there would not be the possibility of error), but neither must anything come between them, (for what could this be but more language?). The gulf between possibilities and actual doing continues to yawn as widely in the later book as in the earlier one, even when *agreements in usage* and *rules* have replaced *forms* and *logical forms*. (Analogously, learning how to use a hammer does not mean that it is settled how we will actually use it, or that we will always use it "rightly.")

What we would *like* to put between language and its application in many instances is "immediate experience" or some kind of an "inner process." For example, I see a house and have the "experience" of it before I call it a *house*. Or I *understand* a command before I obey it. Or I think before I speak. There are, Wittgenstein says, occasions on which we can sensibly say such things, but to suppose that there must always be such an intermediary experience or process is only to insist on a certain picture which prevents "seeing clearly." There is no necessity for *anything* between language and its application—nothing that *has* to be there. (And, in addition, since we have also had to learn the language activities in which such words as "experience," "understand" and "think" occur and must finally use *these* words directly, we have not evaded the principle that nothing in the end can come between language and its application.)

We can see also in this principle the shift in philosophic perspective for which Wittgenstein is perhaps most thoroughly responsible—the shift from the Cartesian emphasis on problems of knowledge to the new emphasis on problems of language. The era when epistemology was at the center of the stage comes to an end with Wittgenstein, and the old problems appear in new guises, neither primarily epistemological or ontological, but linguistic. The change was already present virtually *in toto* in the *Tractatus*, for the ontological realm there is only a reflection of a certain conception of language. The epistemological dilemma of modern philosophy moves off the stage, for, as against traditional empiricism, the whole side of "content" or "immediate experience" is simply put to one side as inexpressible, while, as against traditional rationalism, we have a metaphysical system which denies its own possibility, and that too finally is dismissed as a "phantasm."

To many it will appear that Wittgenstein has turned the attention of philosophy away from understanding the world and human life more profoundly to studying simply words. And why should we look at "mere words" when it is the world and life which concern us most? But with the actual philosophical study of language the word "mere" drops out, and we discover that there is nothing more profound than language and that in language alone the world and life have their full meaning.

Appendices

THE STRUCTURE OF THE *TRACTATUS*

The curious numbering system of the *Tractatus*, dividing the book into seven principal sections in each of which—(except the last which contains only one sentence admonishing silence)—the text serves as a commentary on a single leading proposition, raises a number of critical problems. Chief among these is Wittgenstein's device of using 0's in the numbering at the beginnings of the sections. In two cases in particular there are many such 0-numbered entries: between the entries numbered 2 and 2.1 there are three and a half pages of entries numbered with 0's, while between 4 and 4.1 there are more than six pages of such entries.

A careful examination shows that the use of the 0's in the numbering can best be understood in the light or Wittgenstein's view that only propositions about facts (positive and negative) have sense. In one respect this rules out the whole *Tractatus* itself from having sense. (6.54) But if we recall that the *Tractatus* also deals with *pictures* and *propositional signs*, which themselves *are* facts, (2.141, 3.14B) (and with *thoughts* and *propositions* as being necessarily related to pictures and propositional signs), then it becomes evident that the specific matters which are unsayable are what are presupposed by these facts, and it is propositions about these which are especially singled out by being numbered with 0's.

In the light of this it will be found that the 0-numbered entries fall into three broad categories of what is unsayable:

1 — Everything below the level of facts, or states of affairs is unsayable because unpicturable. (2.1, 3.001) This involves specifically the whole metaphysical treatment of objects, because objects can only be named in factual propositions and not in addition named "metaphysically."

2 — Everything about the relation between propositions and the world which does not treat propositions as propositional signs and hence as facts is unsayable because propositions cannot picture themselves. (3.331, 4.0411, 5.54)

3 — Everything below the level of logical and mathetical propositions
again is employed *in* logic and mathematics but cannot be named
apart from this. (4.1272)

When Wittgenstein is talking about *objects*, (2.0's) *thoughts in general* (3.0's) the *general relation of language to the world*, (4.0's) *indices
of names*, (5.0's) and *numbers*, (6.0's) he is either talking about presuppositions of facts, logic and mathematics or making general non-
factual statements about language or about the relation of language and
the world. The 2.0's terminate with the beginning of the discussion of
pictures, the 3.0's with the beginning of discussion of propositions as
propositional signs, the 4.0's with the beginning of the discussion of
propositions as *pictures of reality*, the 5.0's with the beginning of the
discussion of propositions as *truth functions* and the 6.0's with the
beginning of the discussion of the *propositions of logic*.

The *Tractatus* may be seen as having the following structure un-
folding the nature of propositions:

1 — *the world as the totality of facts* (1.1)
2 — *pictures as pictures of facts* (2.1)
3 — *propositions as signs* (3., 3.1)
4 — *propositions as pictures of reality* (4.01, 4.021)
5 — *propositions as truth functions* (5.)
6 — *logical, mathematical and scientific propositions and ethical
    pseudo-propositions* (6.1, 6.2, 6.3, 6.4)
7 — *silence*

Within this framework the book breaks into two main divisions: the
first comprising the sections numbered 1, 2 and 3 and the second the
sections numered 4, 5, 6 and 7. The second half beginning with the
4's (which was very likely written first), is something like a treatise on
propositional logic, while the first half, (very likely written second),
is the metaphysical basis for this. The two branches of philosophy mentioned by Wittgenstein in his 1913 *Notes on Logic* (*Notebooks*. p. 93)
—logic and metaphysics—are the subjects of the two halves of the book,
in the reverse order.

The connection between the first three sections of the book and the
last four involves a particularly important transition (a kind of a "half-
step," as in the chromatic scale). This is the jump from a thought as
"a logical picture of facts" (3.) to a thought as "a proposition with a

sense." (4.) This transition, reminding us of Aristotle's transition from the passive intellect to the active intellect, signals the difference between a thought as *registering* the way things are and a thought as *asserting* the way things are.

More speculatively (and whether Wittgenstein intended this or not), it is also illuminating to look at the seven sections of the book in the way suggested by the following diagram:[1]

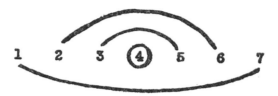

Certain symmetries between the two parts then appear:

1 and 7 — *world as totality*   *silence*
2 and 6 — *ontological presuppositions*   *logical framework*
3 and 5 — *"sense functions"*   *truth functions*
    4   —   *nature of language and philosophy*
                 elementary propositions
                 4.0312 — central thesis of book

This way of looking at the book has the advantages that it brings out interesting relations between the two parts, (presuppositions of logic and logic itself), and it also puts entry 4.0312, which contains what Wittgenstein calls "My fundamental idea" (*Mein Grundgedanke*), where it belongs — at the center.[2]

---

[1] This diagram was suggested to me, (though in no way in connection with Wittgenstein), by reading Charles A. Muses's *Illumination on Jacob Boehme, The Work of Dionysius Andreas Freher*, (N.Y.: Columbia, Kings Crown, 1951), p. 139.

[2] Max Black observes in his *Companion to Wittgenstein's "Tractatus"* "It is odd to find this 'fundamental thought' appearing . . . in such a subordinate position in the text." (p. 174) This is an inescapable reaction if we do not see it as at the *center*.

APPENDIX 2

MULTIPLY-EXTENDED MANIFOLDS

Wittgenstein's conception of space, time and color as multiply-extended manifolds in all likehood has its origin in Russell's *Foundation of Geometry*[1] which contains a detailed discussion of Riemann's original formulation of this idea. Russell, however, criticized Riemann's conception of color as such a manifold on the grounds that *color points:* (1) are qualitatively different from each other and (2) must be able to mix together to produce additional colors. By contrast with this, Russell observed, *spatial points* are all the same and are only distinguished by their positions in relation to each other. (pp. 66-7)

Wittgenstein's statement that "In a manner of speaking objects are colorless" (2.0232) indicates his adherence to the Riemann rather than the Russell view. And in the *Notebooks* he declares:

> That the colors are not properties is shown by the analysis of physics, by the internal relations in which physics displays the colors.
> Apply this to sounds too. (p. 82)

Colors, like spatial and temporal "properties," are to be regarded as "forms of objects," (2.0251) the objects not being themselves colored, but in their various combinations "producing" the material properties (2.0231) which we experience as color phenomena, (the experienced "content," then, like all "content," not being describable or expressible as such, but only by the corresponding structures).

It seems to have been Wittgenstein's idea, as it was Riemann's, that every color can be "located" by giving its coordinates on the three "axes" of hue, saturation and brightness recognized in color theory.[2]

---

[1] *An Essay on the Foundations of Geometry*, (Cambridge University Press, 1897). In the Preface to the *Tractatus* Wittgenstein speaks of the stimulation to his thoughts which he has received from "the writings of my friend Mr. Bertrand Russell." It seems more than likely that this *Essay* is one of the most important of the writings here referred to.

[2] For full discussions of these ideas in color theory see especially: M. Sargant-Florence.—*Colour Co-Ordination*, (London, John Lane, The Bodley Head, 1940). and P. J. Bouma—*Physical Aspects of Colour*, (Eindhoven, The Netherlands, N. V. Philips Gloeilampenfabrieken. English edition. 1947).

In his *Zettel* Wittgenstein even mentions the possibility of a "fourth dimension" for color:

> If we can imagine four-dimensional space, why not also four-dimensional colors, that is colors which, besides degree of saturation, hue and brightness, allowed of a fourth determination. (entry 269)

The idea of a dimensional description for color, as well as for space, which we find in the *Tractatus*, is clearly indicated here.

That the parallel between color and space is intended to be carried out fully is suggested by a sentence in the unpublished *Mathematical Notes*:

> If asked what he considers simple colors, almost everyone will say: red, blue, yellow, green, white and black.

This sentence is illuminating because it suggests that Wittgenstein adhered to the Goethe-Hering-Mach four-color theory (as against the Young-Helmholtz-Clerk Maxwell three-color theory) and, in addition, that he also regarded white and black as colors. Taking this in conjunction with the "dimensional" description we must suppose that he believed that the six simple colors could be given by various combinations of the three dimensional coordinates, in somewhat the same fashion that the six possible combinations of any three dimensional spatial coordinates give the six possible degrees of freedom of a body or the six possible "directions" in three-dimensional space. (Any color might then be represented by the six possible combinations of three color-coordinates—the coordinates a, b, c, for example, giving the possible combinations abc, acb, bac, bca, cba, and cab—a formulation which would hold no matter what specific axes of reference were chosen.)[3]

The analogy between this and the phenomena of sound has often been drawn and appears also to have been in Wittgenstein's mind. The three dimensions of sound—loudness, pitch and timbre or quality—may

---

[3] Just how this was to be worked out we can only guess. Conceivably black and white might constitute the "brightness axis," red-green the "hue axis" and blue-yellow the "saturation axis." It is far from clear, however, that all sensed colors could then be represented by appropriately chosen coordinates on these three "color axes." And Wittgenstein's later realization that such an "atomistic" description could not handle a continuum of gradations of brightness, for example, speaks against it. (cf. *Some Remarks on Logical Form.* Aristotelian Society Supplement, vol. 9. 1929.)

be conceived as paralleling the three dimensions of color, pitch being comparable to hue, timbre to saturation and loudness to brightness. Co-ordinates or objects with the "form of sound" will then give any sound in terms of *these three axes,* as objects with the "form of color" give any color in terms of the color axes and objects with the "form of space" any spatial point or shape in terms of the space axes. (In the case of time or temporal durations presumably there would be the op-tion of a one-dimensional before-and-after description or a two-dimen-sional past-present-and-future one, or perhaps some combination of the two.)

Whether Wittgenstein's notion of a possible situation being *pro-jected into* a proposition in the form of a sense (3.11) requires that, instead of this, the points be considered as "projective points" with a minimum of four points needed to determine a line (state of affairs), as in projective geometry, is not clear. A picture of a cube is described in the *Tractatus* as a fact, (5.5423) and it is possible that a cube itself is to be regarded as a fact, in which case one of its lines might be taken as a single state of affairs, representable by four such projective points. If this is the notion of objects intended, the minimum number of names in an elementary proposition would have to be four, and we would require a fourth color determination and a fourth sound determination if the analogy with spatial lines in projective geometry were to hold.[4]

What is most important about Wittgenstein's conception of "mul-tiply-extended manifolds" in any case is that they are given com-binatorially, each perceivable quality in each manifold being repre-sented by one combination of "all possible combinations" of the suitable objects. Space, time and color are such "combinatorial manifolds," dif-ferent because involving different kinds of objects, but similar because every phenomena in each case is describable merely by a linear com-bination of names. (If four objects are needed, as in projective geom-etry, then there will be twenty-four possible combinations, although, also as in projective geometry, only six might give operable values.)

Wittgenstein's objects, as dimensional coordinates designated by simple signs or names, do not, of course, individually correspond to

---

[4] "Music, theoretically considered, consists altogether of lines of tone. It more nearly resembles a picture or an architectural drawing than any other art crea-tion; the difference being that in the drawing the lines are visible and constant, while in music they are audible and in motion." Percy Goetschius—*Exercises in Elementary Counterpoint,* (N.Y., 1910), p. 1.

anything phenomenal at all; only their combinations correspond to what we experience as various spatial, temporal or color phenomena. Hence there is no more sense in talking about whether objects "exist" than there is in talking about whether what corresponds to a single generalized coordinate in physics "exists." We simply do not encounter these coordinates singly; and it is only combinations of objects which exist and do not exist (*Bestehen* and *Nichtbestehen*), and they exist and do not exist as the propositions which represent them have existence (*Existenz*). As Wittgenstein puts it:

A proposition determines a place in logical space. The existence (*Existenz*) of this logical place is guaranteed by the mere existence (*Existenz*) of the constituents—by the existence (*Existenz*) of a proposition with a sense. (3.4)

THE *TRACTATUS* AND THE PLATONIC *METHEXIS*

One of the most important problems of the Platonic dialogues is the question of how there is a "participation" (sharing—*methexis*)[1] of the realm of sense particulars in the realm of Ideas. A parallel question in the *Tractatus* is how *things*, which are changeable and complex, function as *objects*, which are unchangeable and simple.

Wittgenstein has two closely related answers: that it is "essential" to things that they can be parts of structure (2.011) and that, while they have a "form of independence," this is limited by their formal possibilities of combination. (2.0122) (In this they parallel *words*, which also have meanings "independently" of each other, but *only on the condition* that they have the same meanings when they are in the structural arrangements of propositions.)

That what is being referred to is a *thing*, and not an *object*, is shown by a "certain indeterminacy" in the proposition in which it is referred to. (3.24C) This indeterminacy is the mark of "thingness," while full determinacy marks objects. And this provides a way of looking at the difference between Wittgenstein's and Plato's conceptions of form. For Wittgenstein *form* means, in the first instance, "possibilities of combination" of objects (2.0141) and, in the second instance, given along with this, "all possible combinations or structures." (2.033) For Plato, the idea (*idea* or *eidos*) meant, of course, the "class nature" of the object. (Classification is arbitrary and conventional for Wittgenstein up to the point where analysis discloses what "corresponds to a logical form." (3.315). In the *Tractatus* classes are not needed in logic (5.454) or in mathematics. (6.031))

The statement that it is "essential" to things that they can be constituents of states of affairs may be taken to mean that it is *common* to all things that they can enter into structural combinations. This nature of things is disclosed, as essence in general is disclosed, (3.3421) by what is possible in each individual case. The *form* of things, on the other hand, is simultaneously a "form of independence" (in so far as things enter into

---

[1] For Plato's use of the term *metecho*, meaning *to partake of* or *have a share of*, see Fridericus Astius—*Lexicon Platonicum sive Vocum Platonicarum Index*, (Leipzig, 1836), vol. 2, pp. 325f.

situations and not states of affairs) and "form of dependence" (in so far as they enter into *all possible situations*, and hence by this are connected with states of affairs). The expression "all possible" here tells us that things are connected with *a priori* forms, though in an "independent" way.

The two-sidedness of Wittgenstein's account is evident: on the one hand we find what is *essential* for things by finding out what is possible for them individually; and, on the other hand, their relations to forms are given *a priori* when we see them as entering into *all possible* situations, given when all objects are given. (2.014)

A similar question can be asked of both Wittgenstein and Plato: Do things participate in the same form by virtue of a commonness (*koinonia*) which they share, or do they share such a commonness because they participate in the same form? In each case the answer would seem to be "Both," for these are simply two ways of looking at the same matter—in terms of actual possibility and in terms of *a priori* possibility. On the one hand, not all possibilities are realized in actuality, but, on the other, those that *are* realized *are* possibilities only because they *are* instances of all possibilities. In Wittgenstein's terminology, "essence" does not coincide with "form," but unless we have one we will not have the other.[2]

---

[2] A decisive difference in the later philosophy is the decision to talk only about "actual possibility," surrendering ideal or *a priori* possibility. Language-games fall somewhere between descriptions of what might actually occur and idealized simplifications; any notion of "all possible language-games" is decisively rejected. (*Philosophical Investigations*. sect. 23)

APPENDIX 4

WITTGENSTEIN AND KANT ON *OBJECTS*

A thorough comparison between the early philosophy of Wittgenstein and the philosophy of Kant is much needed to establish the intellectual tradition to which Wittgenstein belongs. The parallels between the two philosophers are sufficiently striking to suggest, merely on internal evidence, that Wittgenstein was familiar with Kant directly and not merely through Schopenhauer. The *Tractatus* deals with many Kantian themes in a thoroughly Kantian way, although at the same time rejecting Kant's fundamental "transcendental idealism" in favor of a Fregean-inspired "transcendental realism," (cf. 5.64 where "pure realism" is reached by way of solipsism).

The place where the divergence comes out perhaps most fundamentally is in their respective treatment of *objects*. At first sight Wittgenstein's distinction between *things* and *objects* reminds us of Kant's distinction between the *empirical object* and the *transcendental object* (especially as this is developed in the second edition of the *Critique of Pure Reason*). And, in addition to this, Wittgenstein's distinction between the configuration of objects producing material properties (2.0231) and producing purely determinate structures (2.0272) reminds us of Kant's distinction between the phenomenal and the noumenal.

Wittgenstein's objects, however, differ fundamentally from both Kant's *transcendental object* (which is conceptual) and Kant's *thing-in-itself* (which is existential). They are not like Kant's "transcendental object = X" because they are not the concept of an object (for Wittgenstein "object" is a "pseudo-concept" (4.1272)). And they are not like the *thing-in-itself* because for Wittgenstein existence does not attach to individual things or objects, but only to a logical place guaranteed by the *existence (Existenz)* of a proposition (3.4) and to the *existence (Bestehen)* of a combination of objects in such a logical place. (Even if we regard Wittgenstein's *content*, or the sheer inexpressible given, as the same as Kant's *thing-in-itself*, the difference still remains that Wittgenstein's *content* appears as the immediately experienced qualitative phenomena and not "things.")

While Kant and Wittgenstein are both concerned with the "conditions of objectivity" they see these in radically different ways. Kant's objects are necessary correlates of the synthetic activity of a perceiving and knowing subject—or, to use Kant's favorite expression, conditions for the "transcendental unity of apperception." Wittgenstein, on the other hand, specifically repudiates the grounding of objectivity in what is required for the activity and unity of a subject, by denying that there *is* any thinking or representing subject. (5.631)[1] For Wittgenstein objects are eternal *substance*, not conditions for knowing, but themselves known (2.0123) and not necessary for the activities of a subject, but for the structures of the world and of thought and language.[2]

The crux of the difference lies in Kant's view that

> the combination (*conjunctio*) of a manifold in general can never come to us through the senses, and cannot therefore be already contained in the pure form of sensible intuition . . . of all representations *combination* is the only one which cannot be given through objects. Being an activity of the subject, it cannot be executed save by the subject itself. . . . Combination is representation of the *synthetic* unity of the manifold. The representation of this unity cannot, therefore, arise out of this combination.[3]

A few pages further on Kant speaks of "apperception and its synthetic unity" as the "source of all combination." Two views are brought together here by Kant. On the one hand, he recognizes that combination cannot be given "through the senses," but, on the other, he then supposes that it must, therefore, be an "activity of the subject." Wittgenstein agrees with the first (in so far as he sees all "content" as unknowable and inexpressible) but rejects the second (since for him "combination" belongs to objects independently of any subject). In the *Tractatus* combination is known and given because the possibilities of representation are determined, not by the activity of a subject, but by the internal properties of objects themselves. (2.01231)

---

[1] It should, of course, be borne in mind that in the *Tractatus* there is a metaphysical subject, which expresses only that "the world is my world" and an ethical subject, about which nothing can be said.

[2] The objection that in the *Tractatus* objects must be known through pictures so that we are involved in a vicious circle, since there are no pictures without objects and no objects without pictures, is settled implicitly by Wittgenstein in favor of the "priority of objects" since thoughts are pictures of facts (3.) (or combinations of objects) *before* anything is known about them.

[3] Kant—*Critique of Pure Reason*. trans. Kemp Smith, (N.Y., 1950), B 130-131.

Kant believed that there were two, and only two, alternatives, for he says:

> There are only two ways in which synthetic representations and their objects can establish connection, obtain necessary relation to one another, and, as it were, meet one another. Either the object alone must make the representation possible or the representation alone must make the object possible. In the former case this relation is only empirical and the representation is never possible *a priori*. This is true of appearances, as regards that (element) in them which belongs to sensation. In the latter case representation in itself does not produce its object, for we are not here speaking of its causality by means of the will. None the less the representation is *a priori* determinant of the object if it be the case that only through the representation is it possible to *know* anything as an object.[4]

Wittgenstein's way of conceiving of objects avoids Kant's choice here. For him objects are neither sense-given (for they are *known*), nor determined *a priori* by representation, (for they are the *substance* of the world). They are "substantial metaphysical unities"—just what Kant had rejected when he rejected Leibniz's "dogmatic metaphysics." But there is a difference now, for the *Tractatus's* metaphysics are only a heuristic device to teach us to see the world rightly. (6.54)

Wittgenstein can dispense with Kant's "synthetic activity of consciousness" because his objects themselves already provide all the possible and necessary forms of "synthetic unity." The *Tractatus's* objects themselves combine in all the ways which Kant supposed require the activities of a subject. They have spatial, temporal, colored, etc. forms (2.0251) (corresponding to Kant's forms of intuition), and they also have logical form (all that is needed in place of Kant's categories of the understanding if we add also Wittgenstein's "forms of description" as they appear in science).

The *Tractatus* might be described as something like Kant's first *Critique* transposed into a propositional and realistic key, but with all the differences that this implies. The *propositional bond of sense* (mirroring the internal structural nature of the world) replaces Kant's *epistemological bond of synthetic unity* (the necessary correlate of the

---

[4] *Ibid.*, A 92, B 125. For an illuminating discussion of the significance of this passage in Kant's philosophy see Robert Paul Wolff—*Kant's Theory of Mental Activity*, (Harvard Univ. Press, 1963), pp. 94-99.

activities of a subject). *Form* and *structure* are thus given back to the objective world, a world now stripped of its relation to subjectivity *except at one point*. Whether this undoes Kant's Copernican revolution, stands Kant on his head, or performs some other intellectual gyration beloved of historians of philosophy remains to be seen. What does seem likely to be the case, however, is that Wittgenstein will be seen to have as much claim to be a true descendant of Kant as any of the rest of Kant's vast philosophical progeny.[5]

---

[5] Wittgenstein's later philosophy, of course, resembles the shift from the First Critique to the Second Critique, even down to the "priority of the practical reason" (i.e. to the priority of language-activities to the requirements of theory). Wittgenstein unfortunately did not live to write his Third Critique.

APPENDIX 5

WITTGENSTEIN AND BUDDHIST LOGIC

Although only a small fragment of the main texts of classical Hindu and Buddhist logic have been translated into European languages, recent work by Sanskritists and Orientalists, some of whom are also students of contemporary Western philosophy, is opening up these vast regions of human thought to Western scholars. In the field of Indian logic there are important studies of two basic works—the *Nyaya-sutra* (The Logic Sutra) (2nd century A.D.) and the *Navya-nyaya* (The New Logic) (11th-14th centuries).[1] And in the parallel field of Buddhist logic there are equally important studies of the logicians Nagarjuna (2nd century A.D.) and his follower Aryadeva[2] and of Dignaga (5th century) and his followers Dharmakirti and Dharmottara.[3]

In the field of Buddhist logic especially important is a study by a Pali scholar who was also a student of Wittgenstein's, having attended Wittgenstein's classes at Cambridge in the years 1945-47—*Early Bud-*

---

[1] See especially Satischandra Chatterjee—*The Nyaya Theory of Knowledge*, (Univ. of Calcutta, 1950); D. H. H. Ingalls—*Materials for the Study of Navya-nyaya Logic*, (Harvard Univ., 1951); Bimal Krishna Matilal—*The Navya-nyaya Doctrine of Negation (The Semantics and Ontology of Negative Statements in the Navya-nyaya Philosophy)*, (Harvard Univ., 1968); S. S. Barlingay—*A Modern Introduction to Indian Logic*, (Delhi, 1965); and B. L. Atreya—*The Elements of Indian Logic*, (Moradabad, 1962).

[2] See especially Richard H. Robinson—*Early Madhyamika in India and China*, (Univ. of Winconsin, 1967); T. V. Murti—*The Central Philosophy of Buddhism*, (London, 1955); Giuseppe Tucci—*PreDignaga Buddhist Texts on Logic from Chinese Sources* (which contains a translation of Nagarjuna's *Vigrahavyavartani* from Chinese and Tibetan texts and also of Aryadeva's *Satasastra*), (Oriental Institute, Baroda, 1929); Th. Stcherbatsky—*The Conception of Buddhist Nirvana*, (which contains translations of Nagarjuna's *Madhyamika-Sastra* and a commentary on it by Candrakirti (7th century A.D.)), (Shanghai, 1940).

[3] Th. Stcherbatsky—*Buddhist Logic*, (2 vols.), ('S-Gravenhage, 1958); Saktari Mookerjee—*The Buddhist Philosophy of Universal Flux—An Exposition of the Philosophy of Critical Realism as Expounded by the School of Dignaga*, (Univ. of Calcutta, 1935). For the place of Buddhist logic in the general history of Buddhist philosophy see especially Junjiro Takakusu—*The Essentials of Buddhist Philosophy*, (Hawaii, 1949), and Yamakami Sogen—*Systems of Buddhist Thought*, (Univ. of Calcutta, 1912). And for the relation between the Brahmanic and Buddhist logics see Dharmendra Nath Shastri—*An Outline of Critique of Indian Realism—A Study of the Conflict between the Nyaya-Vaisesika and the Buddhist Dignaga School*, (Institute of Indology, Delhi, 1964).

dhist Theory of Knowledge by K. N. Jayatilleke, (London, 1963). In this illuminating work early Buddhist epistemology and logic is looked at in the light of Western analytic philosophy, helping to break the spell of the Hegelian-Bradleyan approach to Buddhist philosophy so characteristic of an earlier generation of scholars.[4]

One of the themes of Buddhist logic discussed at length by Professor Jayatilleke is the so-called "four-fold logic" believed to have originated with Sanjaya Belatthiputta (possibly a contemporary of Buddha's).[5] Sanjaya may have been the first to formulate the four possibilities of *existence, non-existence, both* and *neither*, which figure prominently in the logic of Nagarjuna as well as in later Buddhist logic. Professor Jayatilleke rejects the view that these "four forms of predication" or "four logical alternatives" violate the Aristotelian law of noncontradiction and holds instead that *not-p* here is to be taken as the contrary, and not the contradictory, of *p*. The law of non-contradiction, he maintains, holds among the "four alternatives," prescribing that *only one* of the four may hold, while the law of the excluded middle also holds, prescribing that *at least* one of the four must hold.[6]

While this may go part of the way toward reconciling Buddhist "four-fold logic" with Western logic, it may be wondered if this is not done at the expense of the metaphysical significance of the former. If we list the four "possibilities" of

(1) *p*
(2) *not-p*
(3) *both p and not-p*
(4) *neither p nor not-p*

it may strike us that all four of them figure in the *metaphysics* of the *Tractatus*.

(1) *p* is what is the case, the *world* as *positive facts*
(2) *not-p* is the *world* as *negative facts*
(3) *both p and not-p* is *reality*, the existence and non-existence of states of affairs

---

[4] Professor Jayatilleke is in no way responsible for the comparisons which are made here. While his book makes references to Wittgenstein, these are not in connection with the "four-fold logic."

[5] See A. B. Keith—*Buddhist Philosophy in India and Ceylon*, (Oxford, 1923), p. 302.

[6] Jayatilleke, *op. cit.*, Chapter vii, *Logic and Truth*.

(4) *neither p nor not-p* is *substance,* or what the language of the *Tractatus* itself talks about, that which neither exists nor does not-exist.

If we stop trying to squeeze these four "alternatives" themselves into truth functions, it is apparent that we need *all four* of them for the *metaphysics* of the *Tractatus before we can have any truth functions at all.* If in some way we could not employ these four "alternatives," the *Tractatus's* metaphysics itself could not be formulated. Thus even though *p and not-p* appears as a *contradiction* once we have truth functions, in a prior sense *p and not-p* is just what is meant by *reality* as Wittgenstein uses this term (*Wirklichkeit*). (2.06) And thus also even though throughout the book he speaks about *objects* and the *nature of objects,* this way of speaking itself is finally pronounced non-sensical, (6.54) and we recognize that nothing either true or false can be said about objects, and indeed they *neither exist nor do not-exist.*

Whether at least some of the Buddhist logicians had in mind that all four "logical alternatives" must always by invoked in any metaphysical system, or whether they believed that it was necessary to choose one of the four remains a subject for further study. Possibly they intended *both and neither.*

Sources of the Epigraphs

The sources of the epigraphs which appear at the beginnings of the chapters in this book are as follows:

CHAPTER 1

Dimitrije Mitrinovic writing under the pseudonym of *M. M. Cosmoi* in an article entitled "World Affairs" in *New Britain* for May, 1933.
Heracleitus (frag. 2) as trans. by G. S. Kirk and J. E. Raven in *The Presocratic Philosophers* (Cambridge, 1957), p. 188.
The fragment comes from Sextus Empiricus (*adv. math. vii* 133), and I have accepted the reading favored by Felix M. Cleve in *The Giants of Pre-Sophistic Greek Philosophy* (The Hague, 1965), p. 93.
Kena Upanishad I-5 in S. Radhakrishnan—*The Principal Upanishads* (N.Y., 1953), p. 582.

CHAPTER 2

L. C. Beckett—*Movement and Emptiness* (Wheaton, Ill., 1968), p. 14. The phrase quoted occurs in the following context: "Reality underlies many coats of paint, and we gaze at the spectacle before us as we gaze at abstract pictures—putting our own interpretation. But that does not exempt us from trying to find out what lies behind this coat of many names."
Gottlob Frege—*The Basic Laws of Arithmetic*, trans. Montgomery Furth (Berkeley, Calif., 1964), pp. 15-16.
Gottfried Leibniz—Correspondence with De Volder, Letter IX in *Philosophical Papers and Letters*, trans. Leroy E. Loemker (Chicago, 1956), vol. 2, pp. 873-4.
Chuang-tzu—in *Chuang-tzu—Taoist Philosopher and Chinese Mystic*, trans. Herbert A. Giles (London, 1961), p. 74.
William Blake—"A Vision of the Last Judgment" in *Poetry and Prose of William Blake*, edited by David V. Erdman (N.Y., 1965), pp. 544-55.

CHAPTER 3

Laotzu—*Tao Te King*. Chinese-English edition, edited by Paul Carus (Chicago, 1898), Chpts. 45 and 11, pp. 216 and 161, for the two references.
Astasahasrika (Conze 71, Mitra 205). This passage is quoted in Richard H. Robinson—*Early Madhyamika in India and China* (Madison, Wis., 1967), p. 179.
Gaurinath Sastri—*The Philosophy of Word and Meaning—Some Indian Approaches with Special Reference to the Philosophy of Bharthari* (Calcutta, 1959), p. 95.

CHAPTER 4

Max Müller—*Three Introductory Lectures on the Science of Thought* (Chicago, 1909), p. 67.
Charles S. Peirce—"The Ethics of Terminology"—in *Collected Papers* (Cambridge, Harvard Univ. Press, 1932), vol. 2, p. 129.
Wittgenstein—*Notes on Logic*, (Sept., 1913), in *Notebooks*. p. 99.
Mimansa—trans. N. V. Thadani—(Bharati Research Institute, Delhi, 1952), Chpt. iv, part ii, p. 85.
Gaurinath Sastri, *op. cit.*, p. 67.

CHAPTER 5

Moritz Schlick—*Form and Content, An Introduction to Philosophical Thinking* in *Gessamelte Aufsätze 1926-1936*, (Vienna, 1938), p. 178.
Bertrand Russell—*The Philosophy of Logical Atomism* in *Logic and Knowledge* (London, 1956), p. 238.
Gottfried Leibniz—"Extracts from Leibniz," Appendix to *A Critical Exposition of the Philosophy of Leibniz* (London, 1949), p. 245.
St. Augustine—*De Civitate Dei*, xi, vi, trans. J. Healey (London, Everyman, 1945), p. 317.
John Ruskin—"Ethics of the Dust," quoted in Ernst Lehars—*Man or Matter* (London, 1951), p. 118.

CHAPTER 6

John Wilmot, Earl of Rochester—"Upon Nothing" in *The Complete*

Poems of, edited by David M. Vieth (New Haven, Yale Univ., 1968), p. 119.

Laotzu—*op. cit.,* Chpt. 43, p. 216.

Viseha-cinta Brahma-pariprccha, Takakusu *Tripitaka,* xv, 50 and 82, quoted by Arthur Waley in "Texts from China and Japan" in *Buddhist Texts Through the Ages,* edited by E. Conze, J. B. Horner, D. Snellgrove and A. Waley (N.Y., 1954), p. 279.

Nagarjuna—(13. 3-4) *Prasannapada,* pp. 240-41, quoted in Robinson, *op. cit.,* p. 41.

Persian Proverb—in S. Haim—*Persian-English Proverbs* (Teheran, 1956), p. 416. This is given as the English equivalent of a proverb which would be literally translated: "What is in the pot will come into the ladle."

CHAPTER 7

Pascal—*Pensées* with an English Translation, Brief Notes and Introduction by H. F. Stewart (London, 1950), p. 95. The French reads: "Chaque chose est icy vraye en partie, fausse en partie. La verité essentielle n'est pas ainsy: elle est toute pure et toute vraye."

Aristotle—*Poetics,* xx, 12, (1457a), in S. H. Butcher—*Aristotle's Theory of Poetry and Fine Art* with a Critical Text and Translation of *The Poetics* (London, 1898), p. 77.

Prabhatchandra Chakravarti—*The Linguistic Speculations of the Hindus* (Univ. of Calcutta, 1933), p. 110.

Seneca (quoting Euripides)—*Ad Lucilium Epistulae Morales*—Letter 49 in Loeb Library edition translated by Richard M. Gummere (London, 1917), vol. 1, p. 331.

Soren Kierkegaard—*Philosophical Fragments or a Fragment of Philosophy* by Johannes Climacus, translated from the Danish with Introduction and Notes by David F. Swenson (Princeton Univ., 1936), p. 33 footnote.

CHAPTER 8

Wittgenstein—*Notebooks.* p. 82. These marvelous lines, written with the exuberance of youth, express the eternal freshness and newness of the spirit. In the *Notebooks* they are followed by: "I want to report how *I* found the world./What others in the world have told me about

the world is a very small and incidental part of my experience of the world./*I have to judge the world, to measure things.*"
Schopenhauer—*The World as Will and Representation*, trans. from the German by E. F. J. Payne (Indian Hills, Col., 1958), vol. 1, p. 5.
Charles Peirce—"Partial Synopsis of a Proposed Work in Logic" in *Collected Papers, op. cit.*, vol. 2, p. 45.
Drg-Drsya Viveka—An Inquiry into the Nature of the Seer and the Seen, text with English trans. and notes by Swami Nikhilananda (Sri Ramakrishna Asrama, Mysore, 1931), p. 33.
Jalaluddin Rumi in *Rumi Poet and Mystic*, trans. R. A. Nicholson (London, 1950), pp. 38-9.

CHAPTER 9

Samuel Beckett—quoted in Israel Shenker—*Moody Man of Letters* in New York *Times*, May 6, 1956, sec. 2, p. 1.
Zohar—I am unable to find the exact source of this quotation in the five-volume Sperling and Simon trans. of *The Zohar* (London, 1949). It may be paraphrased from a number of different places.
Simone Weil—*The Notebooks of*, trans. Arthur Wills (London, 1956), vol. 1, p. 99. Because of the suggestion of a "causal nexus" the quotation is not altogether *a propos*, but it does suggest the complete gulf between fact and value which we find in the *Tractatus*.
Stage directions for the medieval morality play *Adam*—quoted in E. K. Chambers—*The Medieval Stage* (Oxford, 1925), vol. 2, p. 80. These directions begin: "A Paradise is to be made in a raised spot, with curtains and cloths of silk hung round it at such a height that persons in the Paradise may be visible from the shoulders upwards."
E. Alexis Preyre—*The Freedom of Doubt* (N.Y., 1953), p. 68.

CHAPTER 10

Hermann Weyl—*Philosophy of Mathematics and Natural Science*, based on a translation by Olaf Helmer (Princeton, 1949), Appendix B, p. 237.
Gottfried Leibniz—*Collected Papers, op. cit.*, vol. 2, 889.
Plato—*Theaetetus* 179C, trans. B. Jowett—*Dialogues of Plato* (N.Y., 1937), vol. 2, p. 181. The passage is translated by S. W. Dyde (Glasgow, 1899), as follows: "But his present feelings, out of which arise

sensations and corresponding opinions, it is not so easy a matter to convict of error; perhaps I am wrong in thinking it to be even possible."
Simone Weil—*The Notebooks of*, translated by Arthur Wills (London, 1956), vol. 2, p. 410.

CHAPTER 11

Max Müller—*The Identity of Language and Thought* in *op. cit.*, p. 54. Müller marshals an impressive array of opinion to support the thesis of his title. The *Tractatus* does not presuppose this "identity," but only a structural identity.
Paul Klee—*Schöpferische Konfession* (1920) in Will Grohmann—*Paul Klee* (N.Y., n.d.), p. 99.
Henri Poincare—*Value of Science* (N.Y., 1907), p. 142.
Samuel Beckett—*Malone Dies* in *Three Novels* (N.Y., 1959), p. 308.
Wittgenstein—*Notebooks*. p. 52.

CHAPTER 12

Wittgenstein—Letter to Ludwig Ficker in Paul Engelmann—*Letters from Wittgenstein with a Memoir* (N.Y., 1967), p. 143. This quotation shows what distinguishes Wittgenstein from any kind of positivism. As Engelmann puts it: "Positivism holds—and this is its essence—that what we can speak about is all that matters in life—Whereas Wittgenstein passionately believes that all that really matters in human life is precisely what, in his view, we must be silent about." (p. 97)
Philolaus—fragment 3—Diels—*Die Fragmente der Vorsokratiker* (Berlin, 1951), vol. 1, p. 408. The translation is that of Kathleen Freeman—*Ancilla to the Pre-Socratic Philosophers* (Oxford, 1948), p. 74. The Philolaus fragment must be understood against the background of Pythagoreanism. See J. E. Raven—*Pythagoreans and Eleatics* (Cambridge, 1948), and J. A. Philip—*Pythagoras and Early Pythagoreanism* (Toronto, 1966).
Laotzu—*op. cit.*, Chpt. 78, p. 270.
The Platform Scripture—The Basic Classic of Zen Buddhism—trans. Wing-tsit Chan (N.Y., 1963), Chpt. 17, p. 51.
Parva Gallina Rubra—quoted in A. R. McIntyre—*Curare—Its History, Nature, and Clinical Use* (Chicago, 1947), p. 209.

CHAPTER 13

Henry Adams—*The Education of, An Autobiography* (Boston, 1918), Chpt. xxx, p. 441.

Samuel Beckett—*Dante . . . Bruno, Vico . . . Joyce* in *Our Examination Round His Factification for Incamination of Work in Progress* (London, 1961), p. 3.

Paul Valery—*Commerce*, I, p. 21, quoted by Preyre, *op. cit.*, p. 49. In the English translation of Valery's *Art of Poetry* by Denise Folliot, (N.Y., 1958), this appears as: "Each and every word that enables us to leap so rapidly across the chasm of thought, and to follow the prompting of an idea that constructs its own expression, appears to me like one of those light planks which one throws across a ditch or a mountain crevasse and which will bear a man crossing it rapidly. But he must pass without weighing on it, without stopping—above all he must not take it into his head to dance on the slender plank to test its resistance! . . . Otherwise the fragile bridge tips or breaks immediately, and all is hurled into the depths. Consult your own experience; and you will find that we understand each other, and ourselves, only thanks to our *rapid passage over words*." (pp. 55f.)

Eric Gutkind—*The Body of God—First Steps Toward an Anti-Theology*, edited by Lucie B. Gutkind and Henry Le Roy Finch (N.Y., 1969), p. 53.

Giorgio de Chirico—from a manuscript from the collection of the late Paul Eluard included as Appendix A in James Thrall Soby—*Giorgio de Chirico* (N.Y., n.d.), p. 245.

John Huss—quoted in W. Gurney Benham—*Putnam's Dictionary of Thoughts* (N.Y., 1930), p. 607b. Huss's remark is said to have been called forth by the sight of a child bringing up its stick to add to the fagots, in ignorant imitation of the men assigned to build the fire by which Huss was to be burned.

Bibliographies

(A complete Bibliography of Writings by and about Wittgenstein in different languages and including books, dissertations, articles and chapters, compiled by K. T. Fann, will be found in the *International Philosophical Quarterly*, Vol. VII, No. 2, (June, 1967), pp. 311-339, and is also published as a separate reprint.

The following bibliographies list only complete books in English, omitting all articles or chapters in books and publications in other languages. Also omitted are books specifically dealing with Wittgenstein's later philosophy. Books are listed under four sections: (1) By Wittgenstein, (2) About Wittgenstein in General, (3) About the *Tractatus* and (4) Background.)

I. Books by Wittgenstein

(In the order in which they were written, omitting the various unpublished sets of lecture notes)

Notebooks 1914-1916. Edited by G. H. von Wright and G. E. M. Anscombe with an English translation by G. E. M. Anscombe. Oxford: Basil Blackwell, 1961. (Includes *Notes on Logic* (Sept., 1913); *Notes Dictated to Moore in Norway* (April, 1914) and some extracts from Letters to Russell, 1912-21.)

Tractatus Logico-Philosophicus with an Introduction by Bertrand Russell. Translated by C. K. Ogden. N.Y.: Harcourt Brace and Co. and London: Kegan Paul, Trench, Trubner and Co., Ltd., 1922.

Tractatus Logico-Philosophicus. A new translation by D. F. Pears and B. F. McGuinness. London: Routledge & Kegan Paul and N.Y.: The Humanities Press, 1961. Second impression with a few corrections, 1963.

"Some Remarks on Logical Form" in *Proceedings of the Aristotelian Society*, Supplementary Volume 9 (1929), pp. 162-171.

"Lecture on Ethics" (1930) in *The Philosophical Review*. Vol. LXXIV, No. 1 (January, 1965), pp. 3-12. Also included here—Friedrich Waismann's *Notes on Talks with Wittgenstein*, pp. 12-16.

Philosophische Bemerkungen. (1930). Edited by Rush Rhees. Oxford: Basil Blackwell, 1964.

The Blue and Brown Books — Preliminary Studies for the "Philosophical Investigations." (1933-35). Edited with a Preface by Rush Rhees. Oxford: Basil Blackwell, 1958.

Lectures and Conversations on Aesthetics, Psychology and Religious Belief. (1938) Compiled from Notes taken by Yorick Smythies, Rush Rhees and James Taylor. Edited by Cyril Barrett. Oxford: Basil Blackwell, 1966. University of California, 1967.

Remarks on the Foundations of Mathematics. (1937-44). Edited by G. H. von Wright, R. Rhees, and G. E. M. Anscombe with an English translation by G. E. M. Anscombe. Oxford: Basil Blackwell, 1956.

Philosophical Investigations. (1945-49). Translated by G. E. M. Anscombe. Oxford: Basil Blackwell, 1958.

Zettel. (1945-48). Edited by G. E. M. Anscombe and G. H. von Wright. Translated by G. E. M. Anscombe. Oxford: Basil Blackwell and Berkeley, Cal.: Univ. of California, 1967.

On Certainty. (1950-51). Edited by G. E. M. Anscombe and G. H. von Wright. Translated by Denis Paul and G. E. M. Anscombe. Oxford: Basil Blackwell, 1969. N.Y.: J. and J. Harper, 1969.

Moore, G. E. — "Wittgenstein's Lectures in 1930-33," in *Mind* Vol. LXIII, Nos. 249 and 251 (Jan. & July, 1954) and Vol. LXIV, No. 253 (Jan., 1955). Reprinted in Moore's *Philosophical Papers.* London: Allen and Unwin, 1959.

II. About Wittgenstein in General

Engelmann, Paul. *Letters from Ludwig Wittgenstein with a Memoir.* Translated by L. Furtmüller. Edited by B. F. McGuinness. Oxford: Basil Blackwell; N.Y.: Horizon Press, 1967.

Fann, K. T. (edt.) *Wittgenstein, the Man and His Philosophy.* An Anthology. A Delta Book. N.Y. Dell, 1967.

Hallett, Garth. *Wittgenstein's Definition of Meaning as Use.* N.Y.: Fordham, 1967.

Hartnack, Justus. *Wittgenstein and Modern Philosophy*. Translated by Maurice Cranston. N.Y.: Anchor Books, 1965.

Hudson, W. D. *Ludwig Wittgenstein. The Bearing of His Philosophy upon Religious Belief*. London: Lutterworth, 1968.

Malcolm, Norman. *Ludwig Wittgenstein — A Memoir*. With a Biographical Sketch by G. H. von Wright. London: Oxford Press, 1958.

Mauro, Tullio de. *Ludwig Wittgenstein, His Place in the Development of Semantics*. Foundations of Language, Supplementary Series. Vol. 3. N.Y.: Humanities Press and Dordrecht, Holland: D. Reidel, 1967.

Pitcher, George. *The Philosophy of Wittgenstein*. Engelwood Cliffs, N.J.: Prentice-Hall, Inc. 1964.

Rhees, Rush. *Discussions of Wittgenstein*. N.Y.: Schocken, 1970.

Shibles, Warren. *Wittgenstein Language and Philosophy*. Dubuque, Iowa: W. C. Brown Book Co., 1969.

van Peursen, C. A. *Ludwig Wittgenstein. An Introduction to His Philosophy*. Translated from the Dutch by Rex Ambler. N.Y.: E. P. Dutton, 1970.

Winch, Peter, (edt.). *Studies in the Philosophy of Wittgenstein*. London: Routledge & Kegan Paul and N.Y.: Humanities Press, 1969.

III. About the *Tractatus*

Anscombe, G. E. M. *An Introduction to Wittgenstein's Tractatus*. London: Hutchinson University Library and N.Y.: Humanities Press, 3rd Edition, 1967.

Black, Max. *A Companion to Wittgenstein's "Tractatus."* Ithaca, N.Y.: Cornell University Press, 1964.

Copi, Irving M. and Beard, Robert W., (edt.). *Essays on Wittgenstein's "Tractatus."* N.Y.: Macmillan Co., 1966.

Favrholdt, David. *An Interpretation and Critique of Wittgenstein's Tractatus*. Copenhagen: Munksgaard and N.Y.: Humanities Press, 1965.

Feibleman, James K. *Inside the Great Mirror. A Critical Examination of the Philosophy of Russell, Wittgenstein and their Followers.* The Hague: Martinus Nijhoff, 1958.

Ganguly, Sachindranath. *Wittgenstein's Tractatus, A Preliminary.* Visva-Bharati, Santiniketan: Centre of Advanced Study in Philosophy, 1968.

Griffin, James. *Wittgenstein's Logical Atomism.* Oxford: Clarendon Press, 1964.

Maslow, Alexander. *A Study in Wittgenstein's "Tractatus."* Berkeley and Los Angeles: University of California Press, 1961.

Morrison, James C. *Meaning and Truth in Wittgenstein's Tractatus.* The Hague and Paris: Mouton, 1968.

Plochman, George Kimball and Lawson, Jack B. *Terms in Their Propositional Contexts in Wittgenstein's Tractatus. An Index.* Carbondale, Ill.: Southern Illinois University Press, 1962.

Stenius, Erik. *Wittgenstein's Tractatus. A Critical Exposition of Its Main Lines of Thought.* Ithaca, N.Y.: Cornell University Press, 1960.

IV. Background

Angelelli, Ignacio. *Studies on Gottlob Frege and Traditional Philosophy.* N.Y.: Humanities Press and Dordrecht, Holland: D. Reidel, 1967.

Frege, Gottlob. *The Basic Laws of Arithmetic. Exposition of the System.* Translated and Edited with an Introduction by Montgomery Furth. Berkeley and Los Angeles: University of California Press, 1964.

Frege, Gottlob. *The Foundations of Arithmetic. A logico-mathematical enquiry into the concept of number.* English translation by J. L. Austin. N.Y.: Philosophical Library, 1950.

Frege, Gottlob. *Translations from the Philosophical Writings of.* Edited by Peter Geach and Max Black. Oxford: Basil Blackwell, 1960.

Grossmann, Reinhardt. *Reflections on Frege's Philosophy.* Evanston, Ill.: Northwestern University Press, 1969.

Hertz, Heinrich. *The Principles of Mechanics Presented in a New Form*. Preface by H. von Helmholtz. Authorized English translations by D. E. Jones and J. T. Walley with a New Introduction by Robert S. Cohen. N.Y.: Dover, 1956.

Klemke, E. D. (edt.). *Essays on Frege*. Urbana, Chicago, and London: University of Illinois, 1968.

Lichtenberg, G. C. *The Reflections of*. Selected and Translated by Norman Alliston. London: Swan Sonnenschein & Co., Ltd., 1908.

Lichtenberg, G. C. *The Lichtenberg Reader* — Selected Writings of Georg Christoph Lichtenberg. Translated, Edited, and Introduced by Franz H. Mautner and Henry Hatfield. Boston: Beacon, 1959.

Lichtenberg, G. C. *A Doctrine of Scattered Occasions*. Reconstructed from His Aphorisms and Reflections. Bloomington, Ind.: Indiana University Press, 1959.

Moore, G. E. *An Autobiography*, in P. Schilpp, (edt.). *The Philosophy of G. E. Moore*. Library of Living Philosophers. Vol. IV. Evanston and Chicago: Northwestern University Press, 1942.

Russell, Bertrand. *Autobiography of. 1914-44*. Boston: Atlantic Monthly Press, 1968. (Contains several letters of Wittgenstein.)

Russell, Bertrand. *An Essay on the Foundations of Geometry*. Cambridge: At the University Press, 1897.

Russell, Bertrand. *Logic and Knowledge. Essays 1901-1950*. London: George Allen and Unwin, 1956.

Russell, Bertrand. *My Philosophical Development*. With an Appendix, Russell's Philosophy by Alan Wood. N.Y.: Simon & Schuster, 1959.

Russell, Bertrand. *The Principles of Mathematics*. Cambridge: At the University Press, 1903.

Schlick, Moritz. *Gesammelete Aufsätze, 1926-1936*. Vienna: Gerold & Co. 1938. (Contains *Form and Content, an Introduction to Philosophical Thinking*, three lectures delivered at the University of London in November, 1932.)

Schoenman, Ralph (edt.). *Bertrand Russell — Philosopher of the Century*, Essay in His Honor. Boston: Atlantic Monthly Press, 1967.

Sternfeld, Robert. *Frege's Logical Theory*. Foreword by George Kimball Plochmann. Carbondale and Edwardsville: Southern Illinois University Press, 1966.

Walker, Jeremy D. B. *A Study of Frege*. Ithaca, N.Y.: Cornell University Press, 1965.

Watson, W. H. *On Understanding Physics*. Cambridge: At the University Press, 1938.

INDEX
of
REFERENCES to the *TRACTATUS*

INDEX
of
NAMES OF PERSONS

INDEX
of
SUBJECTS